MOVING BEYOND WORDS

BY THE SAME AUTHOR

Revolution from Within
Outrageous Acts and Everyday Rebellions
Marilyn: Norma Jean

MOVING BEYOND WORDS

Gloria Steinem

BLOOMSBURY

First published in Great Britain 1994

Copyright © 1994 by Gloria Steinem

The moral right of the author has been asserted

Bloomsbury Publishing Ltd, 2 Soho Square, London W1V 5DE

A CIP catalogue record for this book
is available from the British Library

10 9 8 7 6 5 4 3 2 1

ISBN 0 7475 1713 4

Printed in Great Britain by Clays Ltd, St Ives plc

The author is grateful for permission to reprint the following copyrighted material:
"Nobody Wrote a Poem" from *Piece of Time,* by Carrie Allen McCray (a Crimson Edge Chapbook by Chicory Blue Press, 1993). Copyright © 1993 by Carrie Allen McCray.
Excerpted lines from "Prologue" are reprinted from *Undersong, Chosen Poems Old and New,* Revised Edition, by Audre Lorde, by permission of W. W. Norton & Company, Inc. Copyright © 1992, 1982, 1976, 1974, 1973, 1970, 1968 by Audre Lorde.
Excerpt from "We Alone" in *Horses Make a Landscape Look More Beautiful, Poems,* by Alice Walker, reprinted by permission of Harcourt Brace & Company. Copyright © 1984 by Alice Walker.

FOR MY SISTER
SUSANNE STEINEM PATCH
WITH LOVE, GRATITUDE, AND HOLIDAYS

Contents

Preface

Add Water

I was hoping this would be an easy book. Having taken a long time with the last one, *Revolution from Within,* I thought this could be a collection of already published articles. All I would have to do was write a short introduction and a transition or two, and I would have what E. M. Forster called "a miscellany of occasional writings" and my contemporaries refer to as refrying the beans.

But more than a year later, it has become a book of mostly new writing. Three of its six parts appear here for the first time. Three of them had a seed, seedling, or partly grown plant in a previously published article, but they too have acquired new prefaces along with new ideas and examples within their texts. As a result, each of these six parts has become rather like a condensed book, often with its own introduction. Since there seems to be no genre for this, I've found myself explaining it this way: If you added water to any of these parts, it would become a book.

To show you how each essay assumed a life of its own, the short introduction became "Doing Sixty," which is now the last part of this book. In retrospect, I realize it is the culprit whose energy forced me to deviate from my plan. Not only did it take on a length and independence that refused to introduce anything—except perhaps the future—but it kept inviting me to return to it long after I thought I had finished. Instead of watching previous states of mind jostle against each other and make a different kind of sense together, which is the pleasure of a collection, I found this newer state of mind refusing to take a back seat, and insisting on pushing everything else a little further. Though some of this urge came from the many years I spent more absorbed in activism than writing, which did indeed leave me with an unwritten book in every toe, elbow, and tooth, its content was a practical example of growing more radical with age.

Though I once would have treated Freud's writings as a secular bible, in much the way an atheist debater might try to impress a fundamentalist audience by using biblical references she or he doesn't believe for a minute, this new state of mind insisted on reading Freud in the way all writing deserves: as if we found it in the street and were reading it for any kind of sense, insight, sincerity, or value. Getting rid of the Great Man scrim was a revelation, and the result was both funny and frightening.

When I first interviewed Bev Francis, the strongest woman in the world, I was viewing fitness as personal and Bev as exceptional, but this newer state of mind saw the politics of muscle, and also a history of my own that I hadn't been ready to look at before.

Instead of thinking like an isolated dissident within the media's ranks, as I had been when I first wrote "Sex, Lies, and Advertising," I began to see the ways in which people and interests within the current system are also trapped by it, and therefore to glimpse why and how it could be changed.

When I first wrote about women in America's families of inherited wealth and power, I discovered the masculinization of wealth as the other end of the feminization of poverty—that neither could be solved without attacking the other. Though that remains true, my current state of mind has less tolerance for abstractions. I began to imagine what might happen if the strength of women who haven't had the restrictive social training to be ladies could be shared with women who could seize control of upper-class resources—on behalf of both.

Instead of expanding a report on women's economic development groups that had been planned for the collection, I began to notice that readers of its proposed table of contents received "economics" like a sleeping pill, and the phrase "economic development" with all the enthusiasm usually reserved for a hydroelectric dam. Using my own experience as an economics-impaired person, I tried instead to arrive at a way of demystifying economics, of treating the subject with more enthusiasm and less respect. Now "Revaluing Economics" is the main event, and the new women's development groups are its postscript.

Nonetheless, I didn't realize my original plan was out the window until I found myself eight months later, surrounded by stacks of Freud's old or newly published writings, books by a new generation of researchers who have begun to investigate instead of simply accepting his case histories, and a growing list of phone numbers of scholars who are looking at the impact of his work rather than his myth. The more I learned, the more I was amazed, appalled, and addicted to following up this or that clue, and different versions of the same event. As the mythical Phyllis Freud's biographer, I was in the middle of defending the abandonment of the seduction theory —that is, Freud's trading of his theory about the sexual abuse of children for his theory of children's fantasy of abuse—when I realized what furious fun Jonathan Swift must have had while writing "A Modest Proposal." It sent me back to reread that lethal satire, an alarmingly rational proposal for eating Irish babies as a way of solving many problems, from hunger and the size of the criminal population to abortion and helping men to become "as fond of their wives, during the time of their pregnancy, as they are now of their mares in foal, their cows in calf, or sows when they are ready to farrow, nor offer to beat or kick them (as it is too frequent a practice) for fear of miscarriage."[1] Read this to melt the time between Swift's eighteenth century and today—and to feel even less like excusing Freud with the "product of his time" argument, remember that Swift wrote it more than a century before Freud was born. While exploring the potential of scholarly footnotes and concocting such words as *testyria* and *androphobia,* I began to understand why the great writer Vladimir Nabokov had such a good time doing even the index of *Pale Fire*.

As I saw Phyllis Freud becoming the longest part of the book, I finally began to relax and enjoy whatever form the rest would take. In the hope that it might have the same effect on you (though its footnotes take some getting used to), I placed it first. I don't know if fury can compete with necessity as the mother of invention, but I recommend it. Once finished, I felt as spent and happy as Bev Francis after a workout.

Of course, the process isn't over. Writing a book is like trying to stop a river. I still worry that putting "sixty" in the title of the last essay may have the same effect on younger readers that it would have had on me. At their age, my generation regarded people over sixty, or even forty, as another species—and planned our lives poorly as a result. But I hope this essay will help younger readers to see a long and adventurous life ahead, to worry less about early successes, failures, or advice to "settle down" (which, as it turns out, we never do), and to regard older people as potential friends and colleagues. I want to thank two friends in their twenties, Amelia Richards and Rebecca Walker, who served as test readers with this goal in mind.

Most of all, I hope it's helpful to my beloved age peers, in whom I have the greatest faith. If our generation could survive coming of age in the 1950s, we can survive anything.

You may be a better judge than I of what these six disparate parts have in common. In retrospect, I see that they're all walking around a familiar subject, and looking at it from a different perspective. Another shared image might be opening the other eye. We have for so long looked at most subjects through male eyes that remedial vision (which for women, would mean looking at the world *as if women mattered,* and for men, *as if they were women*) brings a new perspective. It may not completely change what has always been before us, but it adds new depth, and a sense of the periphery which, as in a cell or a sprout, is where growth takes place. "Even to see the peripheries," as Joanna Russ has reminded us, "it seems you have to be on them, or by an act of radical re-vision, place yourself there."[2] All the parts and sub-parts share the structure of the essay—that elastic but still distinct form that invites a writer to begin in a personal place and come to a larger point. Finally, I hope all are accessible, for the older I get, the less patience I have with writing that is designed to keep people out.

As for adding water, that's something each reader will do in her or his own way. Readers' interests have been well represented so far by Suzanne Braun Levine, my friend and colleague who read and helped clarify each part in various versions; Amelia Richards, who has literally lived with this book and enhanced it in many ways—as have Diana James, Mary Beth Guyther, Franklin Thomas, Esther Broner, William Goldman, Koryne Horbal; and other friends, especially Wilma Mankiller, Rebecca Adamson, Marilyn Waring, Hazel Henderson, and John Kenneth Galbraith, who cast an eye over an amateur's economics, and those whose scholarship is credited within the notes to the Freud section. I'm also grateful to my editor, Alice Mayhew, who is so smart that she creates the luxury of talking in code, and her assistant, Sarah Baker, who eased the deadline problems created by this book's changing form.

How these unexpected events continue is up to you. For me, they may be training for what's to come, for I start a new decade with this book. On both counts, I can't wait to see what happens.

1. Jonathan Swift, *The Portable Swift,* edited by Carl Van Doren (New York: Penguin Books/ Viking Portable Library, 1988), p. 556.
2. Joanna Russ, *How to Suppress Women's Writing* (Austin: University of Texas Press, 1983), p. 132.

I have met brave women who are exploring the outer edge of possibility, with no history to guide them and a courage to make themselves vulnerable that I find moving beyond the words to express it.

Preview Issue of *Ms.* magazine, 1972

Now we have the dreams and tools to move beyond words and history, beyond the possible to the imagined, and into a life both ancient and new, where we will look back to see our present dreams trailing behind us as markers of where we have been.

Speech for Take Our Daughters to Work Day, 1994

What If *Freud* Were *Phyllis?**

*OR,
The Watergate
of the Western World

How Phyllis Freud
Was Born

Progress is nothing but the victory of laughter over dogma.

BENJAMIN DE CASSERES

Like all of us, Phyllis Freud was born of two parents. Her mother was an improvisation I used to do at lectures in the 1970s, which finally grew into an essay called "If Men Could Menstruate." It illustrated a lesson I was just then learning: that anything a powerful group has is perceived as good, no matter what it is, and anything a less powerful group has is not so good, no matter how intrinsically great it might be. Thus, menstruation, something even self-respecting and otherwise body-proud women are often made to feel ashamed of, would suddenly become terrific—providing only men had it.

Think about it:

There would be ceremonies to mark the onset of this envied beginning of manhood.

Men would brag about how long and how much.

A National Institute of Dysmenorrhea would spend millions on researching monthly discomforts.

Sanitary supplies would be federally funded and free.

Men would claim greater sexual powers, heightened intellectual skills, and improved athletic abilities at their "time of the month."

Corporate consultants would charge double for greater intuitive powers in those sensitive days at the onset of their cycles, and . . .

Well, you get the idea. You can improvise on this reversal, too, and can also meet Phyllis's mom, who's still around[1]—though as you'll see, Phyllis has appropriated some of her ideas, as daughters are wont to do.

Phyllis's father, the American Psychiatric Association, is more distant and difficult to explain; fathers so often are. In 1981, when I first met the APA, this very establishmentarian, overwhelmingly white organization had 24,000 members, 89 percent of them male; thus, it was hard to imagine that such a group could have anything to do with a feminist fantasy of men menstruating. As Freud himself had warned his colleagues: "We must not allow ourselves to be deflected . . . by . . . the feminists, who are anxious to force us to regard the two sexes as completely equal in position and worth."[2]

In fact, the illicit meeting took place only because I was asked to speak unofficially (very unofficially) at an APA convention by one of its internal caucuses, Psychiatrists for Equal Rights, a group started mostly by women APA members. They needed an outside agitator to help with their project of getting the APA to move its national meetings out of states that hadn't ratified the Equal Rights Amendment, thus putting its money where its mouth had been since 1974, when it voted to endorse that constitutional amendment.* (I don't mean to be a nudge, but do read that footnote.) Led by two feminist psychiatrists, Jean Shinoda Bolen and Alexandra Symonds, this caucus of well-organized subversives had been mailing out studies that showed equality to be necessary to women's mental health (which was the carrot that had persuaded the APA's board of trustees to endorse the ERA in the first place). They were also circulating reports on the numbers of women who were deserting traditional psychiatry for group and other less Freudianized therapies, plus petitions signed by individual psychiatrists who pledged not to attend meetings in unratified states (which combined into the economic stick they hoped would persuade the rest of the APA to stand up and show the world that psychiatry had changed).

All this organizing paid off. About fifteen hundred psychiatrists left their scheduled events to cram into a hotel conference room for our unofficial meeting. I did my best to explain how much their support would mean to women as a departure from Freudian tradition—not only on equality but on activism itself.† In fact, the psy-

---

* (Good. You're looking down here. You'll need the habit—you'll see why.) The Equal Rights Amendment would make discrimination based on sex as unconstitutional as that based on race, religion, or national origin. Its exact words are: *Equality of rights under the law shall not be abridged by the United States or any state on account of sex.* Radical, huh?

† "Politics spoils the character," Freud once wrote to a friend.[3] Governments could do little more than keep the lid on rape, murder, and the inevitable "conflicts among the ego, id, and superego which psychoanalysis studies in the individual—the same events repeated on a wider stage," as he elaborated in *Civilization and Its Discontents.* Whether it was Marxist revolutionaries in Russia or Woodrow Wilson and the League of Nations, he was critical of those foolish enough to try to make social revolutions; especially feminists, who he thought

chiatrists who came were mostly women and men who were trying to change their profession, and they turned the post-lecture discussion into a spirited organizing meeting. They, too, had been experiencing a contrast between the content of their training and the needs of their patients, and they wanted to take on the gender politics that were causing so much of the pain they witnessed. By the next day, the energy of this diverse and hopeful group had seeped into other meetings, and the APA trustees had actually voted to support the boycott.

Of course, this didn't happen without controversy. Jean Shinoda Bolen and I inadvertently hit a professional nerve when we suggested publishing the registration lists for the next national meeting —which was already scheduled for unratified Louisiana—so patients would know whether or not their psychiatrists were supporting this ERA boycott and be able to act on that knowledge should they so choose. What seemed a consumerist suggestion was such a reversal of the usual power relationship between (overwhelmingly female) patients and their (overwhelmingly male) psychiatrists—if only because it highlighted the usually forgotten fact that the patient was actually the employer—that it turned out to be one of the most controversial things either one of us had ever said in our long lives of controversy.* Nonetheless, the wind of change was coming from other parts of the mental health profession too. In supporting the pro-ERA boycott, the APA would be joining the American Psychological Association, the National Association of Social Workers, and most other associations of mental health professionals.

Unfortunately, what Jean called the "morning-after syndrome" set in once the APA trustees got home from San Francisco. They were countered by colleagues who hadn't been at that mind-changing

---

were opposing biology itself. As he wrote to his fiancée: "nature" intended woman, "through beauty, charm, and sweetness, for something else."[4] He also told her: "you write so intelligently and to the point that I am just a little afraid of you."[5] (Down here, we dish the real stuff.)

* Though the APA registration lists were never made public, the controversy got picked up by the press. Some women and pro-equality men did query their psychiatrists as a result and reported responses that were, shall we say, illuminating. As I write this in 1994, the APA has grown to 38,000 members, three fourths of whom are male—while three fifths of their patients are female. Still sounds like a case for consumerism to me. As Ethel Spector Person has reported from her psychiatric practice and research, the desire of more women patients to go to women professionals has resulted in "the increasing difficulty finding a well-trained woman therapist with open therapy time. No comparable problem exists when placing a patient in therapy with a man."[6]

convention and who pressured them to overturn their decision—which they did. The next convention was held in very unratified New Orleans.

Nonetheless, the sight of at least some psychiatrists willing to support equality in an activist way had given me hope. Marching outside the convention in demonstrations organized with spirit and humor, for instance, there had been a few dignified, tweed-jacketed men carrying signs with slogans like: "Warning: Your Psychiatrist's View on ERA May Be Dangerous to Your Mental Health"; "APA Stance on ERA Is Depressing"; and even "APA Is Schizoid About ERA." It must have been in that romantic moment that something new was conceived.

By the time the APA was planning its 1983 convention, however, the ERA had missed its ratification deadline—and by only three states. At a minimum, nine years of women's nationwide hard work would have to be done over again. Whether feeling guilty or just extending an olive branch in general, the APA invited me to speak, this time as part of the official program. However, any hope of diminished controversy was dispelled when the APA's Committee on Women asked me to address a subject on which they were trying to get APA permission to survey its membership: the alarming number of psychiatrists who took advantage of power and privacy to exploit their patients sexually.[7] Not only a betrayal of professional trust, this was an act with some of the implications of incest, since by psychoanalytic definition, the analyst became a parent in the patient's eyes.* Though Dr. Nanette Gartrell and others leading the survey project were the ones taking the professional risk, I could see this wasn't going to be easy for an outsider either.

As you can imagine, I spent some anxious days. Clearly, I was going to need all the research I could get, plus accounts from the

* These abuses were so common that in 1972, Phyllis Chesler reported in her landmark book, *Women and Madness:* "There are even therapists who 'specialize' in treating *other* therapists' 'guilt' or 'conflict' about having sexual relations with their patients." By 1986, when the national survey initiated by Dr. Nanette Gartrell and her APA colleagues was finally finished and released—with money they had raised privately, since the APA had stalled and never approved the survey—65 percent of psychiatrists, responding anonymously, said they had treated patients who had been sexually involved with a previous therapist. Though 87 percent of those psychiatrists said sexual contact was always harmful to the patient, only 8 percent had reported it.[8] Since then, the APA's *Principles of Ethics* have been tightened to forbid psychiatrist-patient sexual contact, but the APA still doesn't require reporting, within its own ranks or otherwise. What requirements do exist have been instituted by state law, the political system Freud spurned.

few women with the courage to go public with their experiences—and also any bridge-building devices I could think of. Even if psychiatrists were willing to listen to an outsider, what could I say that would help them look at the world through the eyes of their female patients, many of whom said they felt doubly and triply disempowered: by their gender, by their position as patients, by the knowledge of their deepest selves this process had invited them to give, and by whatever trouble had caused them to seek help in the first place. How could these guys walk in women's shoes, much less, as it were, lie on their own couches?

That's when I realized that the menstruation fantasy of the 1970s must have been gestating with the 1981 APA experience all along. Because suddenly there she was, full-blown as if born from the head of Athena, an entirely new creature—Viennese accent, cigarette holder, tailored suit, and all—*Dr. Phyllis Freud.*

I noticed immediately that she looked a lot like Margaret Thatcher, with her assertive style, but wore Gertrude Stein's timeless long skirts and capes. Also that Phyllis wasn't at all nervous about confronting an audience of male psychiatrists. On the contrary, like Norman Mailer at a Ladies' Literary Luncheon, Dylan Thomas before an audience of Wellesley girls, Mick Jagger looking over a new crop of groupies, or Clarence Thomas instructing his staff, she seemed perfectly confident that anything she chose to say to them would be an honor, indeed a gift.

Clearly, this was a woman whose very existence could help members of that august and authoritative body imagine how they would feel if:

- society and psychiatry were reversed so that *women* were 89 percent of APA members and *men* were three fifths of their patients;
- female psychiatrists and psychoanalysts were imbued with the philosophy of this female Freud, the founding genius who had proved that men's lack of wombs made them anatomically inferior and terminally envious;
- men who dared protest were doubly pathologized by a diagnosis of womb envy, thus it was a belief system with *no way out;*
- Freudian thought was accepted as a semiscientific rationale for men's lower status in a matriarchal society—not just within the profession but within the culture at large.

Once at the APA, I had time only to introduce Dr. Phyllis Freud briefly and do a few reversals as a preface to the main purpose of the speech. Nonetheless, she did break the ice, turn the tables, create some laughter and, I think, some empathy too.

Perhaps her outrageous presence also loosened tongues. The post-lecture discussion turned into something far more revelatory than the usual sober, APA-type exchange. A first volley came from a psychiatrist who rose to object to *my* objections to having sex with patients. "You don't understand," he said plaintively. "My patients behave very seductively with me." It took me a minute to realize that he was not only admitting something but defending it.* In the ominous silence that followed, someone else stood up to praise the APA for having expelled a member who published an article in support of "overt transference" (sex with patients was apparently common enough to warrant a euphemism of its very own), in which he maintained that psychiatrist-patient sex could be therapeutic— for the patient, of course. Then several others explained that the psychiatrist in question had got in trouble mainly for going public with those ideas, not for acting on them. Suddenly, professional reserve broke down. Those psychiatrists who seemed as surprised as I was by the attitudes of their colleagues began saying things like "I can't believe you call yourself a psychiatrist!"

From that moment on, I didn't need to say another thing. Professionals were discovering what many patients had known all along: the abuses of power going on behind closed doors.

In the decade since then, I've gained a lot of faith in reversals—of all kinds. They create empathy and are great detectors of bias, in ourselves as well as in others, for they expose injustices that seem normal and so are invisible. In fact, the deeper and less visible the bias, the

* Later, I learned that his attitude wasn't rare. Even when warning against sexual contact with patients in the prestigious *Psychoanalytic Quarterly,* Leon J. Saul seemed to worry more about the analyst: "Let the analyst beware. In the face of sexual love needs, let him recall the Lorelei and Delilah and the many other beauties who have revealed that appearance need not be reality. . . . No matter how obvious Eros may be, hostility is the inevitable middle link." Some psychiatrists had decided that sex with patients might be OK or even "good" under certain circumstances. Their arguments included the idea that sexual surrogates were harder to find for female patients than for male ones (supposing that surrogates were a good idea in the first place). In both cases, the psychiatrist was presented as risking himself for the patient's benefit and as the exploited one.

more helpful it is to take some commonly accepted notion about one race, class, ethnicity, sexuality, ability—whatever—and see how it sounds when transferred to another. Consider the implications of simple examples:

What if white actors and writers, sports stars and politicians, criminals and preachers, were identified first by their color, as their black counterparts so often are?

What if heterosexual male teachers were prejudged as sexual abusers of children, in the way that gay males often have been (which would make more statistical sense, since heterosexual males are the majority of abusers of both girls and boys)?

What if the jogger who was raped and brutally beaten in Central Park had been a black woman instead of a white one—would she have made the national news? Would she have even made the local news?

Suppose everyone who wasn't bisexual were suddenly labeled "monosexual"?

Of all reversals, however, the sexual ones may be the most necessary. Gender is the remaining caste system that still cuts deep enough, and spreads wide enough, to be confused with the laws of nature. To uncover the difference between *what is* and *what could be,* we may need the "Aha!" that comes from exchanging subject for object, the flash of recognition that starts with a smile, the moment of changed viewpoint that turns the world upside down.

While getting to know Dr. Phyllis Freud in her new, full-grown incarnation, for instance, I've found that she has inspired all kinds of learning moments in my day. There are now reality checks when I think about the news: *What if a female chief of state had thrown up on the Japanese and fainted as President Bush did?* There is education when I'm looking at entertainment: *What if movies about "masochistic" women who are portrayed as falling in love with their torturers were about Jews who fell in love with Nazis? What if TV jokes that are told about dumb blondes were told about dumb blacks?* There are also reminders that sexual politics are still deep enough to be called "culture" or "religion": *Why do I hear only women struggling with combining career and family? If men could get pregnant, would abortion be a sacrament?* I've found that Phyllis—however inadvertently—is a better therapist than Sigmund ever was.

But my purpose in creating Phyllis Freud has one thing in common with the technique of psychoanalysis as it exists today: something I greatly admire. An analyst in training has to go through years of his or her own analysis before being certified, thus making psychoanalysis the only profession I know of that has incorporated the technique of reversal into its very identity. Each professional must experience the process through which he or she will later lead others. This opportunity to walk a mile in somebody else's shoes—or lie on the same couch—may not always help, but at least it lessens the danger of doing harm. I think more of us should try it.

As a journalist, for instance, I discovered that I got better at my job the moment I was written about. Understanding the weight of words in print, feeling their ability to hurt and haunt when they were careless or inaccurate, helped me to become more responsible in writing about others. I've come to believe a dose of activist reversal might improve almost anybody's work. Journalism schools could require students to pick from a hat the name of a professional reporter, submit to an interview with all the usual research, and be profiled for an article that would stay in the research files for all future reporters to use—and might even end up as an obit. Applicants for television jobs could wake up one morning to find cameras and TV reporters on their doorsteps, waving microphones and shouting questions about some real or imagined misdeed. *20/20* could do an exposé on the producers of *60 Minutes*—and vice versa. The host of one tabloid TV show could be the subject of another. Professionals dealing with children could be treated like their charges for a while—for example, disbelieved about sexual abuse, forced to live in foster homes, and generally regarded as property. Or how about requiring cops and judges to spend a few days in the jails they send others to? Or new health professionals to wait for examinations in too-short gowns, coax medical records out of Kafkaesque bureaucracies, and spend a week in a hospital bed? What if would-be politicians had to listen to campaign speeches every day and then be denied at the end of their training whatever they'd been promised at its beginning? Suppose psychiatrists had to have shock treatments before prescribing this electroconvulsive therapy, in order to show the skeptical patient just how "harmless" it was?

Well, you see the possibilities.

But here's a clue about what's coming. Sigmund Freud himself, the Father of Psychoanalysis, may have been the only man in his trade to exempt himself from therapy. Indeed, he continued all his life to ignore colleagues who could have supervised his analysis. He also destroyed his personal and professional papers several times in his life, plotted when he was an obscure twenty-eight-year-old to leave any future biographers in the dark, kept his emotional life hidden, and falsified details of his dreams when he did write about them so they couldn't be analyzed. Why? Because he insisted he'd analyzed himself.*

His story not only was accepted but became part of the birth myth of psychoanalysis.† At the same time, Freud denied that self-analysis was possible for anybody else and advised even practicing psychoanalysts to reenter analysis (especially if they were to have any position of responsibility in Freudian organizations, in which case he often analyzed them himself—a means of quality control if you feel kindly toward him, and emotional control if you don't). But the real reason that Freud refused to have himself or his dreams analyzed, according to Carl Jung, then still his most trusted disciple, was his objection, " 'But I cannot risk my authority!' " It was a revelation that Jung said sounded the death knell of Freud's power over him. "Freud was placing personal authority above truth." ‡ [16]

* Now that Freud's unedited letters to his bosom buddy Wilhelm Fliess have been published, we know that during this period of his putative self-analysis he was writing: "My self-analysis once more is at a standstill. . . . My analysis remains interrupted. . . . True self-analysis is impossible, otherwise there would be no illness. . . . Still groping about, entirely in the dark. . . . My self-analysis is at rest in favor of the dream book." [9] Later, when challenged about whether the first generation of analysts had undergone analysis, Freud said he had insisted on it, but that he retained the "right to an exceptional position." [10] He also tried to buy and burn the Fliess correspondence—probably for a lot more reasons than this one.

† "It is hard for us nowadays to imagine how momentous this achievement was," wrote Ernest Jones, Freud's official biographer. "Yet the uniqueness of the feat remains. Once done it is done forever. For no one again can be the first to explore these depths." [11] Kurt Eissler, founder of the Freud Archives, presented this self-analysis as even more heroic: "His findings had to be wrested in the face of his own extreme resistances—the self-analysis being comparable. . . to Benjamin Franklin's flying a kite in a thunderstorm in 1752, in order to investigate the laws of electricity. The next two persons who tried to repeat his experiment were both killed." After Freud's death, Jones wrote: "Copernicus and Darwin dared much in facing the unwelcome truths of outer reality, but to face those of inner reality costs something that only the rarest of mortals would unaided be able to give." [12]

Freud's self-analysis was a source not only of his personal myth but supposedly of his famous discoveries; for instance, infantile sexuality. Since, by his own admission, his wife wouldn't let him into the nursery to observe their children, and since his only child patient (called "Little Hans" in his famous case history) was treated long distance through the child's father, he seemed to get his first insight into childhood sexuality from a sample of one—his own. As Frank Sulloway reported on the myth in *Freud: Biologist of the Mind,* "only by first overcoming his own infantile sexual repressions was Freud then able to elucidate the truly dynamic nature of the unconscious mental life that is common to all human beings." [13] But as Sulloway and others reported, Freud also claimed to be the only person who noticed that infants masturbated. (Wait. It gets better.)

‡ There was an additional twist. Jung believed that Freud had withheld the details of a dream because they betrayed an affair between Freud and Minna Bernays, the unmarried sister of

So there was no reversal for Freud, no brake on hierarchy, no putting himself in the patient's shoes. On the contrary, as Sándor Ferenczi, one of his most brilliant and compassionate disciples, noted in a clinical diary he kept toward the end of Freud's life, a diary that wasn't made public until 1985 and was only recently published in English, Freud said, "Patients are a rabble. Patients only serve to provide us with a livelihood and material to learn from." He described Freud as "levitating like some kind of divinity above the poor patient, reduced to the status of a mere child. . . ."[17] Especially in later years, this attitude seemed to engulf his colleagues. As Freud put it, "Does one know today with whom Columbus sailed when he discovered America?"[18]

But there's another aspect here that has been neglected, even by Freud's critics. It goes deeper than a problem of his honesty as a professional. There was no help for the poor guy himself. Never in his life did he seem able to go back and air out the secret compartments of his early life, see that what had happened to him was separable from the experiences of others and perhaps not synonymous with the human condition; no chance to unfreeze the patterns that shaped his view of the world and later became canonized as his theories. Does that seem odd to say about a man who is supposed to be the Big Therapist in the Sky? Listen to Freud quoted by Giovanni Papini, an Italian writer who said he interviewed him five years before his death: "I taught others the virtue of confession and

---

Freud's wife, Martha, who lived in the household, helped with the six children, and often traveled with Freud. Jung said Minna herself had felt guilty and consulted with him about the affair. According to Oskar Rie, a Freud family friend and pediatrician, "For children, Freud went with Martha; for pleasure, he took Minna."[14]

True or not, what's more interesting than the affair—which might turn out to be the most normal thing about Freud—were his Watergate-type efforts to conceal this and other parts of his life, efforts adopted by his followers. Even now, Freud's letters to Minna for the period in question are reported to be mysteriously absent from a numbered sequence at the Library of Congress.[15] In Freud's own time—according to John Kerr's *A Most Dangerous Method*—he and Jung sort of mutually blackmailed each other into a standoff, because the married Jung had an affair with Sabina Spielrein, a patient who was a major influence on Jung. Later, she discussed with Freud becoming his patient, and did become a very personal pipeline of information about Jung. She confirmed his growing independence of Freud's theories—a deviation Freud thought was a son's attempt to kill the father. In fact, his male relationships all seemed to follow his own Oedipal, father-son paradigm. Males who started out as *his* father/mentors were often overthrown with hostility, and Freud himself viewed male followers as loved and obedient sons—until they showed independence. He then turned his vengeance on them, from Adler to Jung, while feeling *they* had victimized *him*. (Didn't I tell you it would be revealing down here?)

have never been able to lay bare my own soul. I wrote a short biography, but more for the purposes of propaganda than anything else. . . . Nobody knows or has even guessed the real secret of my work." * [20] Jung said: "Freud never asked himself why he was compelled to talk continually of sex, why this idea had taken such possession of him. . . . When he spoke of [his sexual theory], his tone became urgent, almost anxious, and all signs of his normally critical and skeptical manner vanished. . . . Apparently neither Freud nor his disciples could understand what it meant for the theory and practice of psychoanalysis if not even the master could deal with his neurosis." [21]

And it's true, he seems never to have asked for or accepted help with any of his array of big-time problems: to name just a few, a need for women's worship, extreme hostility toward his father and father figures in general, a suspicion that any men around him with minds of their own were out to destroy him, and a belief that masturbation and birth control were dangerous but cocaine was just fine.† He went on projecting the fiery outlines of his own experience

* You should know that some say this interview was a hoax. On the other hand, Freud partisans don't seem to think it's bizarre that he said of his "long hard years" of childhood, "I think nothing about them was worth remembering." [19]
† Here's a starter set of a few more: As described in almost every biography, Freud identified with the likes of Hannibal and Alexander the Great, and was depressed when he met anyone whose "impulse, which defies analysis, leads that person to under-estimate me." Why? Because his mother believed her firstborn son, her "Golden Sigi," deserved greatness. As Helen Puner reported in her 1947 biography of Freud, he was the only one of seven children who rated a bedroom of his own; yet he still complained that his sisters' piano practice was disturbing his studies. Though his mother was musical and his five sisters also had talent, he asserted that either the piano went or he did. The piano went—"and with it," as his sister Anna recalled, "all opportunities for his sisters to become musicians." [22] We're talking a major Jewish Prince here. (Or Catholic Prince or whatever—pick your patriarchy.)
   Did Freud, famous self-analyst, examine the narcissism-producing burden of having all his strong mother's ambitions instilled into him? Did he write much about mothers at all? No. He just normalized his own experience. "The only thing that brings a mother undiluted satisfaction is her relation to her son," he wrote. "Even a marriage is not firmly assured until the woman has succeeded in making her husband into her child and acting the part of a mother towards him." [23] As he often stated, mother and son were "the most perfect, easily the most ambivalence-free of all human relationships."
   His endlessly analyzed father-son relationships were all patterned on his hostility to his father—who was distant or worse, depending on what clues you believe. He normalized that too. "Hostility to the father is unavoidable for any boy who has the slightest claim to masculinity." [24] As Jung observed about two cases of Freud's famous propensity to faint, "I was alarmed by the intensity of his fantasies—so strong that, obviously, they could cause him to faint. . . . The fantasy of father-murder was common to both cases." [25] Getting curious? Good.

onto the words and lives of his patients, often turning them into a screen for his theory rather than a source of it. "Anatomy is destiny" could have been joined by "Biography is destiny."[26] That is, Freud treated *his* biography as *our* destiny.

So don't be surprised by the subtitle of Phyllis Freud's biography, or by a certain detective-like quality to the footnotes. After all, we should be more able now to guess what the "real secret" of his work was, and figure out why those "long hard years" were not "worth remembering." More information has become available in the past few years as primary sources have been discovered, and thanks to therapy movements that let us listen to each other instead of to theory, we have a greater understanding of what certain kinds of early wounds tend to look like in later life. Disproving Freud's beliefs has continued as the women's movement has brought women and men one of its most valuable lessons: tell personal truths and challenge general theories. We can laugh and also sympathize.

But to understand that Freud isn't one of the gods who's dead, you have only to pick up a psychology text that still credits "drive theory" (wherein everything is reduced to the urge toward sex or death), or turn on a TV show where women talk about "phallic symbols" (with no idea that there are female symbols of sexual power too), or read that women in pornography or violent marriages "want" to be beaten (with Freud's theory of beating fantasies and female masochism for backup), or notice that even therapists who wouldn't say hello to Freud still behave as if the individual damage they repair is disconnected from what is damaging in society. Even some of his most devoted critics credit him with collective human discoveries as they would nobody else—at least, not without laughter. Marx isn't said to have discovered poverty or class, and we know that Gandhi had many predecessors in nonviolence. Yet Freud is credited with inventing a science called psychoanalysis (which is neither science nor his invention—more like a trademark on a découpage), discovering the unconscious (which is rather like getting the credit for discovering breathing), and bringing sex "out of the closet" (though he put us all in a closet with "SEX" on the door).

Our problem isn't Freud but his existence as a code name for a set of cultural beliefs that serve too deep and convenient a purpose to be easily knocked off. Otherwise, his reputation would have been *bubkes** long ago. But since his persona conjures up so much of the problem, it owes us some of the solution.

So to see how it feels to be on the wrong end of the Freudian myth, as well as to exorcise its power with laughter once and for all, I propose that everyone in the psychology trade, male or female, plus male human beings in general—indeed, all of us in this Freudianized culture—imagine a profession and a society influenced by the work, even the worship, of the greatest, most written about, mythic, and fiercely defended thinker in Western civilization: Dr. Phyllis Freud. Her biographer here is a scholar who has been made somewhat defensive by criticisms of the old matriarch but is still starstruck; has years invested in the Freudian vineyard and isn't about to see them go down the drain; doesn't believe for a minute that anti-Freudian nonsense about childhood sexual abuse being more common than children's desirous fantasies of it; and is confident that serious thinkers see problems as timeless and insoluble, while only superficial ones try to solve them—in other words, the very model of a modern major Freudian.

I can vouch for the fact that everything in Phyllis's life and work springs from something in Sigmund's. Only words having to do with gender have been changed. It may sometimes be anything from painful to impossible to imagine a woman thinking as Freud did, but that should remind us that any imbalance of power can create problems, no matter which way it cuts.† I've added footnotes—a

---

* According to Leo Rosten's *The Joys of Yiddish:* "Something trivial, worthless, insultingly disproportionate to expectations." Don't worry—Freud would have looked down here, too. He was proud that he "never learned or spoke Yiddish." He also wrote *Moses and Monotheism,* in which Moses, with whom Freud greatly identified, turned out to be the illegitimate son of an Egyptian princess, not Jewish at all, and monotheism was an Egyptian creation. (Of course, Freud's mother spoke Yiddish almost exclusively. Hmmm.)

† Here's a recent news item to get you in the mood: " 'It's only natural for the woman to be superior to the man, and it always has been,' says Maria Vazquez, a fruit vendor at the market. 'Isn't it that way everywhere in Mexico?' . . . The people of Juchitan descend from the Zapotec Indians, a tribe whose distaff side is famed among anthropologists for its Amazonian traits. . . . During a railroad strike in the 1950s, women here blocked the tracks and filled their skirts with rocks so the train couldn't pass even if its wheels crushed their bones. . . . As important to Juchitan women's dominance as their physique is their armlock on the local economy. . . . But the iguana trade isn't men's greatest challenge. 'Catching an iguana,' says José Antonio Francisco, 'isn't as hard as catching a wife.' . . . He parks his daughter's stroller in front of the former Juchitan boxing arena. 'The baby won't be disturbed here,' Mr. Francisco says. Indeed, she won't. In a nation of rabid male fight fans, Juchitan is practically the only village of any size without boxing. . . . [Women] are also given to unsolicited and effusive displays of affection toward more diminutive members of the opposite sex. . . . Traffic cop Ricardo Cervantes is also well aware of the ebb and flow of

tribute to a great academic tradition and a story in themselves—
wherever I feared the reader might think Phyllis had gone off the
deep end, or some piece of information seemed to cry out for inclusion, or I just couldn't resist. As in so much of life, the fun is in the
text, and the truth is in the footnotes. Read both.*

My only regret is that Phyllis and Sigmund will never meet.

What If *Freud* Were *Phyllis?* †

I.

If there is anything you do not understand in human life,
consult the works of Dr. Freud.

SHERWOODIA ANDERSON [28]

I*t's* important to understand that when Phyllis was growing
up in Vienna, women were considered superior because of their
ability to give birth. From the family parlor to the great matriarchal
institutions of politics and religion, this was a uniform belief.

---

power in this town. He blocks a busy intersection as a strapping Juchitan woman comes
bobbing along with a case of beer balanced on her head. 'It is a mistake to get in a woman's
way,' he says, 'especially if she's headed for a party.' " [27]

* You can read both together or come back to the footnotes later. To buttress their content,
let me quote *The New York Review of Books,* an intellectual-establishment source no one could
accuse of being feminist. In a November 18, 1993, review, Frederick Crews said new Freud
books reveal: "a figure so radically different from the Freud we thought we knew that readers
may understandably wonder which version comes closer to the truth. But it is really no
contest. Until recently, most people who wrote about Freud in any detail were open partisans of psychoanalysis who needed to safeguard the legend of the scientist-genius-humani-
tarian, and many of the sources they used had already passed through the censorship of a
jealously secretive psychoanalytic establishment, whose leaders have been so fearful of open
historical judgment that they have locked away large numbers of Freud's papers and letters
in the Library of Congress for periods extending ahead as far as the twenty-second century.
. . . Some sensitive documents, having already served their Sleeping Beauty sentences, make
their way into the light."

† OR
THE WATERGATE OF THE WESTERN WORLD

Though she was a genius who was to tower above all others in enlightenment, she was, of course, a product of her time.*

Women's superior position in society was so easily mistaken for an immutable fact of life that males had developed exaggerated versions of such inevitable but now somewhat diminished conditions as *womb envy.*† Indeed, these beliefs in women's natural right to dominate were the very pillars of Western matriarchal civilization—impossible to weaken without endangering the edifice. At the drop of a hat, wise women would explain that while men might dabble imitatively in the arts, they could never become truly *great* painters, sculptors, musicians, poets, or anything else that demanded originality, for they lacked a womb, the very source of originality.‡ Similarly, since men had only odd, castrated breasts which created no

---

* Sound familiar? Here are some other realities of Freud's era: George Sand was born a half century before him and lived a life far more free and unconventional than did Freud himself. U.S. suffragists had issued the Declaration of Sentiments at Seneca Falls eight years before Freud was born. The Free Love Movement—a serious revolt against marriage or any institution that coerced sex—was a public event when Freud began his career. Austrian suffragists, socialists, and reformers were working on everything from women's political rights to organizing workers and prostitutes—as were their counterparts in other countries—and there was an active movement for homosexual rights. Emma Goldman, the anarchist and feminist, was almost Freud's exact contemporary. When she went to talk with him about this new invention called "psychoanalysis," she found it "nothing but the old confessional."

† Modern Freudians *still* won't give up on penis envy. Here are Freud popularizers Lucy Freeman and Dr. Herbert S. Strean in their 1987 book, *Freud & Women:* "Contemporary psychoanalysts . . . agree penis envy is a universal fantasy of little girls at the age of four. . . . If a little girl's emotional needs are understood by a loving mother and protective father, the normal fantasies of penis envy that occur during her phallic stage of sexual development will be accepted, then suppressed . . . and she will be able to love a man not for the physical attribute which, as a little girl, she envied and unconsciously wished to possess, but out of her feelings for him as a total person. She will want him not as a possessor of the desired phallus, but as mate and father of her child. In Freud's words, her original wish for a penis has changed into the wish for a baby."

Here's a professional view on penis envy from the *Psychiatric Dictionary,* Oxford University Press, 1981: "Freud says that when the little girl realizes she has no penis, she reacts either by hoping that some day she will have one or by denying that she does not have one. In the latter case she may be 'compelled to behave as though she were a man.' . . . The wish for the penis is transformed into the wish for a child. 'With this object in view, she takes her father as a love-object. Her mother becomes the object of jealousy.' Advocates of the feminist movement have correctly pointed out . . . the androcentric bias of psychoanalytic theory. . . . No wholly satisfactory substitute has yet been developed, however, in part because of the difficulty of revising assumptions about such concepts as penis-envy without calling into question all of drive theory. At the present time, the clinician is likely to adopt a 'Wait and see' attitude."

Waiting for what?

‡ "A sculptress loses her skill when confronted with the task of modeling the male body," explained Sigmund to the Vienna Psychoanalytic Society, "a girl whom her teacher embraces whenever she successfully accomplishes a task cannot achieve anything anymore." [29]

sustenance, they might become adequate family cooks—provided they followed recipes, of course—but certainly could never become great chefs, vintners, herbalists, nutritionists, or anything else that required a flair for food, a knowledge of nutrition, or an instinct for gustatory nuance. And because childbirth caused women to use the medical system more than men did, making childbirth its natural focus, there was little point in encouraging young men to become physicians, surgeons, researchers, or anything other than nurses and other low-paid health care helpers.*

Even designing their own clothes could be left to men only at the risk of repetitive results. When allowed to dress themselves, they seldom could get beyond an envy of wombs and female genitals, which restricted them to an endless succession of female sexual symbols. Thus, the open button-to-neck "V" of men's jackets was a well-known recapitulation of the "V" of female genitalia; the knot in men's ties replicated the clitoris, while the long ends of the tie were clearly meant to represent the labia. As for men's bow ties, they were the clitoris *erecta* in all its glory. All these were, to use Phyllis Freud's technical term, "representations." †

Of course, one can understand why men would not choose to replicate their own symbols—chicken necks, bits of rope, dumbbells, cigarillos, spring potatoes, kumquats, belfries, and the like—but instead would choose to admire the glories of cathedrals, stadia, and mammoth caves, the ocean, the sky, and other representations of the womb, as well as to replicate the exquisite jewel of the clitoris in the ties that were the only interesting feature of their dress. Nonetheless,

* Women *do* use the health care system about 30 percent more than men do—but you'd never know it from who's in charge. Logic is in the eye of the logician.

† "In her unconscious envy of the penis, many a woman adorns herself with feathers, sequins, furs, glistening silver and gold ornaments that 'hang down'—what psychoanalysts call 'representations' of the penis," explain Freeman and Strean.

   Other phallic symbols, as listed by Freud in *The Interpretation of Dreams*: "Sticks, umbrellas, posts, trees* . . . objects which share with the thing they represent the characteristic of penetrating into the body and injuring—thus, sharp *weapons* of every kind, *knives, daggers, spears, sabres,* but also firearms, *rifles, pistols* and *revolvers* . . . *water-taps, watering-cans,* or *fountains*—or again by other objects which are capable of being lengthened, such as hanging-lamps, extensible pencils . . . *pencils, pen-holders, nail-files, hammers* . . . The remarkable characteristic of the male organ which enables it to rise up in defiance of the laws of gravity . . . leads to its being represented symbolically by *balloons, flying-machines* and most recently *zeppelin airships*. But dreams can symbolize erection in . . . the sexual organ as the essence of the dreamer's whole person and make him himself *fly*. . . . Among the less easily understandable male sexual symbols are certain *reptiles* and *fishes,* and above all the famous symbol of the *snake* . . . [also] *hats* and *overcoats* or *cloaks* . . . *the foot or the hand*. . . ."

you can also understand why stylish husbands of the well-to-do, or wife-hunting young bachelors of the upper classes, preferred to be well dressed by talented *female* designers.*

Clearly, men's imitativeness did not include modesty; on the contrary. As Phyllis Freud was to write decades later in "Masculinity," her great synthesis of a lifetime of learning about male patients: "The effect of womb envy has a share, further, in the physical vanity of men, since they are bound to value their charms more highly as a late compensation for their original sexual inferiority."[31]

In addition, men's lack of firsthand experience with birth and nonbirth—with choosing between existence and nonexistence, conception and contraception, as women must do so wisely for all their fertile years—severely inhibited their potential for developing a sense of justice and ethics.† This tended to disqualify them as philosophers, whose purview was the "to be or not to be" issue, the deepest question of existence versus nonexistence, that dominates serious human discourse. Practically speaking, it also lessened men's ability to make life-and-death judgments, which explained their absence from decisionmaking positions in the judiciary, law enforcement, the military, and other such professions. True, one or two exceptional men might ascend to a position requiring high moral judgment, but they had been trained to "think like a woman" by rare contact with academia or because they had no sisters and their mothers were forced to burden their tender sons with matriarchal duties.

Finally, as Phyllis Freud's clinical findings showed, males were inclined toward meanness and backbiting, the inevitable result of having been cut off from the coveted sources of life and fulfillment to which their mates had such ready access within their bodies. As she wrote: "The fact that men must be regarded as having little sense

* Sigmund cited a few female symbols: anything "enclosing a hollow space which can take something into itself." Also *wood* and *paper*. "Among animals, *snails and mussels* . . . among parts of the body, the *mouth* (as substitute for the genital orifice); among buildings, *churches* and *chapels*."

It's OK if none of this makes sense. According to Freud, symbols allowed psychoanalysts "to interpret a dream without questioning the dreamer, who indeed would in any case have nothing to tell us about the symbol."[30]

† Which makes more sense than Sigmund's conclusion at the age of seventy-six, in "New Introductory Lectures": "We also regard women as weaker in their social interests and as having less capacity for sublimating their instincts than men." This assumption that women were incapable of reaching the highest stage of ethical development—which was, in masculinist thought, the subordination of the individual to an abstract principle—became the foundation of the field of ethics. For an antidote, see Carol Gilligan's *In a Different Voice*.

of justice is no doubt related to the predominance of envy in their mental life; for the demand for justice is a modification of envy and lays down the condition subject to which one can put envy aside."[32]

After life-giving wombs and sustenance-giving breasts, women's ability to menstruate was the most obvious proof of their superiority. Only women could bleed without injury or death; only they rose from the gore each month like a phoenix; only their bodies were in tune with the ululations of the universe and the timing of the tides. Without this innate lunar cycle, how could men have a sense of time, tides, space, seasons, movement of the universe, or the ability to measure anything at all? How could men mistress the skills of measurement necessary for mathematics, engineering, architecture, surveying—and so many other professions? In Christian churches, how could males, lacking monthly evidence of Her death and resurrection, serve the Daughter of the Goddess? In Judaism, how could they honor the Matriarch without the symbol of Her sacrifices recorded in the Old Ovariment? Thus insensible to the movements of the planets and the turning of the universe, how could men become astronomers, naturalists, scientists—or much of anything at all?*

Certainly, careers in business or politics were out of the question. In the Austria of Phyllis Freud's day, men were not allowed a university education and studied only informally as their limited capacity permitted. ("How wise our educators," Phyllis said with her customary courtliness while still a student, "that they pester the handsome sex so little with scientific knowledge!!"[33]) Later, when she visited the United States, she mourned the overeducation of its males, for such intellectual activity could only keep them from assuaging their womb envy by attaching themselves to a woman ("wombed-one," as Freud explained etymologically) and raising the

---

* Sounds pretty good, doesn't it? But Freud never explored the impact of menstruation. He briefly discussed menopause as a time of increased anxiety. Why? Because fear of pregnancy was past, this increased libido in women, and libido was masculine, so *voilà!* an anxious woman. Otherwise, he was only interested in transferring pleasure from the clitoris to the vagina. Perhaps what interested him about *our* anatomy was the part he saw as *his* destiny. Fairness obligates me to admit that males have cycles too. Indeed, everything from dogs to carrots has lunar and diurnal cycles. If men were allowed to celebrate this evidence of interdependence with all living things—instead of covering it with expensive facades of autonomy, control, dominance, and other trappings necessary to keep male-dominant systems going—they could ditch some of that rocklike masculinity. If such a possibility seems too far off to help with antimenstruation bias right now, try this argument: Since in women's "difficult" days before the onset of the menstrual period, the female hormone is at its lowest ebb, women are in those few days most like men all month long.

fruits of *her* womb.* (Even today, many authorities agree with Freud that the high U.S. divorce rate proves the accuracy of her perception. Now that many scholars steeped in "the Freudian family romance" have explained that the cause of crime is not poverty but the breakdown of the nuclear, matriarchal family, even non-Freudians admit that the epidemic of single fathers and working fathers is a danger. After all, if men leave the home, who *will* raise the children? Those who bear them were obviously not intended to raise them, else one sex would be doing all the work. That wouldn't be fair, would it? But I digress.†) In Phyllis Freud's simpler time—for which, if truth be told, even many men feel nostalgia—males were not permitted to engage in commerce, go to court, supervise their households, or educate their children without the permission of their wives or mothers.

Beyond their clear biological, womb-acquiring need to raise children, there were few natural professions for men, but Phyllis Freud, always generous in comparison with other women of her unenlightened era, championed those that had any anatomical basis at all. Work related to fire was one. As she elucidated, men had originally

---

* To Leonhard Blumgart, an American analysand who had dared to become engaged just as he would have to be separated from his fiancée for his analysis with Freud himself, the master wrote: "You Americans are peculiar people. None of you has ever found the right attitude toward your women."[34] At seventy-eight, he told Joseph Wortis, a U.S. psychoanalyst: " 'American women are an anti-cultural phenomenon. They have nothing but conceit to make up for their uselessness. You have a real rule of women in America. You young men go to college with girls, fall in love and marry at an age when the girls are usually much more mature than the men. They lead the men around by the nose, make fools of them, and the result is matriarchy. That is why marriage is so unsuccessful in America—that is why your divorce rate is so high. Your average American man approaches marriage without any experience at all. You wouldn't expect a person to step up to an orchestra and play first fiddle without some training, but the American man steps into marriage without the least experience for so complicated a business. In Europe, things are different. Men take the lead. That is as it should be.'

"Here the browbeaten American meekly inquired: 'But don't you think that it would be best if both partners were equal?'

" 'That,' Freud said, 'is a practical impossibility. There must be inequality, and the superiority of the man is the lesser of two evils.' "[35]

A product of his time? Jung made the same trip to the United States, and wrote home, "Men are as well off here as culture permits; women badly off."

† Of course, it was industrialization that took the father out of the home, made him the sole wage earner, and created the nuclear family. For almost all of human history, the family has been extended and communal—which it still is in many agricultural cultures. Personally, I think we should call the nuclear, two-parent family "the broken family." Men should raise children. Communities should raise children. As the African proverb says: "It takes a whole village to raise a child." But I digress.

learned to put out fire by peeing on it, but in order "to renounce the homosexually tinged desire to extinguish it by a stream of urine,"* they had to learn to control fire in other ways. No wonder little boys loved to play at cooking over fires, and men so often gathered around the campfire while women went hunting. No wonder pyromaniacs were overwhelmingly males who had been frightened early in life by seeing a woman urinate in a way that made it seem only females could withstand the heat of peeing directly on a fire, and no wonder the word "faggot" denoted "firewood" as well as "male homosexual." (It's a continuing tribute to Freud's genius that her insights can be made to explain so much of life and language.)

Weaving was the second naturally male profession she identified. Freud wrote: "It seems that men have made few contributions to the discoveries and inventions in the history of civilization; there is, however, one technique which they may have invented—that of plaiting and weaving. . . . Nature himself would seem to have given the model which this achievement imitates by causing the growth at maturity of the pubic hair that conceals the genitals." Obviously, the male's unsightly penile extension of the clitoris, and the low-hanging testicles which had descended, quite literally, from the ovaries, were in dire need of some camouflage. This led naturally to the masculine talent for weaving. As Freud explained: "Shame, which is considered to be a masculine characteristic *par excellence* . . . has as its purpose, we believe, concealment of this genital unsightliness." But she generously gave men credit for the creative contribution that this endemic shame had forced them to make: "The step that remained to be taken lay in making the threads adhere to one another, while on the body they stick into the skin and are only matted together." † [36]

Given such a powerful wedding of anatomy and aphorism, circumstance and common sense, we can see why Phyllis grew up believing that men's deepest satisfactions lay in manual labor, housekeeping, child care, and, among the upper classes, the social graces of embroidering or playing simple tunes upon the piano. We can understand why Freud herself, a serious matriarch, eschewed such

---

* Straight from an essay written by a seventy-six-year-old Sigmund Freud, "The Acquisition of Power Over Fire": "There can be no doubt about . . . flames as the phallus. . . . The attempt to extinguish fire by means of his own water signified a pleasurable struggle with another phallus." Could you make this stuff up?

† Except for the gender reversals, straight from Sigmund's *Introductory Lectures*. (If you're curious, the words that are reversed, and all the Sigmund references of these immortal Phyllis quotes, are in the numbered end notes.)

male frivolity as music, and clapped her hands over her ears whenever she heard it.* Or why she was not surprised when men among the lower classes so often became prostitutes or—the next thing to it—actors. It was simply accepted for males to be homemakers, ornaments, devoted sons, and sexual companions (providing they were well trained, of course, for though abortion was an honored rite of passage, it was painful and to be avoided; thus, a careless impregnation could be punished by imprisonment).

We can already see that Phyllis Freud's genius was leading her far beyond her training as a nineteenth-century neurologist. Fascinated as she would be for her entire life by "the psychological consequences of anatomical distinctions"—provided, of course, they were of the genital variety—she was able to both perceive and aphorize such consequences brilliantly. Nonetheless, insights into such universal problems as the *womb envy* and *clitoris envy* that limited males, and the *penis anxiety* and *breast-castration anxiety* that haunted even females—whose greatest fear was of becoming males—these would not be her greatest contributions to science. They were already part of the culture, and she had only done the service of giving them a scientific rationale. No, her heroine's journey began with her interest in and treatment of *testyria,* a disease marked by uncontrollable fits of emotion and mysterious physical symptoms, which was so peculiar and common to males that most experts assumed it to be related to the testicles. (Hence its name. You may find it easier to pronounce in its modern spelling, *testeria,* but I have chosen its original nineteenth-century version, with a *y,* in keeping with the Freudian spirit.) It was only while attending lectures in the great asylums of Paris, where she had gone in the hope of alleviating the sufferings of humanity,† that she discovered a few *female* testyrics, who also shared these bizarre and apparently nonorganic symptoms.

* Even Sigmund's worshipful biographer Ernest Jones admits, "Freud's aversion to music was one of his well-known characteristics. One well remembers the pained expression on his face on entering a restaurant or beer garden where there was a band and how quickly his hands would go over his ears. . . ." Just as his sisters had no musical education as a result, neither did Freud's sons and daughters.[37] Some say he liked only *Don Giovanni.*

† As a twenty-nine-year-old physician about to study hypnosis with Jean-Martin Charcot, Sigmund wrote to his fiancée that he would "go to Paris and become a great scholar and then return to Vienna with a huge, enormous halo . . . and I will cure all the incurable nervous cases."[38]

Nonetheless, males made up the huge majority of testyrics. The low regard in which they were held, and their natural status as the more emotional sex, plus the lack of any apparent organic cause for the disease, meant they were often seen as perverse, pretending, or otherwise untreatable—indeed, many medical matriarchs felt victimized and exploited by unruly testyrical patients—but some treatments had been devised. They ranged from simple water cures, bed rest, mild electric shock, and, for the well-to-do, trips to a spa, to circumcision, the removal of the testicles, cauterization of the penis, penisectomy, and other remedies that may seem draconian now but were sometimes oddly successful.* In Paris, Phyllis Freud had also been among the hundreds of women who assembled in lecture halls to see demonstrations of hypnosis—a new technique for treating these mysterious symptoms by reaching into the unconscious—on young and often oddly appealing male testyrics, who were clad in short hospital gowns and brought over from the wards for the purpose. Under hypnosis, they often revealed bizarre fantasies, usually of a sexual nature, which increased the interest of the assembled matriarchs—though, of course, all in the advancement of science.†

What Phyllis Freud had seen in Paris coalesced in her mind with a case of testyria she had heard about in Vienna. An older neurologist colleague, Dr. Josephine Breuer, had discussed her progress in relieving testyrical symptoms by encouraging a patient to explore the memories of earlier painful experiences with which they seemed to be associated—first with the aid of hypnosis, later by just asking for associations to specific symptoms and past events. Actually, this "talking cure" had been improvised and named by the young patient

* For original documents of the period on the sadistic treatment of female patients—from electrical shocks to clitoridectomy and other sex-related surgeries—see Jeffrey Masson's *A Dark Science: Women, Sexuality and Psychiatry in the Nineteenth Century*. For this tradition as adapted in the less surgical Freudian era, see Phyllis Chesler's *Women and Madness*. For the long tradition of treating nonconforming women as "mad," see Elaine Showalter, *The Female Malady: Women, Madness, and English Culture 1830–1980*. Women's own stories of being put in mental institutions as a form of divorce, to take over their property, etc., have been collected and edited by Jeffrey L. Geller and Maxine Harris in *Women of the Asylum: The Unheard Voices of America's Madwomen*.

† A famous painting by Brouillet of such a "Clinical Lesson" shows a large group of men in black frock coats and beards looking on as Charcot demonstrates hypnosis on a beautiful young woman—almost bare-bosomed for no reason, in the best style of a modern advertisement—supported by his arm around her waist as she leans backward in a semiconscious state, all light from the window focused on her blushing skin. Freud hung a copy in his waiting room.

in question, Bert Pappenheim—later to become famous as "Andy O." in his case history—the attractive son of a wealthy family, whom Breuer herself admitted to be "a powerful intellect."

Freud had found Pappenheim interesting on several counts. His strong and inappropriate desire to study at the university, as his younger sister had done, was evidence of classic womb envy. His incapacitating symptoms, which ranged from a chronic cough and near blindness to guilt, shame, humiliation, and a sudden inability to speak German, the language of his childhood, even a suicide gesture—all brought on by his faithful filial attendance at the bedside of his mother while she suffered a long and eventually fatal illness—were classic symptoms of testyria. Indeed, he even evidenced two distinct personalities, neither of which remembered the activities of the other. (Here, some readers may wonder if this is "dissociation" or even "multiple personality disorder," a so-called splitting into separate ego states as the result of extreme child abuse, which anti-Freudians now describe when trying to convince the mental health professions that such sexual and other severe child abuse is more common than any rational woman could credit. Let me make clear: There was *no such evidence in this case*.) Finally, Freud was fascinated with this cure that had been accomplished simply by delving into the mind, often uncovering sexual things: a process to which she herself had always felt mysteriously drawn.

Breuer's success with this case was to become the raw material that Phyllis Freud metamorphosed into her own creation of psychoanalysis—as you will see in any account of Freud's pioneering years.* For her, it was ovarian in many ways. First, her ability to

---

* You probably will. But in the 1970s, Henri Ellenberger, historian of psychiatry, found the records of Bertha Pappenheim's several relapses in a Swiss sanitarium. Since her case history wasn't published until fourteen years *after* her supposedly successful treatment, there was plenty of time to learn this. Even a year after Pappenheim's treatment ended, Freud had written to his fiancée Martha that Breuer said Bertha was still suffering so much that he wished she would die and be released. [39]

To un-reverse this "seminal" saga: Bertha Pappenheim (known as "Anna O." in the case history from which her identity was guessed) experienced these devastating symptoms and was treated by Josef Breuer, an older and admired colleague of Sigmund Freud's. Though she was already suffering from a "monotonous family life and the absence of adequate intellectual occupation," according to Breuer, who respected and believed this intelligent twenty-one-year-old, her devastating physical symptoms developed during the illness of her father, whose bedside she served as a night nurse in a way that seems to have uncovered terrors—of what, we don't know. (Breuer hints: "As I knew, she had felt very much offended over something and had determined not to speak about it. . . . I have suppressed a large number of quite interesting details. . . .") We do learn that she was devoted to and/or

absorb so much about another physician's patient, whom she herself had never treated, showed her talent for creative listening and globalizing individual experiences that would become a keystone of her career. Second, the case indicated Phyllis Freud's unique willingness to look male sexuality in the eye, as it were, for Breuer herself was said by Freud to have abandoned Bert Pappenheim during his treatment, out of shock at his sexual revelations, so inappropriate for a well-bred young man.* Finally, the fourteen years that elapsed between the end of Bert Pappenheim's treatment and Freud's persuasion of Breuer to write up and publish his case history as "Andy O." —published in *Studies on Testyria,*[44] a book under their joint byline —was evidence of Freud's patience and devotion in bringing out the truth.†

---

obsessed with her father; that she had never been in love and that "sexuality was astonishingly undeveloped in her"; that she grew literally ill with guilt at wanting to leave his bedside when she heard music that evoked her love for dancing; and that she actually grew "calmer" after her father's death.[40]

Breuer did indeed first glimpse the cathartic and healing power of digging out and talking about painful memories from this charismatic young woman, who invented the "talking cure" that Breuer told Freud about. In spite of relapses and continued suffering, Bertha Pappenheim became an advocate, activist, and journalist who worked for the rights of exploited women and girls. She was especially concerned with the plight of Jewish females and traveled to Russia and the Middle East to expose the importing of girls for sexual slavery. (As she is often quoted: "If there will be justice in the world to come, women will be lawgivers and men will have to have babies.") After her death, she was the subject of a postage stamp and many international tributes for her pioneering work. She remained an implacable foe of Freud and his uses of her "talking cure."[41]

Nonetheless, Pappenheim remained a success to Freud. "That is the way Freud's mind worked," as his follower Ernest Jones wrote. "When he got hold of a simple but significant fact, he would feel, and know, that it was an example of something general or universal, and the idea of collecting statistics on the matter was alien to him."[42]

* By the official Ernest Jones account, Bertha Pappenheim, or "Anna O.," had so shocked Josef Breuer by referring to her pains as giving birth to his baby that he abandoned her as a patient. The idea was that Breuer lacked Freud's courage to confront sexual matters, and that he treated no other such cases. Actually, Bertha decided to end treatment, and Breuer treated others similarly afflicted. Freud also said that Breuer then went off with his wife— who had been jealous of his seeing this attractive patient every day—and conceived a child. In fact, the child in question was born *before* Bertha's treatment.[43] Thus, Freud has emerged in history as the hero of a case that wasn't his, a cure that wasn't a cure, and a patient who condemned him.

† Josef Breuer called Bertha Pappenheim's experience "the germ cell of the whole of psychoanalysis." Too bad he wasn't ambitious enough to take up this experience, instead of Freud. The same contemporaries who commented on Freud's dogmatism also commented on Breuer's humanity.[45] Read the first two *Studies on Hysteria*—"Anna O.," by Josef Breuer, and "Frau Emmy von N.," by Freud—and it's all there in their own words. Breuer emerges as a kind, intelligent man who may not have disclosed or understood everything but helped a respected patient find her own way into healing memories. Freud comes across as a self-

Of course, Pappenheim later descended into noisy masculinism, which supported Phyllis Freud's diagnosis of womb envy. Though contributing to matriarchal scientific advances would have been honor enough for most young men, Pappenheim had the temerity to be angry when he was recognizable as "Andy O." As a "rescuer" of "exploited" young boys, he even refused to have them psychoanalyzed and insisted that "Psychoanalysis in the hands of the physician is what confession is in the hands of the Catholic priest,"[46] events best interpreted as evidence of his unrequited passion for Josephine Breuer and his feelings of rejection when the attractive older woman abandoned him as a patient.* Finally, Pappenheim's work against the alleged sexual exploitation of young boys ignored the fact that, as Phyllis Freud's theory of infantile sexuality had by then proven in such a revolutionary way, many of those supposed sexual attacks had been desired, invited, or fantasized by the little boys in question.

. . .

important man who announced his devotion to his patient but used the standard hypnotic technique to cover up memories ("My therapy consists in wiping away these pictures . . ."), to play post-hypnotic tricks (he got her to order red wine, when she didn't drink), and to give her a suggestion that she could be hypnotized by no one else. He noted that he had to give her permission to be hypnotized by the *next* doctor—to whom "Frau Emmy" gave "the same performance."

So why, under hypnosis, had "Frau Emmy" kept crying out, "Keep still!—Don't say anything!—Don't touch me!"? Why had she identified with the report of a murdered boy and felt terror at the sight of animals? Why had she seemed desperate for approval yet been described by a daughter as a "cruel and ruthless tyrant"? Why would Freud believe his patients for only one brief period—but otherwise avoid real events? Stay tuned.

* Think there's some exaggeration here? When asked if one of the abused girls she worked with should be taken to a psychoanalyst, Bertha Pappenheim replied: "Never! Not as long as I am alive!" Do modern Freudians accept that as a rational response to her betrayal by Breuer, who, under pressure from Freud, finally wrote the case history in which she was recognized? Nope. They believe Freud's story about Breuer's breaking off her treatment, and treat her as a spurned woman. "Undoubtedly," observe Freeman and Strean, "this was a reaction to her rejection by Breuer."[47]

Was Pappenheim's interest in exploited girls due to their *actual* exploitation? No again. According to Freeman and Strean, Bertha "became interested in volunteer social work, and raised funds to build her own institution for the care of delinquent, retarded, and pregnant, unwed girls and their babies. She obviously identified with the pregnant, unwed girl—as she had experienced herself with Breuer."

Here is a non-Freudian view of Bertha Pappenheim, from a colleague quoted in *Freud's Women*, by Appignanesi and Forrester: "A volcano lived in this woman. . . . She only fought about things that were directly involved in her goals. . . . Her fight against the abuse of women was almost a physically felt pain for her."

It was Phyllis Freud's interest in the success of the "talking cure," plus her experience in that Paris lecture hall, that led to her courageous decision to focus on testyria when she began to practice in the study of the Vienna apartment she took with Martin, her new bridegroom. Though latter-day male liberationists have implied that the large pool of testyrical sons in wealthy families was an economic motive—and though it's true that Freud abandoned research when promotions weren't forthcoming and decided on clinical work for economic reasons; after all, she had kept her fiancé waiting for five years—those concerned with the suffering of male patients should be grateful for her emphasis on less painful, nonsurgical remedies for testyrical sufferings.*

And sufferings there were. They included depression, hallucinating, and an array of ailments, from paralysis, incapacitating headaches, chronic vomiting and coughing, and difficulty in swallowing, to full-scale testyrical fits, imitation pregnancies, and self-injury that included "couvade," or slitting the skin of the penis, an extreme form of womb and menstruation envy that imitated such female biological events.† Even as Freud worked first with hypnosis, then more and more with psychoanalysis (for she had given Bert Pappenheim's "talking cure" a new and scientific name,‡ thus honoring this obscure young man), she theorized about what might be the cause.

Because testyria was particularly common among young men in their teens and twenties, she surmised that homemaking, child rearing, sexual service, sperm production, and other activities in men's natural sphere had not yet yielded their mature satisfactions. Since some young men were also indulging in the dangerous practice of masturbation, they were subject to severe neurosis and sexual dys-

---

* Actually, Sigmund complained that his "therapeutic arsenal contained only two weapons, electro-therapy and hypnotism, for prescribing a visit to a hydropathic establishment after a single consultation was an inadequate source of income."[48] As for nonsurgical, we'll see.

† OK, so I couldn't resist *couvade,* a pregnancy-imitating ritual among men in tribal cultures where pregnancy and birth are worshiped. Women have been made out to be the "naturally" masochistic ones in patriarchal cultures, but doesn't slitting the penis sound pretty masochistic to you? In the case of Freud and his colleagues, the self-cutting and other mutilations they were seeing in their practices sound exactly like what has now been traced to the real events of sexual and other sadistic abuse in childhood: females (and males when they are similarly abused) repeat what was done to them, punish the body that "attracted" or "deserved" such abuse, and anesthetize themselves against pain by dissociating, just as they learned to do to survive the sadistic abuse.

‡ By the time of his *Complete Introductory Lectures,* Freud was defining psychoanalysis as nothing less than "the medical treatment of neurotic patients."

function per se. Among those slightly older and more rebellious or intellectual men, there was also the problem of being too aggressive and womb-envying to attract a mate. Finally, there were the numerous young husbands who were married to women who practiced coitus interruptus as a form of contraception or simple disregard.*

As more young men came to recline on her couch for the increasingly fashionable though not yet respectable process of psychoanalysis, she was impressed with the potential and importance of this work, for, as she observed, "The sexual business attracts people." † 51 Except for an occasional powerful woman whom she diagnosed as "obsessional" or "paranoic," an even rarer female with testyria, and a few poor men whom Freud saw as research subjects, most of her patients were the sons of powerful matriarchs who were grateful for her help with their intelligent but strangely rebellious sons and, it should be said, who could afford her often daily sessions.‡ These patients included a grateful young married man who gave her an elegant leather-covered couch. (Asking patients to lie down was a holdover from electro-galvanic massage and similar treatments Phyllis Freud had tried before—not necessary, of course, but she imagined these upper-middle-class men reclining all day doing nothing, and wanted to make them feel at home. It was such sensitive consideration that led to the now famous innovation of sitting *behind* the patient, thus allowing him [or her] to focus on his [or her] own

* Interesting—this one works both ways. Since coitus interruptus could be defined as *interruptus* by whichever half of the pair has finished *coitus*—if you see what I mean—it needs no reversal. Anyway, Sigmund, one of the more sexually frustrated young men on record, had been knocked out in Paris when Jean-Martin Charcot and other famous experts openly attributed many hysterical and other female problems to a lack of sex. One even talked about prescribing *"penis normalis,* regularly applied." 49 Of course, this may have been their version of "all she needs is a good fuck"—a tragic remedy if the problem was childhood sexual abuse —but hey, in the land of the frustrated, the sexually obsessed is king.

† Gratifying for a guy who had written to his fiancée: "I consider it a great misfortune that Nature has not granted me that indefinite something which attracts people. I believe it is this lack more than any other that has deprived me of a rosy existence." 50

‡ Sigmund's daughter Anna, the youngest of six children born in eight years, came to resent these rich patients for taking up even the family's summer vacations. As she said, "Just let all millionairesses stay crazy, they don't have anything else to do." 52 Freud required each patient to lease one of his hours and thus to pay whether she (or he) used it or not. However, current Freud biographer Peter Gay assures us: "Freud's dislike of financial compromises had more than the analyst's affluence in view; such compromises endanger the continuity and intensity of the patient's analytic involvement by encouraging resistance. If an analysand falls ill with an ailment that is authentically organic, the analyst should break off the analysis, dispose of the hour, and take the patient back, after his [*sic*] recovery, as soon as time is available."

process of free association.*) The bright and vivacious son of a titled family was so grateful for Phyllis Freud's willingness to listen that he donated a painting to the University of Vienna, thus securing for her a prestigious professorship; an event that might seem out of place now but was well justified then, for the appointment had been delayed by resistance to Freud's revolutionary ideas as well as by anti-Semitism.†

(For the sake of accuracy, I correct here one false conception in the countless representations of the historic analytic setting: the analyst sitting with a notebook. Phyllis Freud herself never took notes, and her brilliant case histories were miracles of memory. As biographer Petra Gay explained, she "cautioned analysts against taking notes during the session, since doing so would only distract their attention. Besides, they could trust their memories to retain what they needed." [55])

Extreme gratitude from her male patients was understandable. Not only was Freud the rare woman who listened *even to men,* but she took what they said seriously, allowed it to become the stuff of her own brilliant theories, even of science. This advanced attitude joins other evidence in exposing the gratuitous womb-envying hostility of masculinists who accuse Phyllis Freud of androphobia.‡ As a young woman, Phyllis had even translated into German the text of Harriet Taylor Mill's *The Subjection of Men,* a tract on male equality that a less enlightened woman would surely have disregarded.§

* As Sigmund Freud put it: "I cannot stand being stared at eight hours a day (or longer) by others." The couch was given to him by a patient named Madame Benvenisti.[53] Of such stuff legends are made.

† This could become a little movie called *The Painting.* Some folks defend Freud's honor by saying the young woman's gift didn't cost enough to be a bribe by Vienna standards. Others say it was the whole ball game. Freud himself said that if this baroness patient had contributed a better painting, "I would have been appointed three months earlier."[54] According to Frank Sulloway's well-researched account in *Freud: Biologist of the Mind,* the questions raised about Freud's work were legitimate and the appointment took only an average length of time. What all Freud's biographers admit, with varying degrees of emphasis, is that it took him an unusual seven and a half years to get through medical school. On the other hand, anti-Semitism was real. Better wait for the movie.

‡ OK, maybe it's not perfect, but you try making up a word for man-hating—also try figuring out why there's no accepted term for the reverse of misogyny.

§ Freud picked up a little extra money by translating John Stuart Mill's *The Subjection of Women* while doing peacetime military service. Thus, he was exposed to ideas of equality early—and rejected them. As he wrote to Martha: "a main argument in the pamphlet I translated was that the married woman can earn as much as the husband. I dare say we agree that housekeeping and the care and education of children claim the whole person and practically rule out any profession; even if simplified conditions relieve the woman of house-

Later, she supported the idea that men could also become psychoanalysts—provided, of course, they believed in Freudian theory and
carried out Freudian practice, just as any female analyst must do.
(Certainly, Freud would not have approved of the current school of
equality that demands "men's history" and other special treatment.)
In her mature life, she was exceptional in her willingness to surround
herself with intelligent and interesting men.* Finally, I'm sure that
if you read carefully each one of Freud's case histories, you will see
the true depth of understanding for the opposite sex.†

Moreover, one can always see women's attitudes toward men in
the way they treat their husbands. It is remarked upon in almost all
biographies that Phyllis Freud was devoted to Martin, who kept the
apartment and the six children quiet for his wife's work, which he so

---

keeping, dusting, cleaning, cooking, etc. All this he simply forgot, just as he omitted all
relations connected with sex. . . . Am I to think of my delicate sweet girl as a competitor?
. . . The position of woman cannot be other than what it is: to be an adored sweetheart in
youth, and a beloved wife in maturity." What especially annoyed Freud was Mill's comparison of sex to race. As Freud wrote: "Any girl, even without a vote and legal rights, whose
hand is kissed by a man willing to risk his all for her love, could have put him right on
this."⁵⁶ (If you're wondering why I reversed John to Harriet, it's because Harriet Taylor was
Mill's wife, who collaborated on this book and rarely gets credit. I couldn't resist.)

* Sigmund did support women's entry into psychoanalytic circles. He even gave each one a
special ring—which is less Bride-of-Christ than it sounds; he gave rings to his inner circle of
male disciples too. Especially in his later life, he was surrounded by intelligent women. The
problem was not the form but the content. For one thing, they usually had to be beautiful.
(When Jung took an old woman as a patient, Freud said he didn't know how Jung could
keep looking at this ugly creature.) For another, female adulation was his refuge from male
competition. Furthermore, it seemed only normal to him that women were required to
subscribe to theories of their own denigration and incompleteness in order to become
analysts or to win his approval. Any dissent was attributed to penis envy, even if the dissenter
—Karen Horney, for instance—was challenging penis envy.

No wonder there weren't many other dissenters. Instead, there were women patients like
Hilda Doolittle (the poet "H.D."), who compared Freud as a healer to Jesus Christ in public
(even though she criticized him in private, as her biographer Susan Sanford has pointed
out); women analysts like Helene Deutsch, who espoused female masochism and conve-
niently resented her mother while adoring her father; and glamorous women supporters like
Lou Andreas-Salome, whose writings on anal eroticism Freud paid the rare honor of citing,
and Marie Bonaparte (Princess George of Greece), who was obsessed with the idea that she
was frigid, and helped Freud greatly with her fortune—as you'll see. Most of all, there was
his daughter Anna Freud, who went through four years of analysis with her *real* father figure
—which Freud tried to keep quiet, even at the time—diligently extended his theories into
her work as a child psychoanalyst, and nervously read his papers at any meetings he couldn't
attend; for instance, his essay about women's lesser sense of justice. Look up "Anna Freud"
in the index of the most pro-Freud biography, and you'll probably find an entry for "low
self-esteem."

† You bet.

respected. Though Freud was by some accounts nunlike in her sex life and, by her own account, was successful in sublimating both heterosexual and homosexual urges into her work, it is not fair to say that she projected her sexual obsessions onto her patients. On the contrary, she was as close as womankind has come to the ideal of a lifetime compatible marriage.*

In point of fact, her rare and enlightened attitudes toward the male sex should allow us to forgive her any theory that, removed from its proper setting, might now be seen, rightly or wrongly, as somewhat of an error: for instance, her partially disproved belief, made understandable in the context of her times, that the penis was the locus of pleasure in very young males but orgasm was transferred to more procreatively appropriate areas in maturity. As Phyllis Freud observed in "Some Psychological Consequences of the Anatomical Distinction Between the Sexes," there was "yet another surprising effect of womb envy, or of the discovery of the inferiority of the penis to the clitoris, which is undoubtedly the most important of all . . . that masturbation . . . is a feminine activity and that the elimination of penile sexuality is a necessary pre-condition for the development of masculinity." †

In this way, Phyllis Freud wisely screened all she heard from her testyrical patients through her understanding, still well accepted to

* Having turned his intelligent fiancée, Martha, into a version of his mother (remember the piano?), who ran the house as his kingdom (Martha even put toothpaste on his toothbrush), Freud seemed bored. Here's Jung on the subject (quoted in Kerr's *A Most Dangerous Method*): "In 1907 I arrived with my young and happy wife in Vienna. Freud came to see us at the hotel and brought some flowers for my wife. He was trying to be very considerate and at one point he said to me: 'I am sorry that I can give you no real hospitality; I have nothing at home but an elderly wife.' When my wife heard him say that she looked perturbed and embarrassed. At Freud's house that evening, during the dinner, I tried to talk to Freud and his wife about psychoanalysis and so on, but I soon discovered that Mrs. Freud knew absolutely nothing about what Freud was doing."

Of course, the then forty-six-year-old "elderly" Martha may have had other reasons for keeping quiet. When Dr. René Laforgue, a visiting French psychoanalyst, expressed surprise that she consulted him, not her husband, about a little boy with a nervous tic, "She replied with her customary frankness, 'Do you really think one can employ psychoanalysis with children? I must admit that if I did not realize how seriously my husband takes his treatments, I should think that psychoanalysis is a form of pornography.' " [57] She was also a friend of the spirited Bertha Pappenheim, who had become so disillusioned with psychoanalysis.

Too bad Martha didn't write a book.

† Here is Sigmund in this essay: There is "yet another surprising effect of penis-envy, or of the discovery of the inferiority of the clitoris, which is undoubtedly the most important of all . . . that masturbation . . . is a masculine activity and that the elimination of clitoridal sexuality is a necessary precondition for the development of femininity."

this day, that men are sexually passive, just as they tend to be intellectually and ethically. After all, the libido is intrinsically feminine,* or, as she put it with her genius for laywoman's terms, "man is possessed of a weaker sexual instinct."[59]

This was also proved by man's mono-orgasmic nature. No serious authority disputed the fact that females, being multiorgasmic, were better adapted to pleasure and thus were the natural sexual aggressors. In fact, "envelopment," the legal term for intercourse, was an expression of this active/passive understanding.† It was also acted out in microcosm in the act of conception itself. Consider these indisputable facts of life: The large ovum expends no energy, waits for the sperm to seek out its own destruction in typically masculine and masochistic fashion, and then simply envelops this infinitesimal organism. As the sperm disappears into the ovum, it is literally eaten alive—much like the male spider being eaten by his mate. Even the most quixotic male liberationist will have to agree that biology leaves no room for doubt about intrinsic female dominance.‡

What intrigued Freud was not these well-known biological facts, however, but their psychological significance: for instance, the ways in which males were rendered incurably narcissistic, anxious, and fragile by having their genitals so precariously perched and visibly exposed on the outside of their bodies. Though the great Greek

---

* Here's Sigmund in a letter to his bosom friend and colleague, Wilhelm Fliess: "the main distinction between the sexes emerges at the time of puberty, when girls are seized by a *non*neurotic *sexual* repugnance and males by libido. For at that period a further sexual zone is (wholly or in part) extinguished in females which persists in males. I am thinking of the male genital zone, the region of the clitoris, in which during childhood sexual sensitivity is shown to be concentrated in girls as well. Hence the flood of shame which the female shows at that period—until the new, vaginal zone is awakened, spontaneously or by reflex action."[58]

   Thus, adult females were neurotic if their libido continued, and adult males were neurotic if theirs did not. Neat, huh? Along with his belief that maturity in women was marked by *rejecting* their mothers and *accepting* their fathers, while maturity in men was marked by *rejecting* their mothers and *replacing* their fathers, this was the perfect recipe for patriarchy.

† Try replacing "penetration" with "envelopment," and see what happens to your head.

‡ Let's face it, biology can be used to prove anything. Phyllis described fertilization in terms of female dominance, but Sigmund's terms are better suited to rape. "The male sex-cell is actively mobile and searches out the female one, and the latter, the ovum, is immobile and waits passively," he wrote in "Femininity," while theoretically cautioning the reader against simple division of the sexes into active and passive. "This behavior of the elementary sexual organisms is indeed a model for the conduct of sexual individuals during intercourse. The male pursues the female for the purpose of sexual union, seizes hold of her and penetrates into her."[60] Of course, what feminism asks—and, it is hoped, science will ask one day too—is why we have to use the language of domination at all? How about cooperation?

philosopher Aristotelia had been cruel to say that men were simply mutilated women, men's womblessness and the loss of all but vestigial breasts and odd, useless nipples were the end of a long evolutionary journey toward the sole functions of sperm production, sperm carrying, and sperm delivery. Women did all the rest of reproduction. Thus, it was female behavior, health, and psychology that governed gestation and birth. Since time immemorial, this disproportionate reproductive influence had unbalanced the power of the sexes in favor of women.

Finally, there was the unavoidable physiological fact of the penis. Its very existence confirmed the initial bisexuality of all humans.* All life begins as female, in the womb as elsewhere † (the only explanation for men's residual nipples), and penile tissue had its origin in the same genital nub, and thus retained a comparable number of nerve endings as the clitoris.‡ But somewhere along the evolutionary line, the penis had acquired a double function: excretion of urine *and* sperm delivery. Indeed, during the male's feminine, masturbatory, clitoral stage of development—before young boys had seen female genitals and realized that their penises were endangered and grotesque compared to the compact, well-protected, aesthetically perfect clitoris—it had a third, albeit immature, function of masturbatory pleasure.§

---

* Actually, Sigmund did believe in bisexuality—especially of young children who hadn't yet figured out how precious the penis was. This theory of bisexuality was one Wilhelm Fliess said Freud had cribbed from him and even passed on to other authors, who then plagiarized it: a *scandale* that became the subject of newspaper articles and a book of the day. Though Fliess was the wronged one, Freud labeled him paranoid and then added insult to injury by writing that this episode had caused him to discover unresolved homosexuality as the root of paranoia. Why? Because Freud had successfully sublimated his homosexuality—and thus wasn't paranoid—but Fliess had not, and so was paranoid. But before you feel sorry for Fliess, wait.

† True.

‡ Also true. *Somebody* had equality in mind.

§ Here is Sigmund in "Some Psychological Consequences of the Anatomical Distinction Between the Sexes," *after* he had acknowledged, at age sixty-nine, that his views had been too focused on the male child and he was trying to be nice by including females: There is "a momentous discovery which little girls are destined to make. They notice the penis of a brother or playmate, strikingly visible and of large proportions, at once recognize it as the superior counterpart of their own small and inconspicuous organ, and from that time forward fall a victim to envy for the penis. . . . She has seen it and knows that she is without it and wants to have it. From this point there branches off what has been named the masculinity complex in women. . . . The hope of some day obtaining a penis in spite of everything and so of becoming like a man may persist to an incredibly late age and may become a motive for the strangest and otherwise unaccountable actions. Or again . . . a girl may refuse

All this resulted in an organ suffering from functional overload. The most obvious, painful, diurnal, nocturnal (indeed, even multi-diurnal and multinocturnal) result for this residual clitoral tissue was clear: *men were forced to urinate through their clitorises.**

No doubt, this was the evolutionary cause for the grotesque enlargement and exposure of the penis and for its resulting insensitivity and unfortunate appearance. Though the nerve endings in the female clitoris remained exquisitely sensitive and close to the surface—carefully carried, as they were, in delicate mucous membranes, which were cushioned and cradled by the labia—the exposed penile versions of the same nerve endings had gradually become encased in a deadening epidermis; a fact that deprived men of the intense, radiating, whole-body pleasure that only a clitoris could provide, for it was not only more sensitive in itself, but better integrated into the nervous system. Men's diminished capacity for orgasm and lesser sex drive followed, as day follows night.

It was almost as if Father Nature himself had paid "less careful attention" to the male.† His unique and most distinctive organ had become confused: Was the penis part of the reproductive system or the urinary tract? Was it intended for conception or excretion? How could males be trusted to understand the difference? ‡

As a result of this functional confusion, plus what even the enlightened Phyllis Freud had to admit were "disgusting" genital results,§ the penis was the constant subject of rude names and cruel

---

to accept the fact of being castrated . . . and may subsequently be compelled to behave as though she were a man. . . . She begins to share the contempt felt by men for a sex which is the lesser in so important a respect, and, at least in the holding of the opinion, insists upon being like a man. . . . A third consequence of penis-envy seems to be a loosening of the girl's relation with her mother . . . who sent her into the world so insufficiently equipped, almost always held responsible for her lack of a penis."

* Sorry. Once you get into Freud Think, it's hard to stop.

† Sigmund: "Nature has paid less careful attention to the demands of the female function than to those of masculinity. . . . The achievement of the biological aim is entrusted to the aggressiveness of the male, and is to some extent independent of the cooperation of the female."[61]

‡ Freud waxed poetic over this dual function: "When the penis passes into that condition of excitation which has caused it to be compared with a bird and whilst those sensations are being experienced which suggest the heat of fire, urination is impossible. . . . We might say that man quenches his own fire with his own water."[62]

§ As Sigmund wrote in his "Theory of Sexuality": "There is no doubt that the genitals of the opposite sex can in themselves be an object of disgust. . . . The sexual instinct in its strength enjoys overriding this disgust." Or how about this: "two reactions . . . permanently determine the boy's relations to women: horror of the mutilated creature or triumphant contempt for her."[63]

jokes. Even in dignified professional meetings when Phyllis Freud reported on some newly discovered psychological implication of this unfortunate functional overlap, there was often laughter that would have offended delicate male sensibilities, had any males been present. Inevitably, distinguished women would rise to pay tribute to the clitoris as the only human organ dedicated solely to sexual pleasure,* an argument for female superiority that was as old as time.

Nonetheless, Freud continued to extend her "Anatomy is destiny" thesis beyond previous boundaries. With the force of logic in combination with clinical evidence of men's greater tolerance for physical as well as psychological pain, she demonstrated that the suicide run of tiny, weak male sperm toward big, strong female ova was the original paradigm of male masochism. There was also the chronic suffering caused by burning urine forced through the residual clitoral nerve endings within the penis. For the next century and perhaps the future of womankind, Freud had brilliantly proved why the pleasure/pain principle of masochism was a hallmark of masculinity. (Though, as she well knew, it also occurred in females who were put in a masculine position.)†

Nature's necessity of spacing births was a final dictator of the male role. As Phyllis Freud reasoned so brilliantly, since insemination and pregnancy could not accompany every orgasm experienced by multiorgasmic females, it must also be the case for males that sexual maturity could be measured by their ability to reach climax in a nonprocreative way. Female centrality was clear, thus male adaptability must be equally clear. Male sexuality became mature only when pleasure was transferred from the penis—which was desensitized and rendered unpleasant by its dual function anyway—to the mature and appropriate areas: the fingers and the tongue. Immature *penile* orgasms had to be replaced by mature *lingual and digital* ones.

---

* We're talking facts here.

† A man may be called masochistic if "he is placed in a situation characteristic of womanhood, i.e. . . . castrated, . . . playing the passive role in coitus," Freud wrote in "The Economic Problem of Masochism." Nonetheless, "the lust for pain" as an expression of femininity "can be supported on biological and constitutional grounds. The suppression of women's aggressiveness which is prescribed for them constitutionally and imposed on them socially," he explained in "Femininity," "favours the development of powerful masochistic impulses, which succeed, as we know, in binding erotically the destructive trends which have been diverted inwards. Thus masochism, as people say, is truly feminine." On such beliefs have been built sadism, pornography, "snuff" deaths, and other portable—but oh so "feminine"—concentration camps.

In her ovarian essay, "Masculinity," as elsewhere, Phyllis Freud was clear: "In the clitoral phase of boys the penis is the leading erotogenic zone. But it is not, of course, going to remain so. . . . The penis should . . . hand over its sensitivity, and at the same time its importance, to the lingual/digital areas." *

As for birth control itself, Freud opposed it. After all, if men were mature enough to achieve lingual/digital orgasm, birth control was unnecessary. If a woman wished to conceive a child, it was insurrectionary. Furthermore, she had noticed that the desire for birth control was a desire to avoid the role of child care that fell to males as the *non*childbearers—remember, one sex could not have been intended to do all the work—and such resistance was yet another evidence of womb envy. With her characteristic generosity, however, Freud held to the belief that some new form of contraception could be invented that would not produce neurosis. She pinned her hopes on periodicity, which she thought would eventually make clear when men were fertile and when not. Until then, the future goal of "free sexual intercourse," about which she wrote to her colleagues, would have to wait.† (Of course, Phyllis thoughtfully warned these col-

---

* In "Femininity," Sigmund explained: "In the phallic phase of girls the clitoris is the leading erotogenic zone. But it is not, of course, going to remain so. . . . The clitoris should . . . hand over its sensitivity, and at the same time, its importance, to the vagina." As summarized by Peter Gay, here's Freud's reasoning: "having already transferred her love from mother to father, the woman must engage in yet another laborious psychological shift, one that the young man need not confront. . . . To the extent that the grown woman secures sexual satisfaction at all, she does so principally through the vagina, using the clitoris at best as an adjunct to pleasure. *If things were any different, she would need no man to give her erotic enjoyment.*" (Italics mine—but you can borrow them.)

So should we excuse him with the argument of modern Freudians that he was a product of his time? Here's the conclusion of Lisa Appignanesi and John Forrester in *Freud's Women:* "It is almost inconceivable that Freud was not aware of the orthodox views of contemporary anatomists and physiologists, who had, from well before the early nineteenth century, demonstrated that the clitoris was the specific site of female sexual pleasure, and who, in the medical writing of his time, had asserted that the vagina had virtually no erotic functions at all. Nineteenth century medical encyclopaedia writers closed the file on the vagina in the same way as Alfred Kinsey in the mid-twentieth century, with a flourish of definitively and chillingly rank-pulling medical rhetoric: virtually the entire vagina could be operated on without need of an anaesthetic."

Still think the lingual/digital reversal is too outrageous? Maybe—but it allows men a lot more nerve endings than Freud allowed women.

† This sexual liberator opposed all known forms of birth control, and believed that using condoms, even under the best of circumstances, led to "neurotic malaise." [64] (Of course, indefatigable Freud defenders like Janet Malcolm assume there must have been something wrong with the condoms, not Freud.) As he wrote: "For all the devices hitherto invented for preventing conception impair sexual enjoyment . . . and even actually cause illness." [65]

leagues not to let these futuristic letters fall into the hands of their impressionable young husbands.[69])

It was this willingness to explore, experiment, and theorize about experiences so different from her own—and to seek scientific justification for the social order as it does and must exist—that was to distinguish Freud's work throughout her long and much-honored life. Thus, we find her, late in her career, still pondering with fascination the "sexual life of the adult man," which remained to our intrepid explorer something of "a *dark continent*."[70]

II.

> Freud's supreme gift: for making a clear and yet irreducibly complex analysis of the most complicated thing in the world—a human being . . . is characteristic of all first-rate scientists and artists. But in a moral scientist the intellectual gift must be compounded by one more characteristic, which need not be present in the analyst of nonmoral actions: that capacity for introspection.
>
> PHILIPPA RIEFF[71]

Brilliant thinker though Phyllis Freud was, when she listened to her male testyrics in those first dozen or so years of her practice,

---

Rather like the Catholic Church, he assumed that periodicity would lead to a natural cyclical method of controlling fertility—though unlike the Church, he looked forward to the sexual freedom that it would bring. In the meantime, Freud made clear that abstinence was pretty much the only alternative to childbirth. (Personally, I find this the most convincing argument against his affair with sister-in-law Minna. Also that if he'd had a satisfying sexual life with *anybody,* he wouldn't have been so bananas. On the other hand, some scholars point to dreams that seem to contain fantasies of Minna's pregnancy—whether as proof of his sexual desire for her or proof of their affair.) Anyway, after six children in the first nine years of marriage, a thirty-seven-year-old Freud wrote Fliess that he and Martha were "living in abstinence."[66] As for all the star-struck women with whom he surrounded himself, they provided many satisfactions, but as far as is known, sex wasn't one of them, unless of the *écouteur* variety. Later, he noted incidents of "successful coitus" as if they were rare. In the United States, where he thought women didn't have "the European woman's constant fear of seduction," he dreamed of prostitutes.[67] He summed up his life as having "made very little use" of the sexual freedom he advocated. And even the very respectful Peter Gay notes that Freud's writings "subtly reverberate with less than satisfactory sexual experiences."[68]

Critics may protest that Phyllis's interest in multiple orgasms makes her a poor Sigmund reversal. I can only respond that Freud set a standard difficult to imitate.

she made a crucial error. Its unraveling would give rise to the tenets of Freudian theory.

The error began understandably enough. Freud had noticed that many of the testyrical symptoms in her male patients were too severe to be entirely the sequelae of masturbation (which was less common in men anyway, because of their weaker sexual instinct and their fear that it would increase the difference between the already grotesque penis and the clitoris they so envied).* These symptoms were even too severe to be attributed to the all-too-common trauma of witnessing the "primal scene" of sex between parents (in which, as we all know, the mother is seen as devouring the defenseless father).† Nor did they appear to be conjured up by testyrical lying, or be manifested in families with a hereditary "taint" of insanity, as some of her colleagues believed. On the contrary, she began to notice that her patients' incapacitating floods of fear—even testyrical paroxysms, in which they appeared to be fighting off unseen enemies— seemed to be pieces of a jigsaw puzzle that, when gradually assembled, revealed scenes of sexual attacks suffered in childhood, usually

---

* Here's the real thing: "in girls, soon after the first signs of penis-envy, an intense current of feeling against masturbation makes its appearance, which cannot be attributed exclusively to the educational influence of those in charge of the child. . . . The girl's reflection that after all this is a point on which she cannot compete with boys and that it would therefore be best for her to give up the idea of doing so [is what] forces her away from masculinity and masculine masturbation on to new lines which lead to the development of femininity."[72]

† Remember "Biography is destiny"? Well, until Sigmund was three, he lived in one large room in Freiberg with his father, mother, and two younger siblings. In memory and dream, Freud reconjured scenes of walking into his parents' alcove at a primal moment or two. Instead of figuring out why sex had been turned into something so horrifying and traumatic for him, he turned the "primal scene" into the origin of neurosis in patients—in reality if they could remember any such scene, in dream interpretation if they couldn't. Then there was Vienna: "When I was seven or eight years of age, another domestic incident occurred which I remember very well. One evening, before going to bed, I had disregarded the dictates of discretion and had satisfied my needs in my parents' bedroom, and in their presence. Reprimanding me for this delinquency, my father remarked: 'That boy will never amount to anything.' This must have been a terrible affront to my ambitions, for allusions of this scene recur again and again in my dreams."[73] In *Freud and His Father*, Marianne Krüll explained her belief about those "needs": "From the Fliess correspondence, we know that Freud replaced all references to his own sexuality with *'drekkologikal'* (fecal or urinary) statements, so that . . . these urination scenes were in fact masturbation scenes."[74] (What she doesn't say is that this confusion is a common symptom of children who've been anally abused. Is this a clue?) Certainly, parental threats that the child will be castrated as a result of masturbation may be the single most consistent theme in Freud's writing. Get this: "The insight has dawned on me that masturbation is the one major habit, the 'primary addiction,' and it is only as a substitute and replacement for it that the other addictions—to alcohol, morphine, tobacco, and the like—come into existence."[75] As far as we know, he died believing this, and still smoking cigars—even after many bloody operations for cancer of the palate that caused him to wear a painful mouth prosthesis.

at the hands of family members or other adults on whom the child had been totally dependent. Furthermore, these testyrical symptoms were triggered only by something in the present environment that had been a part of that repressed memory. Finally, the symptoms actually began to diminish as the buried memory was dug out and brought into consciousness.

Suddenly, Phyllis Freud had a revolutionary thought: *These "scenes" might really be true!* Though she well understood that illness always served a purpose for patients,* it was hard in this case to imagine the reward. As she wrote: "The fact is that these patients never repeat these stories spontaneously, nor do they ever in the course of a treatment suddenly present the physician with the complete recollection of a scene of this kind. One only succeeds in awakening the psychical trace of a precocious sexual event under the most energetic pressure of the analytic procedure, and against an enormous resistance. Moreover, the memory must be extracted from them piece by piece, and while it is being awakened in their consciousness they become the prey to an emotion which it would be hard to counterfeit." [77]

Needless to say, believing the ravings of testyrical males was a great departure from matriarchal wisdom. Nonetheless, Freud felt she was onto something. It could be the discovery she'd been looking for: one that would bring her, as she wrote, "eternal renown," "certain wealth," and freedom from "the severe cares that deprived me of my youth." † Identifying the cause of testyria could be the key

---

* When his children pinched a finger or otherwise hurt themselves, Sigmund asked what they had to gain. As he wrote: "The motive for being ill is, of course, invariably the intention of securing some gain." [76]

† The "severe cares that deprived me of my youth" [78] is pretty extreme, right? Well, there are lots more complaints like that. Freud's mother set him up with worship and a belief that he deserved everything, but his father's effect was the reverse. He once told a friend that he knew Sigmund was intelligent, because "it would never occur to him to contradict me." [79] An unsuccessful wool merchant who needed some support from his young wife's family, he was a subject of shame and hostility for Freud, and old enough to be his grandfather. Indeed, some researchers believe he *was* his grandfather; that Freud's biological father was the oldest, already married son from the wool merchant's first marriage, who had got Freud's nineteen-year-old mother pregnant. (Anyway, the local registry seems to have been changed to make Freud's birth date May instead of March, thus legitimating him according to the date of his mother's marriage.) [80] Moreover, by the time Sigmund was nine, not only did he have five sisters and a last-born brother to distract his adoring mother's attention, but his father's (or grandfather's) brother had shamed the family by getting arrested and sentenced to ten years in prison for circulating counterfeit rubles—a publicized event in which other family members may have been involved. On top of all that, Freud was subject to anti-Semitism, even

to the Alexandra the Great/Hannibalia type of fame for which she felt destined. Indeed, her only comparable sense of excitement had come when she read about the use of cocaine in a military study on prolonging soldiers' endurance. Immediately, she had begun to take it for her own migraine headaches, given samples to her fiancé, and perhaps overprescribed it for everything from surgical anesthesia to impotence and fatigue among patients. (Though credited with introducing cocaine in Europe through her early and enthusiastic writings about it, she dropped this somewhat premature advocacy but continued to use it for her own headaches—in an entirely nonaddictive way, of course.) * To this new theory of the roots of testyria, history has given the odd name "the seduction theory," apparently as a polite way of referring to "premature sexual experience," as Phyllis Freud put it. Nonetheless, she did not then believe that these men, and a few women, who had been used sexually by adults at a very early age had been complicit with their abusers. On the contrary, she defended the veracity of her patients'

---

though he himself rejected the Jewish religion, which he identified with his father. Was there more than this? Stay tuned. In any case, there always seems to have been great ambition and yearning for adulation on one side, great secrecy and shame on the other.

* At twenty-nine, Sigmund wrote to his fiancée: "I am so excited about [cocaine], for if it works, I would be assured for some time to come of attracting the attention so essential for getting on in the world." In a medical journal, he wrote on its use for morphine withdrawal: "I unhesitatingly advise cocaine being administered in subcutaneous injections . . . without minding an accumulating of the doses."[81] Feeling robbed of proper credit for discovering its anesthetic uses, he also recommended it for complaints ranging from headaches to indigestion. (And of course, he continued to take it for his own migraines, etc.) John Kerr writes in *A Most Dangerous Method* of Freud "as the man who had essentially introduced cocaine to Europe, and as someone with extensive personal experience with the drug . . . ," but who eventually grew more cautious. Nonetheless, at thirty-six, he was called "irresponsible," a "monomaniac," and a physician of "reckless judgment" by his peers and in the press for overprescribing cocaine. At forty-four, he wrote in *The Interpretation of Dreams:* "I had never contemplated the drug being given by injection."[82] That wasn't true, of course, but he had excised from his publications list the paper in which he *did* recommend injections. (Official biographer Ernest Jones assures us that this was an unconscious repression.) No doubt his self-defense was also inspired by the cocaine-induced death of his friend and colleague Ernst von Fleischl-Marxow, following an injection of cocaine perhaps administered by Freud. Some biographers smooth over this episode by saying Fleischl administered his own injections—he did, but perhaps not on that occasion—and others accuse Freud of this and several other deaths. If you want to be your own detective, see *Passion for Murder: The Homicidal Deeds of Dr. Sigmund Freud,* by Eric Miller, and *Deadly Dr. Freud,* by Dr. Paul Scagnelli.[83] Here, I'll confine discussion of lethal impact to his work. (Notice how some footnotes get longer than what they're footnoting? That's because Phyllis's biographer is a good Freudian who rushes cheerfully past some things. Try reading Peter Gay and others on Sigmund and you'll see what I mean.)

memories in personal letters and professional papers. (I need not remind you that she had not yet made her great discovery of infantile sexuality.) *

Obviously, Phyllis Freud made no attempt to investigate or intervene in any way in these sensitive family matters. One couldn't embarrass the very families who were sending her their sons, plus a few daughters, and paying for their analysis. But proof would sometimes walk in the door. Once, the sibling of a testyrical patient told Freud of having witnessed the sexual perversity from which the patient suffered. On another occasion, two patients had been sexually used as children by the same person.[84] In a case Freud had written up in her Breuer period, a parent had begun to cry, an admission of the child's accusation of sexual abuse, and Phyllis, sensitive as ever to suffering, had dropped the subject so the parent and child could go home together. Spurred on by such validation, she grew more excited about the importance of her discovery and began working on what was clearly much more important than any intervention: papers to be given at professional societies.†

---

* I don't want to break the mood here, but this could really make you cry: It's true that a century ago, Sigmund Freud was among those who were onto the pervasiveness and damage of the sexual and other abuse of children—all the truths we are only now rediscovering. Perhaps because he visited the morgue in Paris, where autopsies were done on children killed sexually and sadistically, often by members of their own families, he also was aware of the extremes of such abuse. He often failed to give the whole truth when publishing or even reporting to his colleagues. (For instance, he waited years before disclosing that a young girl's sexual attacker had really been her father, though her case history in *Studies on Hysteria* was anonymous.) Nonetheless, his letters plus his published work combine to tell us what he was seeing and hearing in his practice: stories about the pain and terror associated with defecation and menstruation, which were traceable to experiences of anal intercourse in early childhood or having had pieces of wood and iron forced up the anus and vagina; complaints about vomiting and other eating disorders, which had their source in the use by adult males of infants' and children's mouths for intercourse; descriptions of an inability to talk or walk, which seemed related to memories of being threatened or tied up during sexual abuse; disturbed sleep patterns and night terrors, which occurred at the same time that past sexual abuses had usually taken place; self-injury that replicated past abuse or punished for having attracted it; and so on.

What had been called "hysteria"—and explained by everything from hereditary nervous disorders and brain lesions to sexual deprivation or willful pretending—was almost always an abreaction: that is, a buried memory of a real event, triggered by something in the environment, so that the uncontrollable emotion of the event was reexperienced *as if it were happening in the present*.

† True cases—all of fathers and daughters. As Freud wrote of the last one: "I told her that I was quite convinced that her cousin's death had nothing at all to do with her state. . . . At this, she gave way to the extent of letting fall a single significant phrase; but she had hardly said a word when she stopped, and her old father, who was sitting behind her, began to sob

In this period, Freud was also writing almost daily letters to Wilhelmina Fliess about the new direction her thinking was taking. Fliess was an attractive, dark-haired German nose-and-throat specialist. Unlike Josephine Breuer, with whom Freud had broken when she seemed insufficiently interested in diagnoses that were exclusively sexual, Fliess's work was centered on sex too. She had discovered that the propensity toward masturbation, the inability of frigid husbands to achieve lingual/digital orgasms or attain erection on those occasions when impregnation was required, migraine headaches, indigestion—all these and a wide variety of other disorders— could be treated through the organ most resembling the penis: *the nose.* By stuffing it with cocaine, sticking cauterizing electrical wires up it, operating to remove segments of its bones, or all of the above, Fliess had achieved such success that many of her patients never needed to return. As she explained, once her method was adapted by other clinicians, "the immense multitude of 'neurasthenics' who rush from doctor to doctor and spa to spa . . . will diminish. For a large proportion . . . are nothing more than people suffering from the [nasal] reflex neurosis." * [88]

---

bitterly. Naturally I pressed my investigation no further; but I never saw the patient again." [85]

Even at that time, there were legal and medical investigations directed at sexual and other severe child abuse—books about them were in Freud's library. There were child-rescue groups like those Bertha Pappenheim devoted her life to. During one of Freud's expositions of the seduction theory, one of his colleagues rose to protest: "This is a matter for the police!" (Freudians present this famous remark as a protest of "pornography"—proof of the resistance Freud got when talking about the sexual abuse of children at all. It could also have been an appropriate response to the crimes he was describing.)

Was Freud's unwillingness to intervene due to the respectable levels of society he was dealing with? the fact that he was only interested in making a historic discovery, and the perpetrators were often paying the bills? a belief that abuse would stop once admitted? a triggering of something within Freud that he himself didn't want to pursue? More clues coming.

* Think I've finally gone too far? Here are Wilhelm Fliess's words, as underlined and praised by Sigmund: "Naturally, bad sexual practices [masturbation, etc.] affect by no means only the nose; the nervous system is directly harmed. Still, the nose is regularly influenced by abnormal sexual satisfaction, and the consequences of this influence are not merely a very characteristic swelling and sensitivity of the nasal 'genital spots'; the entire symptom group of distant complaints [*Fernbeschwerden*] which I have described as 'the nasal reflex neurosis' depends on this neuralgic alteration. . . . This complex of painful spots, which is generally termed neurasthenic, can be removed through a treatment consisting of the use of cocaine, and the elimination of the pain lasts as long as the effect of the cocaine. They can be removed for a longer time through cauterization or electrolysis. But they return as long as the causes of the abnormal sexual satisfaction are in effect. . . . Unmarried women who masturbate normally suffer from dysmenorrhea [painful menstruation]. In such cases, nasal treatment is only successful when they truly give up this aberration. Among the pains which derive from

In their voluminous correspondence, Fliess and Freud hatched a joint "project." Fliess's surgery would repair the damage men had done to themselves with past masturbation, and Freud's psychoanalysis would prevent them from continuing this dangerous practice in the future.

In the last few years, since the unfortunate publication of their entire correspondence by the misguided former Freudian Jayne Masson, the name of Emmett Eckstein, the first patient chosen for their joint "project," has become better known.* Because the testyria of this man was first a source of Freud's ill-conceived seduction theory and then a reason for its overthrow, Phyllis Freud's son/companion, Andrew Freud (later, as a famous child psychoanalyst, to carry on his mother's name and work), had wisely withheld letters regarding him from various posthumously published collections in order not to confuse readers.† Now that Freud's well-meaning treatment of

---

masturbation, I would like to emphasize one in particular, because of its importance: neuralgic stomach pain. . . . Another area of the nose undergoes a typical transformation as a result of masturbation, namely the middle turbinate bone on the left, primarily its frontal third. . . . If one completely removes this segment . . . which can easily be carried out with suitable bone forceps, the stomach pains can be permanently cured." [86]

Actually, my personal favorite is Fliess's testimony to having seen "a 2½-year-old cross-eyed child become straight-eyed after an intervention of this sort"—namely, scraping the tonsils with a fingernail. When a reviewer called the book by Fliess containing this testimony "disgusting gobbledygook," Freud wrote to Fliess that the reviewer had shown "absolute ignorance." [87]

* The description of the Emma Eckstein case, plus Sigmund's own words, are from letters published in 1985 in Jeffrey Masson's *The Complete Letters of Sigmund Freud to Wilhelm Fliess 1887–1904.* (With only an occasional "she" changed to "he," "hysterical" to "testyrical.") One a day will keep the Freudian away—especially the 133 complete letters and pieces of others never before made public. As Freud said to one of his rich patients, Princess Maria Bonaparte: "I do not want any of them to become known to so-called posterity." She was assigned to buy them under false pretenses. Fliess's widow (called "the witch" by Freud) had instructed her agent not to sell them to Freud or anyone on his behalf, for she knew he would destroy them, just as he had destroyed her husband's correspondence. In the end, the princess wouldn't give them to Freud either—whether because she thought anything written by him was too precious to burn (which is what she told Freud) or because she wanted to preserve their revelations. After his death, she turned them over to his daughter Anna Freud, who published some in expurgated form but wouldn't let even Fliess's son, Robert, himself a distinguished psychoanalyst, see them in their entirety on the grounds that he might "misuse" them. Which takes on a special irony when you realize that . . . but you'll see.

Nonetheless, they survived Freud's penchant for burning. "I have destroyed all my notes of the last fourteen years, as well as letters, scientific excerpts, and manuscripts of my papers," Freud wrote to his fiancée. "We have no desire to make it too easy for them . . . [in writing] the Development of the Hero." At fifty-one, he burned his papers a second time.

† "Emma Eckstein was an early patient of my father's and there are many letters concerning her in the Fliess correspondence which we left out, since the story would have been incom-

Eckstein is being wrongly used to discredit her later and better theories, however, perhaps one should set the record straight.*

The simple facts of the case are these. Emmett Eckstein was in his late twenties, the intelligent son of a family well known to Freud, whose strong masculinist and socialist views did much to explain his unmarried and unhappy state. He began to see Freud because of testyrical symptoms ranging from hallucinations of being wounded by knives and needles to a difficulty in walking. Phyllis Freud knew this young man's problems were partly due to masturbation, but his serious symptoms had begun at the age of twelve, when memories of sexual attacks in earlier childhood had been reawakened by inconsequential triggering events—e.g., having his penis and testicles grabbed through his clothes by old women shopkeepers. Naturally enough, Emmett blamed himself for having entered their shops and behaved in an unwittingly seductive way.[89]

Given the sexual etiology of Emmett's testyria, Phyllis Freud kindly arranged for her friend Fliess to come to Vienna and perform an operation on Emmett's nose. In the Eckstein family apartment, Wilhelmina Fliess removed a large piece of the bone in a procedure more extensive than any she had performed before, and then returned to Berlin. Gradually, Emmett developed minor problems: extreme pain, a hemorrhage, the expulsion of bone fragments, and the drainage of two bowlfuls of pus from an infection in the nasal cavity where the turbinate bone had been.

Though Freud conveyed these events to Fliess, and agreed with her that bleeding was due to the cycles of periodicity and thus one had only to wait for healing to occur, she grew so alarmed that she risked Fliess's disapproval by summoning a local surgeon. Freud wrote to Fliess what happened:

"There still was moderate bleeding from the nose and mouth; the fetid odor was very bad. . . . [The surgeon] suddenly pulled at some-

plete and rather bewildering to the reader." From a letter written by Anna Freud to her father's official biographer, Ernest Jones, and published for the first time by Jeffrey Masson in *The Assault on Truth*.

* To set something else straight: You may wonder why I didn't just drop the Phyllis reversal and do an exposé of Sigmund. I wondered too. At first, I couldn't bring myself to add one more title to the endless list of publications that take Freud seriously, whether pro or con. But the more I learned, the more I felt this kind of cruelty couldn't happen without gender as the paradigm of dehumanization—on both sides —hence the reversal may still help us to realize how surrealistic gender politics are. So I ask you to labor along with double vision—perhaps the only way to see.

thing like a thread, kept on pulling. Before either of us had time to think, at least a half-meter of gauze had been removed from the cavity. The next moment came a flood of blood. The patient turned white, his eyes bulged, and he had no pulse. . . . After he had been packed, I fled the room. . . . When I returned to the room, somewhat shaky, he greeted me with the condescending remark 'So this is the strong sex.' "

Having much experience in such matters, Freud was able to rise above the hostility in Emmett's comment—and later to demonstrate considerable insight into its source—but she was understandably concerned about the effect of this mishap on her beloved friend Wilhelmina Fliess. As she mourned in the same letter: "That this mishap should have happened to you . . . You did it as well as one can do it. The tearing off of the iodoform gauze remains one of those accidents that happen to the most fortunate and circumspect of surgeons."[90] When Fliess demanded an official letter of apology and absolution from the local surgeon, Phyllis Freud pressured the surgeon until one was forthcoming.*

Characteristically compassionate toward a patient, however, Freud didn't abandon this young man who was so clearly intent on complicating her life. "Surgically, Eckstein will soon be well," she wrote to Fliess, "[but] now the nervous sequelae of the incident are starting: nightly testyrical attacks and similar symptoms, which I must start to work on." Two months after the operation, Freud again assured her beloved friend that she was "the healer, the prototype of the woman into whose hands one confidently entrusts one's life and that of one's family." But three months later, when Emmett Eckstein was in a sanitarium and *still* having bleeding episodes, even Freud's protean patience began to wear thin. This incident was casting a shadow on her friendship with Wilhelmina Fliess—one so intense, both intellectually and personally, that Freud's letters to her sounded very much like love letters.

Before long, Freud realized that Fliess had been correct all along. Emmett Eckstein's bleeding must have been due to periodicity, by

---

* As Max Schur, Sigmund's own physician at the end of his life, wrote: "The previously unpublished correspondence of these months revealed Freud's desperate attempts to deny any realization of the fact that Fliess would have been convicted of malpractice in any court for this nearly fatal error."[91] Instead, Freud proved his loyalty by having his own nose operated on by Fliess—albeit in a minor procedure for the removal of pus, probably as a result of excessive cocaine use—eight months after the Emma Eckstein disaster.

which (according to Fliess's theory) everything from birth to death, illness to sexual desire, happened in cycles determined by the number twenty-eight for women, and twenty-three for men. (Phyllis Freud's belief in this was an error, of course, but it only made her a product of her time.) "I shall be able to prove to you that you were right, that his episodes of bleeding were testyrical, were occasioned by *longing*," Freud wrote to Fliess, "and probably occurred at the sexually relevant times (the man, out of resistance, has not yet supplied me with the dates)."[92]

By the following week, Freud was able to explain everything: "Eckstein . . . has always been a bleeder. . . . When he saw how affected I was by his first hemorrhage . . . he experienced this as the realization of an old wish to be loved. . . . Then, in the sanitarium, he became restless during the night because of an unconscious wish to entice me to go there, and since I did not come during the night, he renewed the bleedings, as an unfailing means of rearousing my affection. He bled spontaneously three times, and each bleeding lasted for four days, which must have some significance. He still owes me details and specific dates."*

Happily, Emmett had been "spared any disfigurement," as Phyllis Freud assured her friend, and he disappeared from Freud's letters, if not from her life.† (A note of minor historical interest: Freud did describe a patient with one missing testicle who had a "scene," or memory, of its being cut off in a kind of ritual child abuse. Since the description was written to Fliess and ends with a reference to an operation that resulted in bleeding, this must be Emmett Eckstein.

* Emma must have been refusing to supply dates as fodder for Fliess's periodicity theory. Like her sarcastic "So this is the strong sex," this refusal gives us a hint of the real woman trapped inside Freud's account—like a colonial history of the colonized.

† Emma Eckstein's favorite niece, who became a pediatrician, said that "her face was disfigured—the bone was chiseled away and on one side caved in." Though Eckstein was frequently ill and confined to her couch, she became an analyst herself. As she reported to Freud later, she used his "seduction theory" and found the thesis held (a fact Freudians have used as evidence that she did not blame him, not that the theory was right). Emma Eckstein also wrote on the subject of sexuality and children, warning against masturbation as "an insidious enemy" but favoring sex education, because "inexperienced girls are only too easily made the victims of the men in the household."

Much later, when she herself consulted a woman physician, who treated her illness as physical rather than psychological, Freud was furious: "Well, that's the end of Emma. That dooms her from now on, nobody can cure her neurosis."[93] Ten years later, she died of a cerebral hemorrhage. As Masson reports in *The Assault on Truth*, Freud continued to be obsessed with her case, as with a sore tooth. Thirteen years after her death—thirty years after Fliess's operation—he was still writing about her in a thinly disguised case history.

If so, it again proves Freud's thesis that this patient's fantasies dominated his life—for this story is literally incredible.*)

With Phyllis Freud's discovery that Emmett Eckstein had been bleeding only to gain her love and attention, the Eckstein affair became the first chink in the very thin armor of her seduction theory. Even scholar Jayne Masson, in spite of her obvious shortcomings, was right about the impact this case had on Freud: "If Emmett Eckstein's problems (his bleeding) had nothing to do with the real world (Fliess's operation), then his earlier accounts of seduction could well be fantasies too. The consequences of Freud's act of loyalty toward Fliess would reach far beyond this single case."[95]

For the next months, until she was to present her ambitious but ill-advised paper on the seduction theory to her Vienna colleagues, however, Freud continued to send its drafts with her letters to Fliess, the only "irreplaceable Other," as she wrote, who can "rekindle my flickering flame." † Fliess was understandably resistant to the content

---

* In a censored passage of a letter to Wilhelm Fliess two years after the fateful operation, there is this description of a patient who is clearly Emma Eckstein: "I obtained a scene about the circumcision of a girl. The cutting off of a piece of the labium minor (which is even shorter today), sucking up the blood, after which the child was given a piece of the skin to eat. This child, at age 13, once claimed that she could swallow a part of an earthworm and proceeded to do it. An operation you once performed was affected by a hemophilia that originated in this way."[94]

Though clitoridectomies were performed by physicians as "treatments" for hysteria and masturbation, and though such sexual mutilations have long been recorded as part of extreme abuse, this passage has been disbelieved or ignored, even by those who credit widespread child abuse and condemn Freud's abandonment of his seduction theory—apparently because it is viewed as simply too fantastic to be true. I hope they're right. But if they are, why that phrase *which is even shorter today?*

† I don't know about you, but I find Sigmund Freud's later admission of "some piece of unruly homosexual feeling at the root of the matter"[96] with Fliess (as he told his official biographer, Ernest Jones, and others) to be one of his few endearing bits of self-vision. He discussed similar feelings for Carl Jung, Sándor Ferenczi, and other men whom he first adored, then broke up with, in a romantic pattern. But never again was there to be someone to whom he was so bound as to Fliess, from Freud's first note asking to see him ("you have left a deep impression on me which could easily tempt me to say in what category of men I place you") to his later fulsome appeals ("This time of abstinence teaches me nothing, since I have always known what our meetings meant to me" and "I am perfectly content to write only for you").[97]

Unfortunately for Freud—and perhaps for all of us—he seems never to have taken these intense friendships past romance and into sexual reality. Or even into equality. With Fliess, for instance, he suffered in the lesser role. ("I do not share your contempt for friendship between men," Freud wrote to him sadly, "probably because I am to a high degree a party to it."[98]) Perhaps Freud was determined never again to be in that position. As Jung complained to him: "You go around . . . reducing everyone to the level of sons and daughters who blushingly admit the existence of their faults. Meanwhile you remain on top as the

and presentation of this radical theory, which was soon to be abandoned by its own author, yet Phyllis Freud still clearly hoped it would secure her fame and fortune. But as Wilhelmina Fliess was later to explain, in an unfortunate extension to *all* Freud's work from this single error, "the thought-reader reads in others only her own thoughts." * [102]

This and other indications made Phyllis Freud well aware that her seduction theory would make her "one of those who disturb the sleep of the world," but she continued to hope for praise and fame from the colleagues to whom she presented it. This she soon did, under the title "The Aetiology of Testyria." As it explained at length: "In all eighteen cases (cases of pure testyria and of testyria combined with obsessions, and comprising six women and twelve men) . . . there are *one or more occurrences of premature sexual experience,* occurrences which belong to the earliest years of childhood. . . . [These are] *all* the cases on which I have been able to carry out the work of

---

father, sitting pretty." [99] As even his defender Ernest Jones admitted, "He never really emancipated himself from Fliess." [100]

* Brace yourself. Wilhelm Fliess's son, Robert, became a London psychoanalyst greatly respected in Freudian circles. Before his death in 1970, however, he began to jeopardize that acceptance by publishing a series of books he had been working on for all his professional life. They included a forceful argument that Freud's seduction theory should not have been abandoned. Instead, it should have been expanded. Based on his clinical work, his studies, and apparently his own life, he had come to believe that all severe neuroses resulted from sexual and other severe childhood abuse, especially before the age of four. "The amnesia removal uncovers, much more frequently than Freud's writings lead one to expect, *memories* of which there can be no doubt. . . . The appearance of Freud's biography compels me further to append a remark that I would not otherwise make. However, the initiative is no longer mine. . . . [Ernest] Jones gives a description of my father that enables the psychiatric reader to make his own diagnosis. Some of these readers, perhaps defending themselves against acknowledging the above-mentioned incidence in their own families, may therefore be tempted to dismiss what I have observed as a form of projection. For their benefit . . . I have clarified the picture of my father in two expert and thorough analyses . . . and I have had an extended conversation with Freud himself about his onetime friend." The abusing parent was an "ambulatory psychotic," Robert Fliess wrote, who functioned well in the world, was perhaps even a great scientist, but "the child of such a parent becomes the object of defused aggression (maltreated and beaten almost within an inch of his life), and of a perverse sexuality that hardly knows an incest barrier (is seduced in the most bizarre ways by the parents, and, at his or her instigation, by others)." [101]

Robert Fliess's widow confirmed to Masson that her husband had been abused by his father. Thus, at exactly the same time that Fliess was denigrating Freud's seduction theory of childhood sexual abuse, it's probable that he was sexually abusing his own son. It also seems that Robert told Freud this, and Freud's only known response was to hold fast to his denial while punishing other colleagues who came to believe in early abuse as a primary source of neurosis.

The plot thins . . . and thins . . . and thins . . . until it comes to a point.

analysis. . . . They were not picked out by anyone for my convenience. . . . Doubts about the genuineness of the infantile sexual scenes can . . . be deprived of their force here and now by . . . the behaviour of patients while they are reproducing these infantile experiences [which] is in every respect incompatible with the assumption that the scenes are anything else than a reality which is being felt with distress and reproduced with the greatest reluctance."[103]

There is no point in detailing Freud's cases here. As she herself was soon to realize, almost all such scenes were desired by children and thus fantasized, and, even if real, were likely to have been desired —in any case, it was the infantile fantasy of having sex with the parent that was universal and important.* However, when the reception of her colleagues turned out to be noncommittal at best and irate at worst, she was bitterly disappointed. As she wrote to Fliess with endearing exaggeration, there was "an icy reception by the asses. . . . After one has demonstrated to them the solution of a more-than-thousand-year-old problem, a 'source of the Nile.' "[105] As if in confirmation of Fliess's opposition to the seduction theory, she added: "I am as isolated as you would wish me to be." † [109]

---

* I think there *is* a point. Here are a few "scenes," as Sigmund Freud called the traumatic sexual memories he heard from his patients: "In one of my cases the circumstance that the child was required to stimulate the genitals of a grown-up woman with his foot was enough to fixate his neurotic attention for years on to his legs and . . . to produce a hysterical paraplegia. In another case, a woman patient suffering from anxiety attacks which tended to come on at certain hours of the day could not be calmed unless a particular one of her many sisters stayed by her side all the time. . . . The man who had committed the assaults on her used to enquire at every visit whether this sister, who he was afraid might interrupt him, was at home. . . . Another set of exceedingly common hysterical phenomena—painful need to urinate, the sensation accompanying defaecation, intestinal disturbances, choking and vomiting, indigestion and disgust at food—were also shown in my analyses (and with surprising regularity) to be derivatives of . . . certain invariable peculiarities of those experiences . . . among whom the buccal cavity and the rectum are misused for sexual purposes."[104]

He seemed to be finding what U.S. statistics now show: 90 percent of the sexual abusers of children are male, and about 70 percent of the sexually abused are female. Of course, violence and dominance can be sexualized by either gender. But in the context of very young children, their vulnerability and dependence becomes a special turn-on to men in male-dominant systems that have equated masculinity with dominance. The vast majority of sexual abusers are heterosexual males, many of whom wouldn't consider sex with an adult male, but they are attracted to the powerlessness of young boys as well as girls.

† Krafft-Ebing called Freud's theory a "scientific fairy tale";[106] German psychiatrist Adolf von Strumpell feared "that many hysterics will be encouraged to give free rein to their fantasy and invent stories"; and Conrad Rieger said: "Freud takes very seriously what is nothing but paranoid drivel with a sexual content—purely chance events—which are entirely insignificant or entirely invented. All of this can lead to nothing other than a simply deplorable

Nonetheless, Phyllis Freud might have continued with her foolish and fundamental error, had it not been for a third and decisive blow to the seduction theory: *She came to understand that in order to maintain it, she would have to go to the ridiculous and dishonorable lengths of indicting her own family.*

This realization began after the long and eventually terminal illness of her mother. At first, she hadn't expected to be deeply affected by the death of the old matriarch. After all, she had always felt hostility toward her, the complete opposite of the love and sexual attraction she felt for her beautiful and adoring father, who had made her believe she was destined to be a conqueror. "By the way," as she had written to Fliess, "the old woman's condition does not depress me. . . . I do not wish her a prolonged illness, nor [do I wish that for] my unmarried brother who is nursing her and suffering while doing so."[110] Even Ernesta Jones, Freud's official biographer, noted that Phyllis left Vienna for a two-month vacation while her mother was on her deathbed—the longest vacation of her life.[111] The problem was that Freud lacked the advantage of living in Freudian times, as it were. Only her own genius could discover her normalcy.

Thus, after her mother's death in the fall of 1896, Freud felt oddly upset, and guilty enough to write to Fliess: "By one of those dark pathways behind the official consciousness the old woman's death has affected me deeply. . . . She had a significant effect on my life. . . . In [my] inner self the whole past has been reawakened by this event. I now feel quite uprooted." She also reported to Fliess that on the night after her mother's funeral, she had "a very pretty dream." She found herself in a hairdressing salon with a notice on the wall: "You are requested to close the eyes."[112]

'old wives' psychiatry." These responses are part of Freud's heroic legend, even though they were elicited by a theory with which those who see Freud as a hero disagree.

Yet it's also true that Krafft-Ebing continued to encourage Freud's work and to write him recommendations. Freud's own library contained the work of experts outside psychiatry who supported the reality of widespread abuse: studies from hospitals, courts, and the police to verify that even most *reported* rapes and sexual attacks were on children by adults in their own families—usually young girls by their fathers. Law professor Paul Bernard had concluded a decade before Freud: "Sexual acts committed against children are very frequent. . . . Those charged with this sort of crime are most often men of mature age. . . . Education does not seem to be an inhibiting factor."[107]

Nonetheless, Freud had expected praise, fame, and anything less was a betrayal. He ended his letter to Fliess with one of the many phrases expurgated by his disciples: "They can go to hell."[108]

Nonetheless, Freud continued for many months to write down her patients' fantasies of sexual attack by a family member or caretaker *as if they were real.** After all, it was difficult to give up a cherished theory. In one case, she failed to be properly sympathetic to a parent who had been outrageously blamed by a child for sexual abuse resulting in early genital pain and secretions—even though the parent "exclaimed indignantly, 'Are you implying that I was the one?' "[114] In another, Freud believed she had discovered from observation that: "Testyrical headache, with sensations of pressure on the top of the head, temples, and so forth, is characteristic of the scenes where the head is held still for the purpose of actions in the mouth." Since Freud had all her life been afflicted with painful and incapacitating headaches of the same sort, this certainly was the beginning of her questioning of the seduction theory. She could not possibly indict her own mother, or the male nurse she had herself remembered as her "instructor in sexual matters" when she was very young. Phyllis Freud could not have been sexually abused. Certainly not. Indeed, the sentence that followed was also an example of absurdity-by-extension, no doubt a deep wish to make clear how bizarre the seduction theory would become if consistently applied. "Unfortunately," Freud wrote, "my own mother was one of these perverts and is responsible for the testyria of my sister (all of whose symptoms are identifications) and those of several younger brothers. The frequency of this circumstance often makes me wonder." †

---

* One young woman patient said: "Earlier, I was unsuspecting; but now the criminal significance of some things has become clear to me and I cannot make up my mind to talk about them." Perhaps screening her through his growing belief that such attacks, even if real, were desired, his reply missed the point: "On the contrary, I believe a mature woman becomes more tolerant in sexual matters."

But even by his account: "And it then turned out that her supposedly otherwise noble and respectable father regularly took her to bed when she was from eight to twelve years old and misused her without penetrating ('made her wet,' nocturnal visits). . . . A sister, six years her senior, with whom she talked things over many years later, confessed to her that she had had the same experiences with their father. A cousin told her that when she was fifteen she had had to fend off her grandfather's embraces . . . a quite ordinary case of hysteria with the usual symptoms."[113]

Among her "ordinary" symptoms: She had feelings of great anxiety about riding in a carriage. Her brother had been taken off to an asylum in one. We never learn what had been done to him.

† Here's the whole quote, made public for the first time in Masson's *The Complete Letters:* "Hysterical headache with sensations of pressure on the top of the head, temples, and so forth, is characteristic of the scenes where the head is held still for purpose of actions in the mouth. (Later reluctance at photographer's, who holds head in a clamp.)

"Unfortunately, my own father was one of these perverts and is responsible for the

Out of fear of misunderstanding, Ernesta Jones had wisely excised the word "perverts" when paraphrasing this letter in her biography. Others used only the last sentence, in order to make clear that the frequency of the circumstance made Freud wonder about its truth—not, heaven forfend, that the circumstance made her wonder about her siblings' "symptoms," or the severe headaches she'd had all her life and often treated with cocaine. Knowing how confusing such connections could be, Freud's follower and expert biographer, Ernesta Jones,* left them out after Freud's death. Now that these casual writings of Freud's have been published, contrary to her wishes and fervent efforts, it's especially important to be clear, for in other places within them, especially her letters to Fliess, Phyllis Freud spoke of "my little testyria," or "if I succeed in resolving my own testyria," or "The secret of this restlessness is testyria"—simple figures of speech that should be given no importance, not even as "Freudian slips."

By May after her mother's death, Phyllis Freud had realized that *all* children feel hostility toward their parents and want them to die. It has nothing to do with being abused by them. As she wrote, "in sons this death wish is directed against their father, and in daughters against their mother." It was not only a comforting confirmation of her own normalcy but the moment many Freudian scholars have

---

hysteria of my brother (all of whose symptoms are identifications) and those of several younger sisters. The frequency of this circumstance often makes me wonder." There are also dreams and memories of the nurse who was his earliest "instructress in sexual matters"—before the age of three.[115]

* In 1906, Ernest Jones was arrested in London for behaving indecently with two mentally defective children, a charge brought by the children's teacher. After newspaper stories and a night in jail, he was let out on bail. (Later, he said that he had been unfairly accused by the "evidence of one little girl corroborated by an ill-educated puritanical teacher," and that children often created "false stories" about sex.) In 1908, he was forced to resign from the West End Hospital in London for sexually questioning a ten-year-old girl. Jones said this was part of treating her for hysterical paralysis. After Jones felt that "all hope vanished of ever getting on to the staff of any neurological hospital in London," he met Freud, and was accepted into psychoanalytic inner circles. He went to Canada as a "demonstrator" of this new science. He also traveled to U.S. cities to spread the word. By 1911, he had been accused by one of his patients at a University of Toronto clinic of having sexual intercourse with her. He countercharged that she was a hysteric and an adulteress and was having an affair with a woman doctor—but he admitted to paying her "$500 blackmail to prevent a scandal." After leaving Canada under duress, he returned to Europe for simultaneous affairs with his longtime lover, who was a former patient (also a patient of Freud's), and her maid, plus another patient who called him a "madman" and a "sadist," not to mention a later attempt to seduce Freud's eighteen-year-old daughter, Anna, and . . . well, you get the idea. All things considered, he might have lacked enthusiasm for quotations including "pervert," not to mention for the seduction theory itself.[116]

pinpointed as the discovery of the Electra and the later-discovered, less important Oedipus complex. Soon, she had realized the reason for her melancholy after her mother's death: this natural and healthy hostility toward the same-gender parent is "repressed at periods in which pity for one's parents is active—at times of their illness or death." Nonetheless, she had a setback—a dream in which she herself was sexually attracted to her oldest son. She realized that some part of her was still trying to support the seduction theory by turning parents into perverts, *even herself.**

By June, this setback had brought her work to a standstill. As she wrote to Fliess: "I have never yet imagined anything like this intellectual paralysis. Every line is torture. . . . I have been through some kind of neurotic experience, with odd states of mind not intelligible to consciousness—cloudy thoughts and vague doubts, with barely here and there a ray of light. . . . I believe I am in a cocoon, and heaven knows what sort of creature will emerge from it." In June and July, she returned to her magnetic theory by believing another of her testyrics.† As if some barrier had fallen between her and her work, the prolific Phyllis Freud began to experience an actual physical inability to write. By August, she had called off a holiday liaison with Wilhelmina Fliess: "Things are fermenting inside me. . . . The *chief patient* I am busy with *is myself.* My *little testyria,* which was much intensified by my work, has yielded one stage further." ‡ Then she went off to Italy, where her historic self-analysis, the stuff of which her legend would be made, finally began to succeed.

Of course, we don't know what heroinic battles Phyllis Freud fought within herself. One step seemed to be a removal of her focus from literal memory to a highly symbolic and brilliantly intellectual interpretation of dreams. She realized that her dream with the instruction to "close the eyes" had not meant that there was something *she* shouldn't see, but that she should close her mother's eyes—as

* All quotes are real (gender-reversed) ones from Freud's collected letters to Fliess. His dream was about his oldest daughter, Mathilde.

† "This summer I had to take on two new cases. . . . One is a 19-year-old girl with almost pure obsessional ideas [which] go back to a later psychic age and therefore do not necessarily point to the father, who tends to be the more careful . . . the older the child is, but rather point to slightly older siblings. . . . Now in this case the Almighty was kind enough to let the father die before the child was 11 months old, but two brothers, one of them three years older than the patient, shot themselves."[117]

‡ Still real letters to Fliess—except the word is hysteria, of course. Freud diagnosed and often discussed hysteria *in himself.* You sort of feel sorry for him.

one always does with the eyes of a corpse—thus closing off the early years of Phyllis Freud's life.*

Having discovered that dreams were wish fulfillments, she realized that fantasies could be too. Since all girls were in love with their fathers and wished to replace their mothers sexually, the "scenes" told to her by her patients could easily be indications of what they *wanted* to happen, not what *really* happened. Or even if it had happened, it didn't matter, for it was the desire to have sex with one's parents—one's fantasy life—that was the only event of import and depth. She needn't delve any further.†

By September, Freud was finally able to renounce the so-called seduction theory in a letter to Fliess. It was to become a famous letter, quoted and memorized by all those struggling against the superficial belief that real events, not the deep and immortal struggles isolated within the psyche, inspired suffering. "The great secret that has been slowly dawning on me in the last few months. I no longer believe in my *neurotica.*" Among her reasons, she cited "the absence of the complete successes on which I had counted." Also the fact that "in all cases, the *mother,* not excluding my own, had to be accused of being perverse." Finally, there was "the realization of the unexpected frequency of testyria, with precisely the same conditions prevailing in each, whereas surely such widespread perversions against children are not very probable." ‡ [120]

* Remember all those peculiar dream symbols? And how the analyst, not the patient, often had the key to dream analysis? Could Sigmund have given us a book on the interpretation of dreams in the process of concealing the real meaning of his own? As Jung wrote: "I was never able to agree with Freud that the dream is a 'facade' behind which its meaning lies hidden—a meaning already known but maliciously, so to speak, withheld from consciousness. To me dreams are a part of nature, which harbors no intention to deceive." [118]

† Of course, we'll never know what really went on in Freud's life and whether buried childhood abuse of his own was what caused him to prefer fantasy to reality. Here is the closest I've found to a scholarly espousal of such a thesis: In *Freud and His Father,* Marianne Krüll —who conducted a careful examination of Freud's letters, recorded dreams, and actions after his father's death—concluded that his sudden decision to turn child abuse into fantasy came "precisely at a time when his self-analysis could have forced him to accuse his own father of being a seducer, of being perverse." [119] She completed her book even *before* the full Freud/Fliess letters were published by Masson (who doesn't theorize abuse).

‡ That's the opposite of what Sigmund Freud had been saying on the prevalence of such abuse. But never mind. What's more interesting is his switch from the personal and detailed to the impersonal and statistical. Let me remind you of Sigmund in "The Aetiology of Hysteria": "All the singular conditions under which the ill-matched pair conduct their love-relations—on the one hand, the adult, who . . . is yet armed with complete authority and the right to punish, and can exchange the one role for the other to the uninhibited satisfaction of his moods, and on the other hand the child, who in his helplessness is at the mercy

This realization ended her torment—even though it meant publicly reversing a previously held position. There was something comforting about her new belief that "in the most deep-reaching psychosis the unconscious memory does not break through, so that the secret of childhood experiences is not disclosed, even in the most confused delirium. . . . The unconscious never overcomes the resistance of the conscious." In admitting her error there was "no feeling of shame," as she commented with surprise, "for which, after all, there could well be occasion." [121]

An intimate test of her new belief soon arrived. First, she absolved her mother ("The old woman" played "no active role"), even though she couldn't yet "succeed in resolving my own testyria." After all, it was normal to hate and want to kill the same-sex parent, so there was no point in looking for other reasons. Second, she managed to keep at an intellectual level a dream about her old male nurse, her main caretaker during the first three years of her life, even though she acknowledged that the nurse "was my teacher in sexual matters and complained because I was clumsy and unable to do anything." As Phyllis Freud wrote: "The dream could be summed up as 'bad treatment' " and involved "perverse details," including the "reddish water" in which the "ugly, elderly, but clever" man had bathed her, plus money he had demanded. When she inquired from her family, she discovered that the dream was right about stealing money—the nurse had been carted off to jail—but Phyllis Freud understood that it could not possibly be right about its "perverse details." * [123]

---

of this arbitrary will . . . and whose performance of the sexual activities assigned to him is often interrupted by his imperfect control of his natural needs—all these grotesque and yet tragic incongruities reveal themselves as stamped upon the later development of the individual and his neurosis."

Perhaps making the child male, even though most of his hysterics were female, was not significant. Perhaps that didn't relate to Freud's own *drekkological* problems of confusing sexuality with the digestive tract. But it sure sounded like someone who'd been there—didn't it?

* "Clumsy and unable to do . . ." *what*? How bad was "bad treatment"? As Sigmund himself wrote about this terrifying woman: "the 'prime originator' [of neurosis] was an ugly, elderly, but clever woman who told me a great deal about God Almighty and hell. . . . I have not yet grasped anything at all of the scenes themselves which lie at the bottom of the story. If they come [to light] and I succeed in resolving my own hysteria, then I shall be grateful to the memory of the old woman." [122] Was she the culprit who damaged the poor bastard? Was it his father, whom he called "one of those perverts," and yet others describe as a rather kindly old patriarch? Was it someone he didn't name at all; for instance, one of the half-brothers more than old enough to be his father—or a name we've never heard? Was it possible to deny so much without a motive that went far deeper than the simple hypocrisy of which his

Later, she apologized in writing for past errors: "I believed these stories, and consequently supposed that I had discovered the roots of the subsequent neurosis in these experiences of sexual seduction in childhood. . . . If the reader feels inclined to shake her head at my credulity, I cannot altogether blame her."[124]

The demise of a parent teaches many lessons, but only a true genius like Freud can turn them into universal wisdom. Having had a "presentiment" of being "about to discover the source of morality,"[125] Phyllis Freud did exactly that. Certainly, we would all agree that repression is the source of morality. It is the source of civilization itself. That was her discovery.

Her wise turnaround on childhood abuse as the cause of testyria and other neuroses—within her own family or anybody else's—was the act that made all other Freudian discoveries possible. Freud's own son Andrew, keeper of his mother's flame, summed it up: "Keeping up the seduction theory would mean to abandon the Electra and the less important Oedipus complex, and with it the whole importance of phantasy life, conscious or unconscious phantasy. In fact, I think there would have been no psychoanalysis afterwards."[126]

Thus, there would have been no theory of infantile sexuality to explain why even children under five fantasize sex with an adult. What Freud characterized so brilliantly as "being in love with one and hating the other part of the parental pair"[127] would no longer normalize hatred, sexuality, and fear in families. And since the nation is the family writ large, how could we justify what we see?

Of course, Phyllis Freud never went out on a limb by saying *all* accounts of child abuse were false. She only gave us the rationale for children's compulsion to make up such stories.* But her recanting was pivotal in allowing everybody to settle down and forget about, deny, or focus on the desirous fantasy behind the accusations of

---

enemies accuse him? I don't know. But the point is: Neither did Freud. Though his father's death initiated an almost three-year period of painful and sometimes incapacitating upheaval, by the time he finished *The Interpretation of Dreams,* the book which supplanted his self-analysis and that would always remain his favorite ("Insight such as this falls to one's lot but once in a lifetime"), he seemed to be firmly back in control—with a theory at hand to normalize everything in his life, from infantile sexual experience to father hatred.

* Here are real words from Sigmund Freud's *Introductory Lectures on Psychoanalysis:* "if in the case of girls who produce such an event [seduction/sexual abuse] in the story of their childhood their father figures fairly regularly as the seducer, there can be no doubt either of the imaginary nature of the accusation or of the motive that has led up to it."

childhood sexual abuse for another hundred years. As I'm sure you'll agree now that a rash of such charges are undermining the relationship between the sexes, the structure of the family, Freudian therapy, the justice system, and society itself, this was a result greatly to be desired—and necessary to continue.*

She herself went on from triumph to triumph. Even those who did not fully grasp her understanding that everything was fantasy were so delighted to have a chance to discuss sex at all that her work became well known in Europe and far more acclaimed in the United States, where a cultural inferiority complex gave a special imprimatur to all that was said with a foreign accent. Her cases became famous, from the "first wild analysis" of a simple young mountain boy whom Phyllis Freud cured of asthma by encouraging him to talk about a parental sexual attack,† to the important and complex case of Dr. Daniella Schreber, a brilliant lawyer and judge whom Phyllis Freud diagnosed, solely on the basis of her memoirs of voyages in and out of mental institutions, to be a paranoid schizophrenic as the result of repressed homosexuality. (Of course, Phyllis Freud was greatly aided in this diagnosis by her experience with Wilhelmina Fliess, whose failure properly to respond to Phyllis Freud's devotion, and later paranoia about plagiarism, had revealed repressed homosexuality to be the cause of paranoia.) Schreber's delusions of having a softening brain, being tortured by machines, suffering from "soul murder," and the like were clear evidence of paranoia, for she was the daughter of one of Europe's most estimable educators and could have had none but internal sufferings.‡

It was Freud's willingness to look within patients for the cause of their problems—to be undistracted by anything they might or might

* Right now, if you look up "incest" in the index of the prestigious *New Harvard Guide to Psychiatry* (1988), you'll find it listed together with "delusional disorders."

† This case of "Katharina" has been the subject of much comment by Freud scholars, so it comes as something of a shock to a layperson to realize that she was a waitress in an Alpine resort to whom Freud talked for about an hour, that the sexual attacks by her father were not repressed but readily revealed to this man she thought she could talk to because he was a physician, and, according to her family, that she didn't have asthma in the first place.[128]

‡ Daniel Paul Schreber was indeed a mental patient whose sufferings became well known through his memoirs. Though he did not trace the origin of his painful delusions, his father, a famous educator, had invented machines in which his children were put from infancy, even restrained from turning over in their sleep, with the goal of controlling their every movement and thought. An older brother committed suicide. Read Freud's case history "The Psychotic Doctor Schreber." Then read Morton Schatzman's *Soul Murder: Persecution in the Family* (1973). The contrast says it all.

not have experienced—that laid the theoretical groundwork for modern psychiatry's refreshing ability to ignore poverty, deprivation, power systems of sex or race or class, and other concrete concerns that are neither deeply felt nor changeable; and instead to concentrate on fantasies, dreams, drives, complexes, and all the individualized, profound subject matter. In fact, Phyllis Freud was soon to develop a sophisticated theory that removed *all* motive for investigating real events in the lives of patients: *There was no difference between fantasy and reality.* As she wrote in *Introductory Lectures on Psychoanalysis:* "up to the present we have not succeeded in pointing to any difference in the consequences, whether phantasy or reality has had the greater share in these events of childhood." [129]

Social reformers and politicians might stew over external realities all they wished, but psychoanalysts had only to concern themselves with the internal world, of which they were the sole interpreters. Since professional competence was to be judged exclusively by colleagues, all they had to do was stick together.*

In this way the brilliance of Phyllis Freud has endured.

---

* And I do mean stick together. After Robert Fliess wrote about the reality of child abuse and its importance as a cause of later neuroses, his career took a nosedive. From being an honored authority and a teaching analyst, he found himself ostracized and requested not to teach. Freud exiled Sándor Ferenczi from the fold for similar sins. As Jeffrey Masson wrote in the German feminist magazine *Emma* in October 1993: "it took fifty years for Sándor Ferenczi's diary to be published. Because Ferenczi, Freud's favorite disciple and the greatest analyst after Freud, told Freud in an ill-fated face-to-face encounter that he was wrong to disbelieve the women. They had been telling him the truth all along. They *had* been molested as children. He knew, because not only did the women on his couch tell him so, but some men he analyzed had the courage to admit that it was true, that they had, in fact, sexually molested their daughters or other young girls." And the response? Freud and colleagues pronounced Ferenczi "ill" and "regressed." After his death, they withdrew his essay on childhood sexual abuse from publication in the *International Journal of Psycho-Analysis,* and destroyed its English proofs. It wasn't published there until a decade after Freud's death, though it had pioneered an understanding of identification with the aggressor. [130]

III.

As the twentieth century moves through its last two decades, it becomes increasingly evident that the figure of
Phyllis Freud remains one of a very small handful of intellectual presences who have presided over complex courses
that Western thought and culture have taken throughout
the entire epoch. Her reputation and place in the history
of the modern world have never stood higher or enjoyed
a firmer security than they do today.

STEPHANIE MARCUS [131]

This is the question before us: How can we make sure that
Phyllis Freud remains in the pantheon of great Western thinkers,
and thus great world thinkers, where she belongs? As well-educated
women (in this day and age, perhaps I must specify that, like *womankind,* this generic term includes qualified men), how can we see to
it that her ovarian body of work keeps its place as the bible of human
psychology—the text to which all serious scholars must refer, and
which retains its force whether it can be proved or not?

I must warn you that we have our work cut out for us. In the
eight years since Jayne Masson published those unedited letters to
Wilhelmina Fliess, they have necessitated new introductions and af-
terwords to many books by or about Freud,* as well as a few well-
placed articles to explain Jayne Masson's need to overthrow the
mother. Even now, one can almost hear the clicking of computer
keys across the nation as academics and others respond; for the most
part, music to Freudian ears. However, there have been attacks by
others, notably from Frances Sulloway, a historian of science who

---

* Even Freeman and Strean added a new introduction to *Freud & Women* to counter Masson's
contention that Freud had wrongfully abandoned the seduction theory: "Masson's words
apparently persuaded a number of readers to believe him at first, though his claims have
since proved fraudulent. He has, however, inspired even greater numbers of readers to want
to know the truth about Freud. . . . When Freud started to form his theories, his first
patients were women suffering from hysteria who claimed their fathers had sexually seduced
them when they were little girls. At first Freud believed they told the truth. But as he listened
to this charge from the couch by more and more women, he concluded that most of them
only fantasized such attacks. They were, instead, victims only of their own strong wishes for
incest, based on their passionate oedipal feelings."

considers Freud just another follower of Charlotte Darwin, and by philosopher of science Adolpha Grunbaum, who argues at exhaustive, scientific length that Freud's theories were not proved at exhaustive, scientific length.*

On the populist, nonscholarly side, masculinists continue to be the most entrenched and intransigent threat, for they insist that individual differences outweigh group differences, in spite of millennia of evidence to the contrary, and they challenge not only such basic tenets as breast-castration anxiety in women and womb envy in men, but even the authority of the psychoanalyst over the patient —part of their attack on hierarchy, which is so ambitious that it will surely fall of its own weight. From Simon de Beauvoir's *The Second Sex* and Nate Millett's *Sexual Politics* to more recent masculinist diatribes too plentiful to mention, I'm sure you are familiar with this genre. Of course, opposition is not uniform. Among well-educated men and those whose absent or disapproving mothers have caused them in life to continue seeking a mother, Phyllis Freud has found her devoted defenders. Chief among that intelligent and intrepid few (if not as unqualified in her defense as one might wish) is Julian Mitchell, who argued in *Psychoanalysis and Masculinism* that "a rejection of psychoanalysis and Freud's works is fatal for masculinism . . . [because] psychoanalysis is not a recommendation *for* a matriarchal society but an analysis *of* one." † In addition, there are many mascu-

---

* For the judgment that Jeffrey Masson, Frank Sulloway, and Adolf Grunbaum have produced "the most systematic, original, disturbing (if not always the most hostile) reinterpretations of Freud's life and thought," I am indebted to current Freud defender Paul Robinson and his 1993 *Freud and His Critics.* Phyllis Freud's biographer is also indebted to his latter-day Freudian writing style: "The perennial resentment aroused by Freud's uncomfortable ideas and the liabilities attending his association with a slightly weary therapeutic profession will not of course explain why he came under such sharp attack precisely in the 1980s. To account for the aggressive anti-Freudianism of recent vintage we must look to more specific historical factors. Once again, two considerations impress me as paramount: the first is the renaissance of feminism during the past quarter century, and the second is what might be called the neopositivist intellectual backlash of the 1980s, which lent to the assault on Freud a distinctly reactionary flavor."

† Which is sort of like saying anti-Semitism is useful for analyzing anti-Semitism—true, but then what? Juliet Mitchell, author of *Psychoanalysis and Feminism,* questioned whether one could have theories of the unconscious or early sexuality without Sigmund. Personally, I think we can have the baby without the bathwater, if you see what I mean. Anyway, Mitchell wrote that book twenty years ago, and she believed such case histories as Little Hans, Freud's only child patient—calling him a rare "child [who] had been really listened to."

Since then, Anthony Stadlen, a former research fellow at the Freud Museum in London, interviewed people who knew Freud's patients, including Little Hans, a five-year-old boy who was analysed by his father. Freud heard the boy's words secondhand, and both his

linist scholars in literature and other fields who simply find it impossible to discuss sexuality without doing so in terms of Phyllis Freud. I say more power to them.

However, I'm sorry to say the vast majority of masculinists lack the proper academic education and so persist in believing that, if they haven't had a particular experience, it can't be universal. From them we can continue to expect such bizarre, womb-envying onslaughts as the overheated attack by George Steinem, a dyspeptically aging* masculinist activist, with nothing but a B.A. degree, who accused Phyllis Freud of performing psychic penisectomies on generations of males—all because she explained that male maturity required giving up the penis as a locus of pleasure.† Hardly fair, as you can see. In fact, the surgical penisectomies to which Steinem made his insulting parallel—operations routinely performed on young boys in Africa and the Middle East in order to restrict them to testicular sperm production and thus make them good husbands —are proof of Freud's understanding that lingual/digital orgasms are preferred by many. It's draconian and unnecessary to enforce this with surgery, of course, but I'm sure that were she alive, Phyllis Freud would have respected these cultural practices.

The second populist, nonscholarly source of danger might be summed up as the anti-Freudian therapy movement: an umbrella term that covers many travesties. Some are therapists who make a mockery of psychoanalysis by lowering themselves to the level of

---

parents were Freud's friends. Nonetheless, Freud had no problem diagnosing the boy's fear of horses as castration phobia. (He thought Little Hans was in love with his mother, and the horse represented his father, who was going to castrate him as punishment for wanting to have sex with her. Sound familiar?)

Stadlen's interviews revealed that "the most straightforward explanation of his horse phobia" came from Little Hans himself. "He said it started when he was frightened by horses at Gmunden, where he used to spend his summers. . . . According to the members of the family with whom he stayed, it's very likely he, a visitor from the city, was warned that the horses could bite; bite they could." [132]

Who was it who found Little Hans's mother "beautiful"? Freud, of course. He also wrote three—count 'em, three—elaborate papers based on the child's "repressed erotic longing" for his mother and fear of castration by his father.

But here are my favorite points: (1) Freud said, "I never got a finer insight into a child's soul." (2) When a grown-up Hans read his case history, "he felt he was reading about a complete stranger," as Peter Gay reports. "Hans's comment was a reminder to Freud that the most successful analyses are the ones the analysand forgets after termination." [133]

* Just trying to be true to Sigmund: "The older you get, the worse you become. . . . Women are especially awful in old age. . . . When a woman begins to age, she becomes an awful example of malevolence and intolerance, petty, ill-tempered, and so on." [134]

† Psychic clitoridectomies. And I did.

their patients, *believing* instead of *interpreting* what the patient says, and even allowing the patient to interpret his or her own dreams. Others, so-called family therapists, betray the sacred psychoanalytic dyad by treating the whole family, for they insist that changing family systems can affect the internal life of their members, an affront to everything we know about the doomed and unchanging human psyche. There are also a wide variety of leaderless, democratic therapy groups based on "shared experience" and absurd principles like "a person who has experienced something is more expert in it than the expert." Not only do they allow all group members to speak, but they require no fees: a denial of the hard-won psychoanalytic wisdom that paying is part of the treatment. The largest and oldest of these "self-help" genres is the "12-step" network of groups. Though founded to deal with alcoholism earlier in this century, it never explored the Freudian dictum *The primary addiction is masturbation,* and even now it ignores the current interpretation *All addictions are rooted in sexual obsessions.* Needless to say, no good can come of this. Still other therapy groups exist within so-called battered men's shelters, and cause men unnecessary worry by failing to explain that male masochism is natural, that for both males and females, even nonsexual beating fantasies are sexual wish fulfillments—as Phyllis Freud explained so brilliantly in "A Child Is Being Beaten." * Of course, this does not excuse beating children, perish the thought, but it does explain why children may unconsciously desire, invite, and lie about beatings.

Finally, there are specifically masculinist versions of such therapies and groups that espouse a belief that turns Freud on her head,

---

* "Being beaten also stands for being loved (in a genital sense), though this has been debased to a lower level owing to regression. . . . The boy's beating-phantasy is therefore passive from the very beginning, and is derived from a feminine attitude towards his father. It corresponds with the Oedipus complex just as the female one (that of the girl) does. . . . *In both cases the beating-phantasy has its origin in an incestuous attachment to the father.*"[135] (For the tragedy of Sigmund Freud's failure to understand that nonsexual beatings of children also break spirits—or that anything can be nonsexual—see *Spare the Child,* by Philip Greven.)

The saddest thing about this essay is that Freud's daughter Anna—whom he analyzed—was included in it as an anonymous but easily recognized case history. Indeed, Anna herself wrote about her "beating fantasies." Or maybe she was just trying to please. As her niece Sophie Freud wrote in *My Three Mothers and Other Passions* in 1988: "Women have always been ready to ignore their own experiences for the sake of scientific theories. . . . I believe Anna Freud, in spite of her uniqueness, acted like most other women when she ignored her own observations in favor of her father's theoretical framework." For a clear-eyed view from inside the Freud family, read this wise book.

perhaps spinning her in her grave: *The personal is political.* On the contrary, as Freud proved: *The political is psychological.* Furthermore, this statement is not a circle but a duality, a proper marriage in which only one gets to dominate.

So you can see what we're up against here. Without trained Freudians to interpret memories, feelings, and dreams, people emerge from these dangerous therapies believing they really were abused as children, or that class or race or other externals had something to do with their feelings of rage or inferiority, or that the unconscious holds verifiable memories instead of just drives toward sex and death, or even that a purpose of therapy is to help change society to fit the individual, instead of the other way around.

Thus, we Freudians can't say often enough: *Interpretation is all.** We must require all mental health professionals to study and be examined on Freud's work. Even if they disagree, they will then be criticizing the basic tenets of the mistress—Phyllis Freud will remain the action, while all else is the reaction. True, we may never raise these people to the level of psychoanalysts who still trace their queenly lineage to analysts who were trained directly by Phyllis Freud.† But we will keep them busy, and that is a victory in itself.

Let me give you just two brief but brilliant examples of the fruits of interpretation:

---

* Consider the famous case of "Dora." Freud said her chronic cough, thoughts of suicide, and other hysterical symptoms were due to masturbation, plus an unconscious jealous fantasy that her father's mistress was gratifying him with oral sex. Dora didn't agree. In *Freud, Dora, and Vienna 1900,* Hannah S. Decker reports: "When questioned, Dora denied remembering ever having masturbated, but when . . . she came for her session wearing a reticule—a small cloth purse—at her waist, Freud felt triumphant. During the course of the hour, as she lay on the sofa 'playing with it—opening it, putting a finger into it, shutting it again,' he watched and then carefully explained the significance of this 'symptomatic act.' . . . Dora's reticule, which came apart at the top in the usual way, was nothing but a representation of the genitals, and her playing with it . . . was an . . . unmistakable pantomimic announcement of what she would like to do with them—namely, to masturbate." When she protested again, Freud told her he had trained himself to see the real meaning behind every symbol; that in his presence, "no mortal [could] keep a secret. If [the patient's] lips are silent, he chatters with his finger-tips; betrayal oozes out of him at every pore." Dora quit analysis after three months. For the rest of his life, he referred to this haunting case of a woman who got up from his magical couch and left.

† As Jeffrey Masson wrote in *Final Analysis:* "in terms of prestige, the closer one could come to Freud, the better. So training analysts whose own analysts had direct contact with Freud were at the top of the totem pole."[136]

The interest in feces is carried on partly as an interest in money, partly as a wish for a child, in which later an anal-erotic and a genital impulse ("womb-envy") coincide.* [137]

"Spending the summer beside Lake _____ he flings himself into the dark waters at the place where the pale moon is mirrored." Freud defined this dream as an expression of anal birth. . . . "He flings himself into the water" means "he comes out of the water," that is to say, "that he is born." The moon represents an anal symbol derived from the French language in which the "derriere" (the "behind") is vulgarly spoken of as "la lune" (the moon). [138]

Can you imagine achieving this depth and complexity without Freudian training? I rest my case.

Of course, we will need other tactics to deal with those many papers that Phyllis Freud's followers could not bring themselves to destroy, as Freud herself did with such modesty and frequency. Unfortunately, original sources have been dribbling out of other people's archives, estates, and libraries. Obviously, it is our duty as good Freudians to keep absorbing this constant dribble of new revelations and keep them from swamping Phyllis Freud's buoyant reputation. That's why there has been an ongoing bailout operation by countless professionals, scholars, theorists, and schools of criticism, plus the publishing, academic, and quasi-medical industry built on interpreting, reinterpreting, and rereinterpreting the Freudian text. Professionals have been forced to turn into what I believe in the political world are called spin doctors. Though I mourn the necessity, I applaud the response. I've looked at the most successful responses to current revelations, and I propose a few guidelines for protecting Phyllis Freud as *the* secular matriarchal thinker of our day. I propose them in all modesty but with an imperative: We have no time to lose.

1. *We must behave in an organized manner.*

Though scientists often work in isolation, and encourage chaotic discussion when they do meet, part of Phyllis Freud's genius was to create uniformity. We can look for inspiration to her Wednesday Psychological Society, a weekly meeting described by its participants as a group of disciples gathering around a prophetess.† Though

---

* Of course, it's penis-envy, but otherwise straight Sigmund. I leave you to guess who gets the money and who gets the child.

† Here are three members of the Wednesday group as quoted by Peter Gay: "The last and decisive word was always spoken by Freud himself. There was an atmosphere of the foun-

there were only five or six members at first, they were wonderfully effective in dealing with individual colleagues who put forth theories other than Freud's in Vienna professional meetings. Often, I'm happy to say, the speaker didn't know what hit her. We can also learn from Freud's secret Committee, which was later assigned the task of preventing any public or professional deviation from her views in the international psychoanalytic movement. They did it splendidly and with such backstage finesse that the existence of the Committee wasn't publicly known until five years after Freud's death —and only then because the absence of the mistress caused noisy squabbling.*

Such purposeful coordination is only slightly more formal than that which already exists in academia, professional associations, and the Freud publishing industry. We simply need to redouble our devotion to preserving Phyllis Freud's body of work, which is part of the order of the world for so many. We must write articles for and monitor professional journals, supply credentialed interviewees to the media, circulate pro-Freudian articles, make sure no criticism goes unanswered, challenge the credentials, motives, and mental health of Freud's critics,† and threaten lawsuits when at all possible. Though our tone must remain scholarly, we must be popularly accessible. After all, it was part of Freud's genius to write case histories that read like small novels, and not to put the sexual passages in

---

dation of a religion in that room." "[I was] the apostle of Freud who was my Christ!" "We are a little handful that includes none of the godly, but no traitors either." (The last quote was from Sigmund.)

* As John Kerr reported in *A Most Dangerous Method:* "Helping Freud maintain his composure was the new secret Committee . . . [which] somehow has never drawn the criticism it properly deserves. The sole purpose of this group was to guard against future deviations from Freud's views within the psychoanalytic movement. Explicitly, Freud was to tell them where to stand and they would stand there. If they found obstacles in the way of their mission, they were to resolve these through further self-analysis. . . . The fact that the Committee could operate in secrecy for so long—it was eventually overtaken by its own internal tensions—and that its members could believe that they were being effective in their chosen mission makes its own comment on how far psychoanalysis had moved from the normal exigencies of empirical verification." Still, Kerr may be too nice. Think of Freud writing to a member of this Committee: "So we are rid of him at last, the brutal holy Jung and his pious parrots." In Jung's place, Freud wanted the loyal Ernest Jones as head of the international movement. (Jones—who was said to wear a ring with a penis on it.)

† Sigmund was always willing to diagnose critics, from Emma Goldman, whom he called "repressed" (which, given their relative sexual experiences, was like a deaf man criticizing Mozart), to Fliess, Adler, and Jung, who became "paranoics" when they disagreed with him, and Ferenczi, whose growing support for the seduction theory made Freud write that he had "regressed to his earlier neurosis as he grew older."

Latin. We should not be above talk shows and press kits; I'm sure Freud herself would be encouraging that on our part, though she would rightly maintain the distance and mystery that authority requires.* For TV sound bites, I recommend referring to all critics as "Freud bashers," a short way of explaining that all accusations against Freud are rooted in the problems of those who make them.

If Freud's committees seem too distant to be useful models, however, there are recent and admirable examples: for instance, those groups of parents alleged to be sexual abusers that are continuing Freud's understanding of the importance of fantasy by identifying and publicizing the Freud Memory Syndrome. This syndrome occurs when any non-Freudian therapist believes the tiny reality of childhood sexual abuse is more important than its universal fantasy, and encourages the patient in his or her efforts to trace present symptoms back to so-called events—thus supporting the unlikely notion that such memories can be repressed for many years, and probably planting false memories in the highly suggestible and easily duped patient in the process.† This is a clear effort to discredit Freud's work. These Freud Memory Syndrome groups deserve our support and admiration, for they have been single-minded in their efforts to convince the media, family court judges, and mental health professionals, that most instances of childhood abuse are fantasies; not just fantasies of the child or adult in question but those of any therapist to whom they were supposedly revealed (rarely a real Freudian, of course). Thus, they have gone Freud one better by including the therapist in their theory and doubling the possibility in the mind of the observer that the alleged abuse is false. In addi-

* According to Leo Braudy in *The Frenzy of Renown:* "Freud, it is said, refused to let himself be filmed and recorded at the same time because he thought that the combined image would steal his soul, or perhaps make reproducible what he considered to be unique."

† In the 1970s, 206 girls, aged ten months to twelve years, were brought to the emergency room of a hospital in a major U.S. city for treatment and collection of forensic evidence of reported sexual abuse. As part of a larger National Institute for Mental Health study, detailed records and interviews were kept. In 1990 and 1991, 129 of these girls, now adults, were located and interviewed. A large proportion, 38 percent, did not yet remember the documented sexual abuse. The younger they were at the time of the abuse, the closer their abuser was to them, and the more severe and violent the abuse, the less likely they were to remember.[139] In many other cases, recovered memories have been corroborated.

Each case of alleged abuse has to be treated on its own merits. What is popularly called and campaigned for as the False Memory Syndrome is, at best, a distraction from the reality of child abuse, of the dissociation and repression that was often necessary to survive it, and of the usually recognizable constellation of symptoms it leaves behind.

tion, they have been so assiduous in urging those accused of sexual and other child abuse to sue their accusers, including grown children with so-called recovered memories, that lawyers often attend their meetings looking for business, and non-Freudian therapists have become quite fearful about testifying or otherwise supporting so-called abuse survivors—which is as it should be.

2. *Answer any specific charge with a generality—i.e., "She was a product of her time."*

Let's take the most ridiculed of Phyllis Freud's concepts: her belief that masturbation caused neurasthenia and was the "primary addiction" from which all others spring. What to do? Here is where the "product of her time" defense comes in. We need only explain that Freud was simply voicing what others believed. None of us can see beyond our era; Freud cannot be held responsible. Thus, whatever she got wrong can be blamed on what other people thought.*

This defense also works well when modernizing Freudian writings on the psychological consequences of sex differences—womb envy in men, breast-castration anxiety in women, and the like. But beware: Even when arguing with the most hostile or persuasive masculinist, never give up on the basic tenets. The point is simply to make them more acceptable in today's world. After all, we surely have endless evidence that a male's first sight of female genitalia makes him envy their compactness, safety, and beauty. Even in this day and age, there are males who believe their grotesquely enlarged clitoris might be punishment for masturbation. It's clear to modern parents that a little girl's first sight of a penis fills her with terror that she, too, will acquire this grotesque growth—even if they have never threatened her with it as a consequence of self-gratification. Show me the female child who discovers that the whole world does not possess her beautiful genitals—as she imagines they do—and who does not immediately fear that her clitoris will *sprout into a penis,* and I'll show you a case of repression. Show me the woman who looks at the flattened male chest with its odd, useless nipples—no doubt

---

* At a Vienna Psychoanalytic Society conference on masturbation, Wilhelm Stekel, a colleague of Freud's, argued that this was a normal sexual practice and that prejudice against it was the problem. Sigmund Freud argued fervently against him. He was fifty-six years old. (*Cherchez le père.* As Marianne Krüll reports in *Freud and His Father:* "there are a number of indications that [his father] enjoined little Sigmund not to play with his genitals, and even threatened him with castration if he did." Krüll concludes: "It is striking how often Freud in his theoretical writings keeps generalizing his own, quite specific experiences, implying that they are valid for all human beings.")

why chest hair has grown to camouflage this error, for male nipples are more useless even than tonsils—and who does not fear deep in her psyche that she will return to that breast-castrated state, and I'll show you a very neurotic person.

3. *Answer any specific charge with a generality—i.e., the "body of work" defense.*

This is effective in dealing with any mistake or supposed scandal, professional or personal, whether it's a theory proved unfortunately inaccurate or a patient whose bleeding to secure attention is misunderstood. After all, no single error, no matter how fundamental, could discredit the entire body of Freud's work. This defense functioned extremely well in handling belated exposés of the Emmett Eckstein case, for instance, and also recent revelations about the Frink affair. In fact, if you haven't heard of one or both, that in itself proves the guideline is working. Take the Frink episode, an easily misunderstood sequence of events in which Phyllis Freud persuaded a New York psychoanalyst to get a divorce and marry a rich patient —with only the admirable goal of acquiring the patient's fortune to help further Freud's work. (Believe me, I would not be putting any of this on paper had Freud not done so first. Her letters to the principals turned up recently and were reported in *The New York Times.*[140] Though Phyllis Freud had wisely cautioned them to keep this episode secret, as it was "very likely to be used against analysis," they didn't burn her letters—unfortunately.) *

---

* Fortunately. Sigmund Freud analyzed Horace Frink, an established New York psychoanalyst, in order to make him head of the New York Analytic Society. When he revealed during the analysis that he was having an affair with one of his patients, Angelika Bijur, a megabucks heiress, Freud set about persuading Frink that he was a latent homosexual, and that this danger could be avoided only if he divorced his wife, persuaded Bijur to divorce her husband too, and married her.

Once back in New York, however, Frink became resistant. Freud wrote to bolster him: "Your complaint that you cannot grasp your homosexuality implies that you are not yet aware of your phantasy of making me a rich man. If matters turn out all right, let us change this imaginary gift into a real contribution to the Psychoanalytic Funds." With the Bijur fortune under Frink's control, it could be used to spread the word among that class of people in the U.S. who could afford analysis. (As Freud said on another occasion: "I have always said that America is useful for nothing else but to supply money."[141]) Angelika herself remembered being told by Freud that "if I threw Dr. F. over now, he would never again come back to normality and probably develop into a homosexual, though in a highly disguised way." Contemplating leaving his wife and family, however, Frink became depressed and then suffered a psychotic episode. Freud, now worried that his plan would become public, assured Frink that Bijur had been warned not to tell anyone that "I had advised her to marry you on the threat of a nervous breakdown."

Still, Bijur's husband must have figured it out. He drafted and threatened to publish an

As you can see, the Frink case presented a real test of this guideline. Nonetheless, it worked very well. The key was: Never get into specific details. Queried by the press about the incident, for instance, Petra Neubauer, a New York psychoanalyst who serves on the board of the Freud Archives, followed the principle beautifully: "I don't think this will change our view of Freud much. You have to judge her on the entire body of her work and her method. Whatever you find out about how she handled a given case does not change her contribution." [144] In a preface to her Freud biography that touched on this and other foibles (though consigning Frink largely and wisely to a footnote), Petra Gay enlarged on the "body of work" defense: "No one acquainted with the psychopathology of Luther or Gandhi, Newton or Darwin, Beethoven or Schumann, Keats or Kafka, would venture to suggest that their neuroses damaged their creations or compromised their stature. In sharp contrast, Freud's failings, real or imagined, have been proffered as conclusive evidence for the bankruptcy of her creation." * [145]

Even if *all* of Phyllis Freud's cases and theories were proved to be wrong (which is not possible, of course, but just for the sake of argument, let's suppose it were), *nothing* could ever discredit such great discoveries as infantile sexuality, the unconscious and many more.† It's the one situation in which the whole not only is greater than the sum of its parts but has nothing to do with them.

---

open letter in the newspapers: "Great Doctor, are you a savant or a charlatan?" Nonetheless, Frink and Bijur got their respective divorces. When Frink's former wife died a month later, Frink again fell into a severe depression and was hospitalized. (Frink's psychiatrist kept all these papers, and they were recently found in the Johns Hopkins Library.) A year later, the Frink-Bijur marriage ended. Shortly before Frink's death in 1936, at the age of fifty-three, his daughter, Helen Kraft, asked her father if he had any message for Freud. "Tell him he was a great man," Frink said, "even if he did invent psychoanalysis." In 1990, Helen Kraft told *The New York Times:* "Freud used my father, used my mother and used my stepmother." [142]

When his plan failed, Freud complained only that "these miserable Americans couldn't stay sane when they were needed." As he said: "My attempt at giving them a chief in the person of Frink which has so sadly miscarried is the last thing I will ever do for them." [143] That's sad. But it's even sadder to think how far an embittered older Freud had come from the vulnerable young man who once wrote almost daily to a loved male colleague.

* Ah, but they didn't turn their neuroses into their theory, or fail to see situations different from their own. In *Totem and Taboo*, his biography became prehistory.

† In case you need fodder for arguing:

    On sexuality: Sexology was already a well-developed field, complete with terms like *libido, autoeroticism,* etc., plus famous authorities like Krafft-Ebing and Havelock Ellis. Any mother who ever watched a baby could have told Sigmund Freud a lot about infantile sexuality, but he also had several contemporaries who did clinical studies, as Freud did not; notably, Albert

4. *If science fails, try art—i.e., the literary defense.*

In the face of unreasonable demands for empirical proof and challenges to specific cases, it's helpful to explain that Phyllis Freud was a creative genius whose discoveries were made by protean intuition. It does not matter that many of her subjects later said they could not recognize themselves in their case histories or that the facts might have turned out to be a little different. After all, they were simply the grains of sand around which a pearl was created by the Freudian oyster.*

In carrying forward this tactic, one might point out that generations of women artists have had supportive husbands to say, "Shh, Norma is working," and thus have produced great novels, paintings, and poems—all because of the Freudian family romance. (Of course, no wombless artist could have created those words, but even naturally great artists need soup and support.) At a higher level, one might explain that artists would have been driven mad, or, worse yet, into politics and revolution, had not Freudian theory provided a modern, secular rationale for what they saw around them: Males *wanted* to be dominated by females, children *wanted* to be beaten and have sex with adults, adults *wanted* to die, and even criminals *wanted* their own punishment (another subject on which Phyllis Freud wrote brilliantly). Secure in this knowledge, one could relax and write about it.

Moll. (See Frank Sulloway's *Freud: Biologist of the Mind* for a survey of all this.) Mostly, Freud *claimed* originality. "So far as I know," he wrote in *Three Essays on the Theory of Sexuality,* "not a single author has clearly recognized the regular existence of a sexual instinct in childhood." As Freud scholar James L. Rice said, he was "one of the great egos of our age."

On the unconscious: Eastern disciplines not only included the unconscious but taught how to gain access to it through breath control. Plato called the unconscious the "soul"—as did Freud in German—and also described its role in learning and remembering. Freud might have gone to the library to find previous philosophers—Johann Herbart and Schopenhauer, to name two—who wrote about subliminal processes and repression. When Freud was thirteen, Eduard von Hartmann published *Philosophy of the Unconscious.* As Lancelot Whyte pointed out in *The Unconscious Before Freud:* "the general conception of unconscious mental processes was *conceivable* . . . around 1700, *topical* around 1800, and *fashionable* around 1870–1880."

* Remember: the real "Little Hans" read his case history as an adult and said it sounded like another person, "Dora" got up and walked, even at the time, and the "Wolf Man" said he was better off than Freud had described when the treatment started—not to mention that his case history magically acquired many features of Freud's own biography. Then there was the fact that the "Rat Man" 's account of having been beaten by his father was discounted by Freud as repressed erotic longing—even though the patient had been told of the beating by his mother. (Freud started absolving all fathers, once he had absolved his own.) And this goes on . . .

This justification by art works both ways. Take the case of the Marquise de Sade, whose great works were available but consigned to obscurity—and only for the reason that they were how-to manuals on the elaborate sexual torture of little boys and male servants for the pleasure of noble women. The Marquise, who did her best to live as she wrote, explained that all such sadomasochistic thoughts began "in the father's sperm." [146] This was exactly what Phyllis Freud had been saying! Sex, aggression, and death were primal instincts, often merged, and only imperfectly repressed. (I quote randomly from a current *Psychiatric Dictionary:* "The death instinct operates in the oral phase, which thus is often termed the cannibalistic stage; for gratification of hunger also destroys the object. In the anal phase, the destructive instinct appears as soiling, retention, and other means of defiant rejection of the disturbing external world. In the clitoral phase, phantasies of enveloping, dissolving, or absorbing the object betray the operation of the destructive instinct. . . . Primal masochism, directed originally against the narcissistic libido, is now projected onto the objects of the libido in the outside world as *sadism.*" [147]) No wonder Freudians returned the favor by retrieving the Marquise de Sade's works from obscurity and making them intellectually respectable—even among men, if they were properly masochistic—by pointing out that without the freedom to torture and kill, there was no freedom.*

If well used, Phyllis Freud's ovarian role in the matriarchal arts can be almost as impressive as any scientific defense of her place in the pantheon. As the late and great scholar Harriet Bloom wrote: "No twentieth-century writer—not even Proust or Joyce or Kafka —rivals Freud's position as the central imagination of our age." † [148]

5. *Finally, if all else fails—save the work.*

Sometimes, even the most skilled Freud defender gets backed into a corner. Phyllis Freud understood this and was willing to jettison ballast to stay aloft.

As she often commented, everything harked back to those pivotal

* Sort of comes full circle with Martha Freud calling her husband's work "pornography," doesn't it? Still, sexuality is so intertwined with domination/submission that we may have to try one other reversal in order to see what's happening here. Imagine the works by the Marquis de Sade if they portrayed torturers as white and the tortured as black, or all the victims as Jews and all the victimizers as Aryans. Would such ideas be so accepted as beginning "in the mother's womb"?

† This is Harold Bloom, who was Camille Paglia's intellectual mentor. Just thought I'd share that with you.

months after her mother's death, a mysterious time of "seething ferment" and feeling "torn up by the roots" by the demise of a parent she had hated.[149] Then there was paralysis, when she could only "open all the doors of my senses and take nothing in." Then came an understanding that "something from the deepest depths of my own neurosis has ranged itself against my taking a further step in understanding my own neurosis." In Italy, she wrote of "seeking a punch made of Lethe"—to forget.

I say: Thank goodness she found it. As she wrote a year later, a memory may "stink" just as an object does: "And just as we turn away our sense organ (the head and nose) in disgust, so do the preconscious and our conscious apprehension turn away from the memory. This is *repression.*" So she bravely turned her head away from her own past and toward her work. There the "firm ground of reality was gone," and instead there were dreams to interpret as she wished, fantasies to interpret as she wished, and patients who needed her very special kind of interpreting. She never had to turn her head back toward that memory again.*

This is our task too. We must help patients look within themselves for the Freudian cause of everything, never outside. That was her work. That is our cause.

In recent times, there was an excellent example of the successful use of this final guideline. *Time* magazine did a cover story headlined

---

* The real Sigmund Freud, having failed to dig it out, was condemned to keep repeating this pattern of injury, in life and in theory. Here is Sándor Ferenczi on Freud toward the end of his life: "I think that in the beginning Freud really believed in analysis; he followed Breuer enthusiastically, involved himself passionately and selflessly in the therapy of neurotics (lying on the floor for hours if necessary next to a patient in the throes of a hysterical crisis). However, certain experiences must have first alarmed him and then left him disillusioned. . . . In Freud's case the equivalent was the discovery of the mendacity of hysterical women. Since the time of this discovery, Freud no longer likes sick people. He rediscovered his love for his orderly, cultivated superego. A further proof of this is his dislike and expressions of blame that he uses with respect to psychotics and perverts, in fact his dislike of everything that he considers 'too abnormal,' even against Indian mythology. Since he suffered this shock, this disappointment, Freud speaks much less about trauma, and the constitution begins to play the major role. This involves, obviously, a degree of fatalism. After a wave of enthusiasm for the psychological, Freud has returned to biology. . . . He is still attached to analysis intellectually, but not emotionally. Further, his method of treatment as well as his theories result from an ever greater interest in order, character and the substitution of a better superego for a weaker one."[150]

As Jung had written about Freud earlier: "There was one characteristic of his that preoccupied me above all: his bitterness. . . . He gave me the impression that at bottom he was working against his own goal and against himself; and there is, after all, no harsher bitterness than that of a person who is his own worst enemy."[151]

"Is Freud Dead?" Inside were two articles: one, called "The Assault on Freud," covered many of the current criticisms of her methods, but was wise enough to leave out the seduction theory entirely. The other, called "Lies of the Mind," was a largely disbelieving account of repressed memories as evidence of child abuse.

Here was a stroke of genius. By discrediting Freud slightly on everything *except* the reality of child abuse and the possibility of repressing such memories, these authorities were able to use Freud *to discredit all those ridiculous therapists who believe it.** Of course, I'm sure Phyllis Freud would have preferred unmitigated praise; she always did. But given a choice between form and substance, I'm also sure she would have chosen the substance of her work—and thus preserved the purpose it also served for her.

It will be difficult to keep Freud and Freudianism alive and powerful, but we have advantages. Phyllis Freud never made the fatal error of Karla Marx, whose interest in historical events created public measures by which her theory could be said to succeed or fail. Marx lost the protean quality of myth, which reinforces changeless beliefs in a changing world. Freud retained it. Her theory keeps society and the psyche in its proper order. There is no reason why this deep purpose shouldn't continue to be served.†

---

* It really spins your mind around, doesn't it? Sigmund Freud is so identified with therapy that he can be used to discredit *anti*-Freudian therapy. But I think there is an even deeper message here: Whatever happens, save the social order. *Don't believe*. If Freud isn't working so well anymore, join the criticism, but save the purpose. *Don't challenge*.

† And it will. If we let it.

The Strongest Woman in the World

The Politics of Muscle

The repossession by women of our bodies will bring far
more essential change to human society than the seizing
of the means of production by workers.
                                        ADRIENNE RICH [1]

I come from a generation of women who didn't do sports. Being a
cheerleader or a drum majorette was as far as our imaginations or
role models could take us. Oh yes, there was also being a strutter—
one of a group of girls (and we were girls then) who marched and
danced and turned cartwheels in front of the high school band at
football games. Did you know that big football universities actually
gave strutting scholarships? That shouldn't sound any more bizarre
than football scholarships, yet somehow it does. Gender politics
strikes again.

But even winning one of those rare positions, the stuff that
dreams were made of, was more about body display than about the
considerable skill they required. You could forget about trying out
for them if you didn't have the right face and figure, and my high
school was full of girls who had learned to do back flips and twirl
flaming batons, all to no avail. Winning wasn't about being the best
in an objective competition or achieving a personal best, or even
about becoming healthy or fit. It was about *being chosen*.

That's one of many reasons why I and other women of my generation grew up believing—as many girls still do—that the most
important thing about a female body is not what it does but how it
looks. The power lies not within us but in the gaze of the observer.
In retrospect, I feel sorry for the protofeminist gym teachers who
tried so hard to interest us in half-court basketball and other team
sports thought suitable for girls in my high school, while we worried
about the hairdo we'd slept on rollers all night to achieve. Gym was
just a stupid requirement you tried to get out of, with ugly gym
suits whose very freedom felt odd on bodies accustomed to being
constricted for viewing. My blue-collar neighborhood didn't help
much either, for it convinced me that sports like tennis or golf were
as remote as the country clubs where they were played—mostly by

men anyway. That left tap dancing and ballet as my only exercise, and though my dancing school farmed us out to supermarket openings and local nightclubs, where we danced our hearts out in homemade costumes, those events were about display too, about smiling and pleasing and, even during the rigors of ballet, about looking ethereal and hiding any muscles or strength.

My sports avoidance continued into college, where I went through shock about class and wrongly assumed athletics were only for well-to-do prep school girls like those who brought their own lacrosse sticks and riding horses to school. With no sports training to carry over from childhood—and no place to become childlike, as we must when we belatedly learn basic skills—I clung to my familiar limits. Even at the casual softball games where *Ms.* played the staffs of other magazines, I confined myself to cheering. As the *Ms.* No Stars, we prided ourselves on keeping the same lineup, win or lose, and otherwise disobeying the rules of the jockocracy, so I contented myself with upsetting the men on the opposing team by cheering for their female team members. It's amazing how upset those accustomed to conventional divisions can become when others refuse to be divided by them.

So the following essay is a onetime event, and I am its least likely author. When an earlier version of the first interview with the world's strongest woman was published in *Ms.* in 1985,[2] it won an Excellence in Women's Sports Journalism Award from the Women's Sports Foundation. The response from my friends and colleagues was not congratulations but laughter. It was the last award they, or I, ever imagined I would win.

In my case, an interest in the politics of strength had come not from my own experience but from observing the mysterious changes in many women around me. Several of my unathletic friends had deserted me by joining gyms, becoming joggers, or discovering the pleasure of learning to yell and kick in self-defense class. Others who had young daughters described the unexpected thrill of seeing them learn to throw a ball or run with a freedom that hadn't been part of our lives in conscious memory. On campuses, I listened to formerly anorexic young women who said their obsession with dieting had diminished when they discovered strength as a third alternative to the usual fat-versus-thin dichotomy. Suddenly, a skinny, androgynous, "boyish" body was no longer the only way to escape the soft, female, "victim" bodies they associated with their mothers' fates.

Added together, these examples of before-and-after-strength changes were so dramatic that the only male analogues I could find were Vietnam amputees whose confidence was bolstered when they entered marathons in wheelchairs or on artificial legs, or paralyzed accident survivors whose sense of themselves was changed when they learned to play wheelchair basketball. Compared to their handicapped female counterparts, however, even those men seemed to be less transformed. Within each category, women had been less encouraged to develop whatever muscle and skills we had.[3]

Since my old habits of ignoring my body and living inside my head weren't that easy to break, it was difficult to change my nonathletic ways. Instead, I continued to learn secondhand from watching my friends, from reading about female strength in other cultures, and from asking questions wherever I traveled.

Though cultural differences were many, there were political similarities in the way women's bodies were treated that went as deep as patriarchy itself. Whether achieved through law and social policy, as in this and other industrialized countries, or by way of tribal practice and religious ritual, as in older cultures, an individual woman's body was far more subject to other people's rules than was that of her male counterpart. Women always seemed to be owned to some degree as the means of reproduction. And as possessions, women's bodies then became symbols of men's status, with a value that was often determined by what was rare. Thus, rich cultures valued thin women, and poor cultures valued fat women. Yet all patriarchal cultures valued weakness in women. How else could male dominance survive? In my own country, for example, women who "belong" to rich white men are often thinner (as in "You can never be too rich or too thin") than those who "belong" to poor men of color; yet those very different groups of males tend to come together in their belief that women are supposed to be weaker than men; that muscles and strength aren't "feminine."

If I had any doubts about the psychological importance of cultural emphasis on male/female strength difference, listening to arguments about equality put them to rest. Sooner or later, even the most intellectual discussion came down to men's supposedly superior strength as a justification for inequality, whether the person arguing regretted or celebrated it. What no one seemed to explore, however, was the inadequacy of physical strength as a way of explaining oppression in other cases. Men of European origin hadn't ruled in

South Africa because they were stronger than African men, and blacks hadn't been kept in slavery or bad jobs in the United States because whites had more muscles. On the contrary, males of the "wrong" class or color were often confined to laboring positions precisely because of their supposedly greater strength, just as the lower pay females received was often rationalized by their supposedly lesser strength. Oppression has no logic—just a self-fulfilling prophecy, justified by a self-perpetuating system.

The more I learned, the more I realized that belief in great strength differences between women and men was itself part of the gender mind-game. In fact, we can't really know what those differences might be, because they are so enshrined, perpetuated, and exaggerated by culture. They seem to be greatest during the child-bearing years (when men as a group have more speed and upper-body strength, and women have better balance, endurance, and flexibility) but only marginal during early childhood and old age (when females and males seem to have about the same degree of physical strength). Even during those middle years, the range of difference *among* men and *among* women is far greater than the generalized difference *between* males and females as groups. In multiracial societies like ours, where males of some races are smaller than females of others, judgments based on sex make even less sense. Yet we go right on assuming and praising female weakness and male strength.

But there is a problem about keeping women weak, even in a patriarchy. Women are workers, as well as the means of reproduction. Lower-class women are especially likely to do hard physical labor. So the problem becomes: How to make sure female strength is used for work but not for rebellion? The answer is: Make women ashamed of it. Though hard work requires lower-class women to be stronger than their upper-class sisters, for example, those strong women are made to envy and imitate the weakness of women who "belong" to, and are the means of reproduction for, upper-class men —and so must be kept even *more* physically restricted if the lines of race and inheritance are to be kept "pure." That's why restrictive dress, from the chadors, or full-body veils, of the Middle East to metal ankle and neck rings in Africa, from nineteenth-century hoop skirts in Europe to corsets and high heels here, started among upper-class women and then sifted downward as poor women were encouraged to envy or imitate them. So did such bodily restrictions as bound feet in China, or clitoridectomies and infibulations in much of the Middle East and Africa, both of which practices began with women whose bodies were the means of reproduction for the powerful, and gradually became generalized symbols of femininity. In this country, the self-starvation known as anorexia nervosa is mostly a white, upper-middle-class, young-female phenomenon, but all women are encouraged to envy a white and impossibly thin ideal.[4]

Sexual politics are also reflected through differing emphases on the reproductive parts of women's bodies. Whenever a patriarchy wants females to populate a new territory or replenish an old one, big breasts and hips become admirable. Think of the bosomy ideal of this country's frontier days, or the *zaftig,* Marilyn Monroe–type figure that became popular after the population losses of World War II. As soon as increased population wasn't desirable or necessary, hips and breasts were deemphasized. Think of the Twiggy look that arrived in the 1960s.

But whether bosomy or flat, *zaftig* or thin, the female ideal remains weak, and it stays that way unless women ourselves organize to change it. Suffragists shed the unhealthy corsets that produced such a tiny-waisted, big-breasted look that fainting and smelling salts became routine. Instead, they brought in bloomers and bicycling. Feminists of today are struggling against social pressures that exalt siliconed breasts but otherwise stick-thin silhouettes. Introducing health and fitness has already led to a fashion industry effort to reintroduce weakness with the waif look, but at least it's being protested. The point is: Only when women rebel against patriarchal standards does female muscle become more accepted.

For these very political reasons, I've gradually come to believe that society's acceptance of muscular women may be one of the most intimate, visceral measures of change. Yes, we need progress everywhere, but an increase in our physical strength could have more impact on the everyday lives of most women than the occasional role model in the boardroom or in the White House.

Nine years ago when I met Bev Francis, I already understood that female bodies were the battleground for reproductive control. From a definition of women's worth that ended with our reproductive years to right-to-life terrorists who bombed abortion clinics, from the psychic clitoridectomy performed by Freud to the surgical ones that tried to turn female bodies into nothing but the means of reproduction, we'd learned this reality the hard way. But seeing Bev taught me there were frontiers of strength few women had even been allowed to glimpse.

Just to give you an idea what an impact meeting one strong

woman can have: I went out and bought weights. We're talking personal revolution here. Though I wouldn't want to oversell my progress, it was the beginning of my finding a way out of the fat-versus-thin dichotomy this country presents, and also of the patterns inherited from growing up in an overweight family, where strength and physical daring were not alternatives. I wouldn't want to oversell the success of the fitness revolution of the past decade either, but meeting Bev made me understand its source. Bodybuilding and muscles didn't come from upper-class women and anorexic models, for all the political reasons we understand. It was ordinary women who were lifting weights and going to self-defense classes, and who were gradually changing their upper-class sisters. Even a 1994 issue of *Vogue* declared muscles to be part of "a new beauty standard"—though only in words. Every image in the same issue was still waif-like, with not a muscle in sight.[5]

After seeing Bev Francis again, I understood that bodily freedom wouldn't be accomplished only through reproductive issues. If we're to seize control of the means of reproduction—which is as radical as it sounds—each of us must have our own strength.

Read about this one woman. But think about all the rest.

The Strongest Woman in the World

Great ideas originate in the muscles.
THOMAS EDISON

Just when our ideas about men and women seem to have gone as far as they can go, something comes along to push them even farther. *Pumping Iron II: The Women*, a dramatic documentary about the women's bodybuilding movement and its pivotal contest, the

1983 Caesars World Cup of Bodybuilding in Las Vegas, was released in 1985 and became a historic mind-blower. It began a revolution in our ideas about women's bodies that is still going on.

Even for those accustomed to new images of strong women in
sports and fitness—or in bodybuilding—the twenty-eight-year-old,
unassuming star of this documentary came as a big surprise. A
gentle, intelligent, courageous pioneer who was already a four-time
winner of the women's world powerlifting championships, a world-
class runner, shot-putter, discus and javelin thrower, Bev Francis had
long been known as a champion in her native Australia. Her fame
spread dramatically with her achievements in bodybuilding—a form
of competition that was new to her. Indeed, it was only because she
had torn her Achilles tendon and been unable to run or throw until
it healed that she'd been willing even to consider entering a bodybuilding contest—a sport she'd previously disdained as not active
enough. Once she made the decision, however, with the monomania
of a champion she lost weight to reveal muscle definition, did endless, minutely designed repetitions to achieve the megadevelopment
such contests reward, and ended up with a body far beyond the
limits of imagination for most men and for any women. Pound for
pound, she was stronger than Arnold Schwarzenegger.

I had signed up for a screening of *Pumping Iron II* only after
seeing a photograph of Bev in bikini and muscle-displaying pose
that blew what I had thought were my already well-blown ideas
about gender. It made me realize something very new was going on,
and also forced me to face my own bias against bodybuilding.
Whether for men or for women, it seemed useless and narcissistic:
What were all those muscles *for?* The only possible pleasure I could
imagine from such contests was to see men compete on the basis of
appearance alone, as women so often have been encouraged to do in
beauty contests and forced to do in life. Even that hadn't been
enough to send me to see the first *Pumping Iron,* the 1977 documentary that introduced an obscure muscle man named Arnold Schwarzenegger. Though I knew the film had humanized bodybuilding
enough to help it overcome its freak-show image and to set Schwarzenegger on a path that eventually turned him into an international
movie star—and though women's bodybuilding had the added
Annie Oakley appeal of females competing in a male domain—I still
had major misgivings.

As usual, prejudice marks a mental land mine. What I expected was a movie that flattered the masculine style by imitation and encouraged women to play a game they couldn't win. What I discovered was the real-life saga of a woman who was changing the rules and creating shock waves that would eventually reach all of us. Certainly, I've never felt the same about the female body since seeing the strongest woman in the world.

At first, the purpose of this documentary about strong, sleek women assembling to compete for a whopping $50,000 purse—a big change from earlier women's competitions, which had been minor sideshows to male events—seemed to be showing us just how much the routine resembled that of a traditional beauty contest. Hair and makeup assumed great importance. Contestants had to have their bikini tops checked for padding. Even in talk among the strong women themselves, there was a debate about what "femininity" really was. Many of these women had come to "pumping iron" through fitness and beauty routines, school sports, or boyfriends who were bodybuilders, and their pleasure in their own strength was limited by a constant need to prove that muscles were "feminine," that body balance and symmetry were the point, and that they themselves were "real women." Yes, they were bodybuilders, but, they kept reassuring us, they hadn't gone too far.

Even so, the contestants seemed far less obsessed with ideals of gender than the judges (all men but one, the wife of a bodybuilder), whose standards were under fire from reporters, from the more rebellious contestants, and even from one of their own, a younger judge who was protesting what he felt was the surrealistic nonsense of judging athletes for their feminine appearance. Limiting muscle in a bodybuilding contest was, as he put it, like telling women skiers they shouldn't ski too fast.

In self-defense, the judges attributed their concern to public rejection of muscles in women; yet most of the spectators seemed to be ahead of the judges. After all, many women athletes had already increased the public's comfort level with female strength (think of Martina Navratilova and her weight training for women's tennis). So had some pioneer women in bodybuilding. There was Doris Barrilleaux, who discovered in the 1950s that weight training was an efficient way to get back in shape after her children were born. When she was in her forties, she was appalled by one of the early sideshow-variety women's bodybuilding contests, and tried to elevate the sport by founding the Superior Physique Association and a newsletter that reached many women who had been training in the privacy of their own homes or in local gyms. Anthropologist Lisa Lyon bodybuilt her way to victory in the first World Women's Championship in 1979. She also wrote two books about women's bodybuilding, helped to found the National Physique Committee as the women's division of the International Federation of Body-builders (the primary professional men's group), and generally tried to create "a new standard of beauty—a high-tech body." She also posed for *Playboy,* though whether this was a victory for female muscle or for that magazine's traditional effort to show all women as sexually available was unclear.

But the conversations filmed in the gaudy halls of Caesars Palace revealed there was still plenty of free-floating anxiety about how "femininity," ideals of beauty, and the reality of bodybuilding could coexist. There was even an internal split within the world of women's bodybuilding itself. This had first surfaced earlier in the year at the Miss Olympia Contest in Philadelphia (later renamed the Ms. Olympia Contest), with the appearance of contestants like Auby Paulick and Cammie Lusko, who rejected the traditional limits of "symmetry and balance," the code words used in women's bodybuilding for "not too much muscle." Such standards had resulted in bodies that were only a little more muscular than those of gymnasts or dancers. Once women refused to be bound by those standards, they had begun to develop all the muscles their individual bodies could pro-duce, just as male bodybuilders had always done.

Of course, the representatives of this new aesthetic didn't win. Rachel McLish did. A smoothly muscled, sloe-eyed, dark-haired for-mer cheerleader and born-again Christian from Texas, she was much more acceptable to the judges because of her beauty, and also be-cause her muscles didn't stand out to the point of gender bending. On the other hand, those muscular pioneers who lost did greatly increase curiosity and interest among spectators, as did the slightly freakish appeal of the scenes from this contest that were picked up by television.

As Frank Zane, a former Mr. Universe, said to a bystander while watching those newly well-muscled competitors in 1980, "You fa-miliar with Carl Jung?"

"Yeah." The bystander nodded.

"Well," said Zane, "I don't think there's an archetype for this."

By the time of this 1983 Las Vegas contest, prize money was

equal to that of men for the first time, and the controversy was heating up. ("I've argued that there are two types of women and that the solution would be two types of contests," complained an embattled Doris Barrilleaux. "I've met with nothing but opposition.") The flame that had brought this controversy to a boil, however, was the entry of Bev Francis. She had not only weight-trained hard but lost forty pounds from her powerlifting weight of 180. (Because powerlifting doesn't allow the use of momentum, as Olympic weight lifting does, it requires even more brute strength.) This allowed her to look "ripped"—that is, to lose the surface layer of fat that conceals muscle definition—and arrive in Las Vegas at such a peak of muscularity that she seemed to represent another species.

Unlike the other contestants, Bev also had a face without artifice, and one that was no more conventionally beautiful than that of, say, Babe Didrikson, one of the greatest all-round athletes, or Billie Jean King, the pioneer of modern tennis. Moreover, Bev's well-developed neck, intricately muscled stomach, enormous biceps, and tree-trunk-like thighs not only were more impressive than those of the other women but resembled those of the most developed men. Whether the sight turned her sister contestants on or off was hard to tell, but they certainly seemed awestruck, and they treated Bev with a friendly respect. Indeed, one of the film's pleasures was the camaraderie among most of the women, even though they were competitors.

Soon, however, the judges became obsessed with the crisis of standards that Bev Francis's appearance presented. It was obvious that some of them had already made up their minds. The sole woman judge, also a writer about women's bodybuilding, was challenged by a reporter on the impact of Bev Francis's potential victory. "I think it would be a total disaster," she said bitterly, "and I think the sport would totally go in reverse. ... . She doesn't look like a woman. She doesn't represent what women want to look like."

Of course, Arnold Schwarzenegger doesn't look like most men's ideal either, but she had a point. The distance between Bev Francis and her gender's image was certainly greater than the distance between Schwarzenegger and ordinary men. Nonetheless, those of us watching the documentary had an advantage the judges didn't. We knew Bev not as a freak of nature but as a likable, engaging human being. The film had shown her in Australia, where sports had made her a quiet folk hero. We'd watched her with her supportive family, who found her boundary-breaking career a natural extension of her teacher father's love of sports and her mother's early career as a dancer. (In addition to working as a physical education teacher since graduating from college eight years before, Bev Francis also had trained as a ballet dancer.) Most important, we'd heard the simple philosophy that shaped her career as a champion athlete and was obviously carrying over into her bodybuilding work: Accept no limits but those one's own body imposes. In fact, as we listened to her praise the beauty of strength in animals, her subversive ideas sounded like common sense. If male and female panthers and lions and horses develop their muscles in a similar way, she asked, why shouldn't female and male humans? Indeed, why not?

By then, however, the allegiance of most viewers was probably mixed. We'd come to know several of the other contestants, and to like them too. There was Lori Bowen, a shy twenty-five-year-old from Texas, who had been turned on to bodybuilding by her boyfriend and inspired to compete by the example of Rachel McLish. This was her first professional competition, and she needed the prize money to get married, rescue her quiet husband-to-be from his job as a male stripper in a Texas nightclub, and try for a more stable life.

We'd followed the hard work of Rachel McLish herself, fascinating and beautiful in a way that was both conventional and exotic, whose earlier victories had just begun to pay off in product endorsements, posters, and television appearances. Clearly, she could make strength sexy to some men and thus more acceptable to many women.

We'd come to know Carla Dunlap, one of the few black contestants, a former competitive swimmer from New Jersey. We watched her work hard at both bodybuilding and graceful water ballet, and heard her joke in a down-to-earth way about this Las Vegas adventure. Though not as well-muscled as Bev, she was also challenging the judges' definition of "feminine," both in degree of strength and in racial stereotype.

In fact, we'd been an intimate part of the hope and sweat and intensity that had gone into a remarkably unhostile competition among fifteen women and their friends, families, and trainers, and heard real dialogue as concise and revealing as anything that could have been scripted. George Butler, the filmmaker who created both this and the original *Pumping Iron,* was wise enough to resist narration and to let us eavesdrop on this world that was new to most of us, and in transition itself.

In the end, the surprise was less that Bev Francis lost, or even that the judges placed her in a humiliating eighth—to the boos of many spectators—than that Rachel McLish, the more conventional favorite, lost too.

The winner among this glistening array of strong, oiled bodies was Carla Dunlap, a clear compromise between the old and the new. She was more muscled than Rachel McLish, though just as graceful and beautiful; a breaker of racial barriers in this mostly white world; but not even close to the gender-bending body of Bev Francis. Whoever we might have been rooting for, it was easy to celebrate Carla's victory as a pioneer, and as someone we'd come to like. We'd seen her arriving in Las Vegas with her mother and sister instead of the usual professional male trainer, working on her own routine while others were being coached, and befriending and applauding Bev Francis.

Still, the emotional climax of the film was the scene of Bev in her hotel room, trying hard to be cheerful as she talked over the phone to her family in Australia, and ordering from room service all the foods she had been denying herself. Here was one more woman whose clear right to win had been judged less important than her lack of prettiness and her refusal to conform. Though she accepted the judges' verdict with a champion's good grace, her training partner and lover, Steve Weinberger, an American powerlifter, voiced outrage on her behalf. The film ended on his angry question: *Why?*

Of course, we knew why. Yet she had shocked us too. By breaking all past stereotypes—even archetypes, as that Jungian spectator pointed out—she had forced us to ask: *If I had been a judge, what would I have done?*

It was this echoing question that made her the one contestant who would live on in our minds.

By the time *Pumping Iron II* opened in New York, more than a year had passed since its events. Bev Francis and Steve Weinberger had become engaged and were living quietly in Queens. They were also helping each other train for their respective powerlifting competitions. Though Bev hadn't decided to drop out of bodybuilding completely, she had returned to her powerlifting weight, thus tailoring her body to the sport at hand. In spite of her humiliating public defeat for not looking "like a woman," she had just returned to pressing her own boundaries.

But in the long run, she may have won after all. In the two years since her precedent-setting appearance in Las Vegas, many women bodybuilders had been coming into contests heavier, more muscled, less willing to accept social limits on the development of their bodies. Moreover, these more muscled contestants had been scoring higher, as judges' standards began to shift. By being an athlete focused only on achieving her personal best, Bev had changed the context within which other women bodybuilders worked—and even dreamed. I was looking forward to meeting this woman who was enlarging everyone's world by moving the frontier.

On the way to a gym where George Butler had invited me to watch Bev work out, I asked him for the answers to some of my novice's questions. As a longtime bridge-builder between the public and the esoteric world of pumping iron, he explained:

Yes, most women have to train and diet harder than men in order to achieve muscle development and visible definition. With less testosterone to build muscles and a thicker layer of body fat to conceal them, women have to drop far below their normal 20 to 25 percent body fat. Nonetheless, men and women *do* have the same basic muscle groups, as in Bev Francis's example of female and male animals.

Yes, women bodybuilders—like joggers and other very active women who fall below a certain proportion of body fat—may have no menstrual cycles until their activity changes and a greater percentage of fat returns. I wonder: Since sports require muscles and good diets—not unhealthy thinness—could they be one of the healthier forms of birth control?

No, most women who are into weight training don't develop "masculine-looking" muscle. For that matter, most men who pump iron don't look like male bodybuilders. Only a handful of people are likely to have the determination, patience, athletic skills, and genetic makeup to achieve that bodybuilder look. But whether women are seeking unusual muscles or not, weight training has the appeal of efficiency and effectiveness as a form of exercise. Especially when compared to running and other sports that are usually done outdoors, often in isolated places, it also offers personal safety. Already, it's as popular as jogging in the United States, with women a full 50 percent of Nautilus users in gyms and even more women using free weights at home.

No, women bodybuilders don't routinely take drugs, as far as George has been able to tell. Male hormones encourage muscles, but they also produce facial hair and other unwelcome male characteristics. Most of the women in the film, including Bev Francis, denied taking steroids, although many professional athletes do use them, in spite of their dangers. Since tests were not administered in the Las Vegas contest, however, there was no way to be sure. On the other hand, we do know that Bev Francis was almost certainly telling the truth, for as a shot-put and powerlifting champion, she had been taking drug tests for years—unlike most bodybuilders of either sex.

Yes, Bev had been subject to chromosome tests and other insulting challenges to her genetic identity as a woman, and she had passed them all with flying colors. As she said in the book version of *Pumping Iron II:* "I have female responses, I have female hormones in my body, female chromosomes. . . . I'm happy with being a woman. I never wished that I was a boy. I just wanted to do the things that boys were allowed to do."[6] I wonder: Would men who do badly in sports ever be subjected to the same tests as women who do well?

Of course, there were questions that only the future could answer: With some women gaining upper-body strength more like that of men, would sports competition ever switch to categories based on height and weight instead of gender? More important, would muscles and strength become acceptable for females in general?

Finally, George explained, Bev and the others are not "muscle-bound." In spite of the popular idea that muscle development impedes movement and flexibility, he vouched for the fact that Bev was supple and easy-moving in person. "If we all went to a discotheque," he said, "Bev would be one of the best dancers on the floor."

Watching Bev Francis at the gym in lower Manhattan where she and Steve were going through the slow, arduous ritual of machines and free weights when George and I arrived, I saw what he meant. She had an evenly paced, effortless style of movement that was far more androgynous than Rachel McLish's seductive poses or Carla Dunlap's feline stretches, but it was just as graceful—and hypnotic to watch.

Seeing her in contrast to the dozen or so men and women bodybuilders around her, I could appreciate the difference in her motions. Steve, her fiancé, was very good, and so were several of the others. But each of Bev's repetitions was full, controlled, seemingly perfect, and exactly like the one before. In contrast, many of the other athletes seemed erratic, jerky, occasionally out of control. Since the exactly right pattern of each repetition was what gradually built and defined an individual muscle, I began to appreciate the precision and stamina this required.

We'd been standing aside, trying not to break Bev's concentration or that of the men and the women who, whether they knew it or not, were pioneers of a sort, since most bodybuilding gyms had been all-male preserves until a few years ago. When Bev and Steve finally stopped and came over to say hello, she was direct and friendly, but he seemed protective and suspicious, as if he'd become accustomed to people misunderstanding Bev and feared this would happen again. Most men might feel ambivalent about being the lover of the strongest woman in the world, but Steve, who understands her unique accomplishment in a field that is also his own, was clearly proud. Like the Olympic wrestler George Zaharias, who married and did his best to protect Babe Didrikson from the ridicule of an earlier generation, which greeted her athletic feats with charges that she was not a "real woman," Steve has joined Bev in creating what was clearly a mutually supportive world of their own.

One of my first surprises was that I was taller than Bev. That she was only five feet five made her ability to conquer three categories of powerlifting—to bench-press 331 pounds, squat 480 pounds, and dead-lift 476 pounds—even more impressive. Indeed, since the non-Olympic sport of powerlifting required more force than Olympic weight lifting, which involves an overhead, clean-and-jerk motion that rewards agility as well as strength, there was an outsider's pride in both Steve and Bev. She explained the difference with a punning remark about "a lot of the Olympic clean-and-jerks I have met"— the closest she was to come to either complaining or bragging.

George Butler suggested that Bev take me through one round of machine and free-weight exercises so that I would better understand what I was recording, and she cheerfully agreed. As a trained gym teacher, she understood how to scale each weight down to the exact level necessary to test my very modest strength. She also gave easy-to-follow, supportive instructions. I could imagine her as a precise ballet student in her earlier years, and as a patient and supportive coach, once her own career as a world-class athlete was over.

Afterward, at a nearby restaurant where the four of us went to talk over coffee and Italian pastry, Bev made clear that she gave her coach, Franz Stampfl, who had originally trained and encouraged her, much of the credit for her career. He had transformed her from an unconfident eighteen-year-old at the University of Melbourne into a multisport champion. Stampfl was already famous for training Roger Bannister, the runner who broke the four-minute mile, but this seventy-year-old man had been a supporter of women's rights since the 1920s, when he campaigned for legal abortion in his native Austria. As a coach, he had encouraged many women athletes during his career in England and Australia.

"We all have reserves of unexpected strength," Bev explained. "We've all read stories about the woman who lifts a car off her baby, because the adrenaline and desire are there. Franz helped me discover confidence in myself and train in many sports. I loved the variety and only recently started to specialize in powerlifting. Women have had only six world championships in powerlifting; men have had fifteen, but we're getting there. Maybe the Olympics will include powerlifting as a new category."

In spite of her disappointing experience in Las Vegas, Bev found the United States to be more accepting of strength in women than Australia was, though not yet as open as Eastern Europe or the Soviet Union. "My coach created a center of support around me at the university," she said, "but society in general wasn't that open. In the past, the only place where women could show strength was the circus—at least we've advanced from that. But when I was growing up, I wanted to go as far as I could. I wanted freedom. There was a TV ad in Australia that I always hated. It showed a woman dishing out food and saying, 'Feed the man meat.' Why shouldn't I do more than that?

"On the other hand, freedom takes responsibility, and a lot of the girls didn't want that. They always had a way out. If things got too hard for them, they would just stop, and everyone would accept it because 'she's only a woman, she's only a girl.' It's hard to achieve when everybody gives you a cop-out. Every once in a while, I use being a female as an excuse to get out of something, and I always hate myself for it afterwards.

"Most of my life, boys were my friends, not girls, because I was doing things boys understood and girls didn't like. But I never wanted to imitate men. Even when I've competed and powerlifted against men, I didn't work to beat them. I just wanted to beat my own past performance, to push my own limits. Sometimes people think I *am* a man, which I understand because of my developed shoulders and shortish hair. But when I explain that I am a woman and they say, 'No, you're not,' it really irritates me, because I'm an honest person. I'm happy to be a woman. But I try not to show my anger with them, because aggression is a male characteristic, and that's what they expect. I value female responses."

I asked her about her quote in the *Pumping Iron II* book: "I'm not a feminist in the sense that I don't believe women are better than men." Given that feminism means equality, not superiority, I asked if she still felt that way.

"I was responding to early feminists in Australia," she said thoughtfully, clearly trying to sort out her feelings. "Germaine Greer and others seemed to be imitating the worst characteristics of men —'Belly up to the bar' and all that. But I guess the truth is I've been labeled so many things that I'm still afraid of *any* label. I just want to be myself."

It was the response of someone who had always been a loner, and unique. I wondered, too, how much her feelings were colored by the lack of support from some women, by their antipathy to female muscles and strength. Even in talking to friends about Bev and the movie, I had noticed that many men were open to it in a general way, while women fell into two groups: proud and enthusiastic or hostile and turned off—with little in between. Oddly, the division didn't follow the logic of women who did or didn't support equality in other areas. It seemed more visceral than that.

Yet Bev's own interpretation of the film was a very feminist one. "The first *Pumping Iron* was a good movie, and more humorous than this one," she explained, "but I think ours has a significance that goes far beyond the world of bodybuilding. I hope people will think about the variation in female potential. I hope it will make them look beyond the still photographs of women bodybuilders and athletes that sometimes fall into stereotypes. This movie allows you to know the people inside the image and to see how diverse, and *human*, women are."

Certainly, the world was beginning to accept a few strong women. After that afternoon with Bev, I saw two television commercials: one was for a light beer, a funny scene in which a very pretty Lori Bowen picked up comedian Rodney Dangerfield with one hand; in the other, for a diet cola, a glamorous Rachel McLish gave bodybuilding tips to beefcake actor Lee Majors.

But there were still racial limits. Though Carla Dunlap had great beauty as well as the speech skills of an actress, she had been offered no television commercials. The dozens of bodybuilding magazines had also declined to put her on the cover. This first black woman bodybuilder was a champion in a very white and biased world. While waiting for Bev in the gym, for instance, I'd been told that some bodybuilding fans insisted Carla Dunlap found it "too easy" to build muscles, implying there was a racial difference in strength or the amount of work required: a version of the comments one sometimes heard about why, say, many boxers were black. Clearly, the answer had to do with poverty, not race—once, most boxers were Irish or Italian—but in terms of overcoming racial bias in bodybuilding, there was a long way to go.

As for the acceptance of strength in ordinary women of all ages and groups, the answer was still blowing in the wind.

But no matter how friendly or frightening this new territory might be, Bev Francis had been its first explorer.

It's rare that I have an opportunity to go back to the subject of a story and find out what happened afterward. It had been almost a decade since Bev changed my ideas about what a woman's body could look like, but I found her again. She and Steve Weinberger, now her husband, were running a successful weight-training gym on Long Island.

The low building behind a row of tacky shops was hard to find, and seemed a sad contrast to the settings in which I'd first seen her. Once past its unpromising exterior, however, I was again in an island of calm and professionalism of the sort that I remembered Bev carrying around with her like an aura. I waited while she and Steve finished a businesslike discussion in their unbusinesslike sweat suits, noting again the absorption with which they listened to each other. The sign over the door said BEV FRANCIS GOLD'S GYM—Gold's being the chain from which they'd bought the franchise—and Steve seemed as proud of that as he had been of Bev's career when we first met. They were still a self-contained team.

Steve greeted me as if I were someone who had shared past glories and tribulations, and perhaps had passed a test. This time, he didn't stay with us protectively but left Bev to show me around their domain. "There aren't any glamorous leotards or aerobics here," she explained as she walked me through a large area filled with rows of weight-training machines, "just serious people who want to get in shape." Turning the corner, we came to a still bigger area, added on in a T-shape. It doubled the original space, and Bev said the addition had been necessary to handle the increase in clientele after they took over. Even on this weekday afternoon, before the after-work hours when most people arrive, there were a dozen sweat-suited exercisers at the machines, including several women. Bev noted that as one of the rare weight-training gyms to bear a woman's name, it made women clients feel welcome.

She and Steve had continued to compete, she explained, and to travel as experts in the international subculture of powerlifting and bodybuilding, but the gym was as much their home as was their house nearby. Most of their time was spent in this space, which had all the glamour of an airplane hangar. In the evenings, they became personal trainers to private clients ranging from neophytes to competitors. It was obviously a source of pride to Bev, who stopped to pick up a scrap of paper from the spotless floor, then to offer me a protein drink from a display case. She evoked images that went beyond gender, managing to seem like a hostess in her own home *and* a boss showing off his factory.

We settled into a barren office decorated only with posters of Bev in an even more massive stage than I remembered. "Those are from a bodybuilding contest in '91—probably my last," she said, following my gaze. "I'm not officially retired, but the fire is gone." Knowing that I was a stranger to this world, she began with her usual patience to fill me in on the novel-like saga of the past few years.

After the Las Vegas contest, a onetime event staged mostly for purposes of making the documentary, she'd gone back to the objective competition of powerlifting and won two more world championships, making a total of six in as many years. Counting her achievements in other sports, that meant she had broken over forty world records. The good news was that she was widely recognized as the strongest woman in the world. The bad news was that there were no other heights to climb. Unless the Olympics Committee added powerlifting to the list of Olympic events—something she doubted would happen, since so many other sports were standing in line—she could only see more of the same ahead. Like Michael Jordan, who had just confounded his fans by retiring from basketball because he had achieved what he set out to do, she felt there were

no more challenges. She had decided to retire after the world powerlifting championship in 1985. "I was never defeated in any powerlifting competition," she explained, "so it lost its spark."

What she hadn't conquered, however, was the bodybuilding
world. To her own surprise, she'd become fascinated with this sport.
Partly, she'd learned just how tough and demanding body sculpting
and "one more rep" could be, the ingenuity and tenacity necessary
to develop each muscle in her body to the fullest. Mostly, she was
tempted by the challenge laid down by Las Vegas—that she could
never win because she didn't have the right "look." In 1986, she
returned to bodybuilding, which was becoming more of a sport in
the United States, where she now lived because of her marriage to
Steve. By 1987, she had come in first in the Women's World Bodybuilding Championship in Canada. She could have walked away as
one of the rare athletes who has won world records in more than
one sport, but she knew the Mr. and Ms. Olympia contests were
actually more important in the context of bodybuilding. Like the so-
called world contests, one of which she had just won, they also
attracted entrants from Germany, Holland, France, England, and
other countries where bodybuilding was a popular sport. She decided she would focus on the yearly Olympia contest—until she won
that too.

"Cory Everson was winning the Olympias by the time I got into
them," Bev explained. "She was very statuesque, very muscular, very
tall—about five feet eight. She had an elegance about her body
because of her tallness, her long legs." In fact, Cory was probably
able to be more muscular and still win because of what Bev had done
to push the frontier. Since the judges seemed to be changing their
standards, Bev decided that if she was "just a little more malleable,
instead of my usual 'This is me, take it or leave it,' " she might win
too. After all, she was still ahead in strength. Why not change her
style just enough to complete and benefit from the revolution she
had started?

"I was much stockier and shorter than Cory," Bev explained, "but
I tried to portray as much femininity as I could in my own context."
That included having her nose made slightly smaller through plastic
surgery. "I didn't have a terrible nose," she said with a smile, "but
I'd always felt it was too big for my face. It was also more masculine,
and my muscles were enough that was masculine about me. Besides,
here I was in the capital of plastic surgery, so Steve said, 'If you don't

like it, change it.' I think it fits my face better now, and it's made me feel more confident. I also let my hair grow longer, put highlights in it, and wore a little makeup. That made me feel good, because all of a sudden I could do something I didn't know I could do. I thought you were born one way, and that was it. I didn't know you could look more like these gorgeous women; that they had little tricks to make themselves look better."

One little trick she wouldn't try was breast implants. "All the top women bodybuilders have implants now. I'm one of the last who doesn't—and who's refused to. That's one of the things that annoys me about bodybuilding. We're not *supposed* to be what conventional women look like, because we've built our bodies. How can you have low body fat and still have big breasts? My sexuality isn't threatened enough for me to stuff things in my chest to look like a woman."

There were such layers of irony here that we paused to discuss them. In *Pumping Iron II,* the judges had checked women's bras for padding and disqualified contestants accordingly. Now they were allowing implants, which were dangerous. It was an anomaly shared with many beauty contests. On the other hand, men weren't questioned about padding their jockstraps, a gender enhancement that was rumored to be rampant. "Masculinity isn't in question," Bev explained. "There are male bodybuilders who are open about being gay—which doesn't matter, as it shouldn't. But why do women come under such suspicion? I was too naive to realize it when I first started this sport, but people assumed I was a lesbian, especially because I had a friend who was a woman bodybuilder and we used to room together and hang out together when we were traveling. She was married, but in retrospect, I realize that didn't matter. We were two strong women together.

"If they think I'm a lesbian, or somebody else is a lesbian, I don't care a scrap. But I'm so tired of being categorized that I even object when Steve sees two women in the gym and says they're a couple— how does he know? How does anybody know? It drives me crazy to be *predicted,* so I try not to predict anybody else."

This continuum of sexism reaches an extreme in a much more invasive end: the testing of women to see if their chromosomes are normal. "In track and field, only women's chromosomes are checked," Bev explained. "Women have been kicked out because they may have XXY when you're only supposed to have XX, though genetically they look and act like women. A Bulgarian woman was forced to retire because she had XXY—so she went home and had a baby. Who decides what a woman is?"

There is also the less-well-known double standard of testing for steroids and other strength-enhancing drugs. "Because they think women can't get hard and muscular without drugs—which is wrong, some women can—" Bev said, "they started by testing all the contestants at every Olympia. Then they substituted random testing, which means you can be tested at any time during the year, without warning. But it's only for the women. The men, they don't test. They did it one year, and everyone looked so crappy they stopped it." This is one more way our own notions about male/female strength differences are being exaggerated by culture. The result is bad for women, because ideas about our lesser strength are confirmed, and bad for men, because it encourages them to use drugs that damage their bodies.

In spite of Bev's efforts to be a little more "malleable" in the way she looked, she had risen from tenth place in 1987 to only third place in each of the following three years. As a natural champion, she couldn't be satisfied with coming in third. She decided not just to outperform her competition but to second-guess the judges. In 1989, the year of Cory Everson's sixth and last win before retiring, there was a startling contrast between Cory, who Bev felt was at her least impressive, and Bev, whose combination of muscle, hardness, and body symmetry seemed to be the best in the contest. Getting the message, Bev decided to try another tactic for the first competition after Cory Everson's retirement. "It was a fresh slate, so I came in trying to portray as much 'Coryness' as I could, within my own framework. I pulled off not just fat but muscle. It's not natural for my body to sit at 135 or 140 pounds; that's just not me. I sit more comfortably at 160 or 165. I looked great at the lower weight I achieved for the contest, but I didn't feel great inside—I felt weak. When I went into that 1990 Olympia, I was the most feminine-looking I'd ever been."

The result was not victory but a hard lesson that Bev wouldn't forget. She came in second to Lenda Murray, a woman who had, in Bev's words, "the exotic look, complete with implants, good balance, a small waist, and big shoulders." She was also more muscular than Bev had allowed herself to become. Indeed, there were critics who said Bev didn't deserve to win even second place. By being untrue to herself, she had been beaten at her own game.

For the next year, she prepared with a different resolve. "They went for the big muscular? Damn, I can give them *bigger* muscular," she thought. "I'll go all-out, because that's what I know how to do." She designed her diet carefully to hold muscle, and aimed to come in twenty pounds heavier than ever before. She also astounded clients in her gym by such training feats as doing thirty repetitions of leg presses of nearly 700 pounds—something they stood around watching in awe. Before the Las Vegas contest, she had leapfrogged a full mile three times a week, but for this contest, she mustered even more of her famous discipline and concentration. For six months, she trained her heart out—and most important, she loved it. At last, she was following nothing but her own instincts. She was doing what had made her a champion in the first place: pleasing herself and testing her limits *just to see if she could*.

There was another edge to this preparation for the 1991 Ms. Olympia. Because she was thirty-six and thinking about having children, it was likely to be her last contest. "Steve's parents were divorced," she explained, "and he wasn't quite as enthusiastic about having kids as I was. But I come from such a great family that to me, it was just as important as winning championships. My parents were proud of me, which made me feel terrific, but I was no more important to them than the other four kids. They realized being a good person was just as important as anything else. I'd like to pass that on. I've done all the things that women don't normally do in their lives. Now I'd like to do something that women normally do."

By the time Bev got to Los Angeles, everything had conspired to make the contest a historic one. It was the first bodybuilding event ever to be telecast live in the United States, and the first one to allow two full days for three rounds of judging. Moreover, word had spread that Bev was training to press the limits. She had become, in her own words, "the biggest, tightest, most muscular woman there. All the women were huge—but I was massive."

Since the other contestants—including defending champion Lenda Murray—might as well have stayed in the dressing room if muscularity was the point, it was no surprise when Bev won the first two rounds by an unusual and definitive four points. With such a commanding lead, no one had ever lost the contest. At the end of the third and last round, the stupendously muscular Bev Francis stood hand in hand with the exotic Lenda Murray as they waited for the judges' decision. In the hall, thousands of people held their breath. So did millions in front of their television sets. If Bev won, she would triumph in her five-year quest for the Olympia title. Moreover, women's bodybuilding would be acknowledging that it had changed forever.

The verdict came. Bev Francis's name was read first—meaning she had come in second. A groan came up from the audience. "I was so confident," Bev remembered, "because I knew I was ahead—and I'd done everything beautifully in the third round. It was all I could do to congratulate Lenda, smile at the audience, and walk off the stage." According to the judges' count, she had lost by one point.

If there was any doubt about the reason for Bev Francis's defeat, it was laid to rest when bodybuilding authorities moved immediately to change competition rules in order to penalize extreme muscularity. Later, when Bev became a token part of a few judging processes herself, she heard how these new standards were discussed and applied. "I listened to all the criteria," she explained, "and they're really weird. The judges would say, 'A woman shouldn't be judged as too muscular if she's carrying what her frame can handle.' Now, obviously, every woman has a different frame. I think my frame can handle a lot more muscle than some others. But from another point of view, if your frame couldn't handle the muscle, how could you carry it in the first place?"

Having advanced the cause of female strength by her gender-bending appearance in 1983, popularized it in *Pumping Iron II,* spawned a new generation of women bodybuilders who pushed boundaries for the next six years—and finally decided to go for broke herself—Bev had become too challenging. She was upsetting enough on her own, but having demonstrated her influence over other women, she had become even more so. Like other areas of work in which the first woman meets resistance, gets a little worn down, but is followed by a second wave that threatens to become a critical mass, bodybuilding as a sport decided to send a wider message by disciplining the pioneer.

In a way, Bev's success as a powerlifter had been analogous to that of a woman entrepreneur or any other independent worker in an area where objective criteria make victory hard to conceal. But in bodybuilding contests, as in corporate and academic settings, victory could be negated—and discipline reasserted—through the highly subjective process by which a winner was selected, whether for promotion, tenure, or a bodybuilding prize. We had come full circle, back to the experience that any high school girl who ever tried out for cheerleader remembers: *being chosen*.

By the following year, the message sent by Bev's defeat had been heard and heeded. Entrants seemed to press no limits. *Flex*, one of many magazines devoted to bodybuilding, described that 1992 Ms. Olympia as "the most lackluster in the contest's 12 year history. Talk of the distaff side of the sport being in crisis was rampant."[7] Though contestants were more muscular than they probably would have been without Bev, they still weren't testing the boundaries. Nonetheless, the judges' standards were questioned as never before. Once the possibilities embodied by Bev had been seen, it was hard to unsee them.

For Bev herself, however, what could have been a megaloss turned out to be less personally damaging than the loss the year before. In some ways, it wasn't a loss at all. "For so long, I'd wanted the Olympia—and then all of a sudden, it didn't mean anything. I knew I was the best there that day, and I didn't win, so what's the point? I'd achieved what I wanted to do. I always wanted to show how muscular a woman could get—and I did that. I wanted people to go 'Ah!' when I walked out—and I got that. If you win titles in bodybuilding, it means they agree with your look. If you don't, it doesn't matter—as long as you're satisfied with what you've done with your own body.

"When I speak to people about bodybuilding," she said, gesturing toward the gym outside our door, "I always say that the worst that can happen to you, even if you never win anything, is that you improve your body—you become better than you were. What's so bad about that?"

There is a quality about Bev that evokes a Zen master. She says things that would seem too simple, were they not coming from someone who has earned the right to say them. No one could have worked harder toward a goal; yet about her unfair defeat, she said, "In the end, it's better to feel at peace with yourself." No one could have created more whole-body transformations over the course of a decade—changes she literally had to eat, sleep, and breathe every day—yet after being denied recognition in what would have been an especially humiliating way for most women, she remained philosophical. Where did all this come from?

It was a question that could have elicited a complicated explanation, but Bev responded with its simple roots in her childhood. "My family were basic people," she explained. "If the world were filled with people like them, it would be a good place. The older I get, the more I appreciate them. We didn't have a lot of money, so very early I got an appreciation of things that were really important—like doing your best at whatever you do, not hurting anyone, and being able to laugh at yourself.

"Beyond that, there was a real spark in me. I always liked to do what the boys did, and I was mistaken for a boy all the time. My sister wasn't as athletic. She was quiet, more malleable—I was rebellious.

"We lived simply, from paycheck to paycheck, but every year we'd go camping—and that was heaven for me. I loved being out in the bush, with no one around, shooting rabbits, building a fire, surviving in nature. It was something that was always in me."

Bev had admired the aborigines of her native Australia and the Native Americans of this continent. She had read about them and wanted to be like them. With her friends in the neighborhood, all boys, she played made-up games of endurance—who could go longest without water on the hottest days (it was always Bev), or who could walk barefoot for the longest distance on the tar roads around Geelong when the sun turned them into bubbling black ribbons of tar (again, it was always Bev). The first restriction she remembered was being told she couldn't continue to take her shirt off in the heat, as the boys did. She thought that was clearly unfair. With a child's sense of justice, she had a vision of a genderless world.

"In some ways, my parents were traditional mother/father figures, with Mom at home and Dad bringing home the paycheck," she said, "but all the boys learned how to cook basic foods, and the girls helped with things like pouring concrete in the backyard. The jobs were all mixed up. Even though Mom was good at sewing and cooking, she helped Dad, just like he had no problem with cooking. My mother was very active, but it was my father who loved sports —for their own sake, not for competition."

The message of uniqueness—of winning just by doing one's personal best—had been instilled in each of the five children. "Our parents just said, 'Whatever you do, do it well.' That made us all secure, because not one of us was better than the next, and yet each was special. My sister and brothers weren't jealous of me, and they're still not. They're proud. I see in so many families that if one person achieves something, the others hold it against them. When good fortune falls on any of us, we're happy. We don't say, 'I wish that was me.' "

Her three brothers were athletic too, though not to the same degree as Bev. In later life, they became a teacher, a banker, and an artist. "They're into this macho image, but they all have a roundness about them," Bev said. "They're not afraid to display their emotions. The guys in this country seem afraid to show their emotional side. My brothers are all funny, and not so different from me and my sister. She became a teacher, like my dad.

"Basically, I feel different from most other women. I feel I don't have to put on an act. If I'm not feminine enough for someone, I don't care, because femininity is different in everyone's mind."

Given this philosophy, who were her women friends? "You'll be surprised," Bev said, "but Rachel McLish has become a good friend." It was true, I hadn't expected to hear the name of this superfeminine bodybuilder who had picked up the lucrative product endorsements denied to Bev because of her muscularity and to Carla Dunlap because of her race. "I could see the media were trying to divide us," Bev explained, "so I wrote Rachel a letter and told her that I appreciated what she'd done with her career. I hadn't been trying to do anything to her in Las Vegas—I was just doing what I did. We're two of the most prominent women in bodybuilding, so I didn't see any reason for us to be at odds.

"Rachel answered, and now Steve and I see her and her husband whenever we're in California. I appreciate that she grew up poor and had to scrap for everything she got. I think her success and her marriage to a successful movie producer has made her feel secure for the first time. We keep in fairly constant contact. I also get along very well with Cory, who won the Olympia six times. They're two of my best friends."

It was interesting to find these women still as uncompetitive as they had seemed in *Pumping Iron II,* especially when compared with their male counterparts. It was also interesting that Bev had been the first to reach out across the divisions that did exist. Perhaps it was her secure upbringing, or her sense of being part of the future. Or perhaps it was her gift of androgyny. Psychological tests show that males with more feminine qualities and females with more masculine ones—in other words, individuals with a greater range of *human* qualities—are more flexible, creative, and have healthier self-esteem, if only because they're not envying what they're missing. Having been lucky enough to escape a lot of gender training, she seemed happy to be who she was. "I've always liked my body," she says. "It seemed pleasing and compact. I've never wanted anything dangling between my legs." Having enjoyed being a female and not felt penalized for it, she hadn't internalized society's low estimate of her group. She could like other women.

Ever since childhood, however, the androgyny of her body and behavior had given her the unusual experience of choosing her gender. In women's rest rooms, for example, she was often greeted by someone explaining kindly that the men's room was next door. "I always understand, and it doesn't bother me," Bev said with her usual calm. "People just aren't used to seeing a female body with this much muscle. I only feel angry when I say I'm a woman and they don't believe me." Like those tests in which drawings of nude males and females wearing opposite-gender headgear (a woman in a football helmet, say, or a man in a bonnet) are presented to children, most of whom label the figure with the gender of the headgear, Bev was living proof that the conventions of gender are often more important than the physical fact of sex. Though she makes no attempt to present herself as a man, Bev's existence outside the narrow range of "feminine" means she is often *perceived* as a man.

Sometimes, she herself has debated which gender it would be wise to be. When her motorcycle headlight failed on a moonless stretch of country road in Australia, for instance, she was confronted with three choices. "I could keep going and risk running off the road into a tree," she explained. "Or I could make clear that I was a woman by taking off my helmet and risk having a car stop for the wrong reason. Or, with my helmet on, I could look like a man and take a chance that drivers might be afraid and not stop at all."

In the end, she decided that looking like a man was the safest alternative. Only after a truckdriver stopped for what he thought was a male motorcyclist in trouble did she judge him to be okay, take her helmet off, and surprise him by being a different gender. "He *was* a nice guy," she said. "He drove slowly so I could use his headlights to get into the next town."

That choice was no accident. "It's always a fear of mine, to be raped. When I see a rape on TV, I go crazy. Having someone else's will forced on you is horrifying. I'm stronger than almost any man, and I have little fear in the street. I would hate to hurt anyone, but if they were going to hurt me, I would hurt them—no trouble. It upsets me that most women can't do that. But if someone has a gun, that's a different story. Still, I know how lucky I am—there are almost no men I'm afraid of.

"I also think basic strength and fitness make you hold yourself differently. You have a different posture and you give off a different aura—you're not helpless or weak. It's so important for women to develop their physical strength so they're not afraid of men. I would get them to weight train, develop cardiovascular fitness, and then I would urge every woman to learn some sort of martial arts.

"I like toughness. Women should be tough. Having a baby is one of the hardest things to do. When women tell me they can't push a weight, I say, 'If you've had a baby, you can do anything.' Muscle isn't a male thing, it's a human thing.

"But I know I have different ideas on sexual identity. For instance, when you meet someone, I don't see why you have to know whether they're a man or a woman. Are you going to treat them differently? You shouldn't."

I walked out of the gym and back into the real world of small suburban shops. Women were doing the daily maintenance chores of carrying grocery bags and picking up the dry cleaning. It was six o'clock, and most shoppers were probably doing family chores after work, yet there wasn't a man in sight. Even Bev Francis, the strongest woman in the world, was now living here. Meanwhile, Arnold Schwarzenegger, the strongest man in the world, had become an international celebrity whose last movie paid him fifteen million dollars. Maybe we as women aren't ready for a Bev Francis either, but suddenly the injustice of it all came together—and seemed overwhelming.

As I drove back, I looked out the window at the fields of Long Island. I could imagine the ghosts of strong women who must have walked and worked them over the centuries, from Native Americans who roamed over this land to immigrants who turned it into fields of potatoes. When had women allowed ourselves to become so afraid of our strength? Somehow, that brought images of my own family to my mind. I saw the sunburned, well-muscled arms of my maternal grandmother, who worked in her vegetable garden and did other hard tasks, yet concealed her strength under long sleeves when she dressed up and wanted to be ladylike. Her working-class husband needed the money she earned, and she wished that he could keep her in leisure, that she didn't have to do such physical chores. I remembered the soft, plump body of my paternal grandmother, whose well-to-do husband supported her intellectual and community work, but whose life was certainly shortened by the absence of all physical activity. Neither woman had lived in a body she could fully enjoy.

I could feel again my mother's soft body. Only from photographs did I know the strong, smiling, basketball-playing young woman she once had been, or could I imagine the confident woman she might have become. I remembered my sister struggling with endless diets to control our family heritage of excess weight, but living in a world where sports or physical activity was so rare that even stepping down on a moving escalator became a frightening feat. I thought of my own years of fierce pride in spurning sports and undertaking nothing except dancing. "If there were an Olympic team for sitting still," I used to say, "I would be on it." The truth is that I was sure my lack of early training would make a fool of me.

With that long-overdue admission, part of the past came back— not as it had looked from the outside but as my body felt it. I saw tree branches up close, with a lake shining in the distance. It was my view from a perch in a favorite tree I'd climbed as a little girl of five or six. Each leaf was distinct, and so was a feeling of freedom—the sort that comes only from what we do for ourselves. I remembered the feel of rough bark as I climbed up high, just to see how far I could go, with no one to impress but myself. *No wonder we hide our strong women,* I thought. *We don't want to be reminded of what we're missing.*

My feeling of anger hadn't been on Bev's account, I realized. She had pressed her limits, and so was content. Moreover, she was in the right place, teaching the women who needed her. I was angry for and at myself, one of the countless women who'd gone along with society's denial that we might find any delight in physical daring. How much of the world had I missed while living in my head? If each cell in our bodies is an outpost of our brains, what might I have learned?

I'll never know who that adventurous little girl might have become. But at least I know she's still there—waiting to enter the present.

Whatever you've imagined your limits of strength and daring to be, the strongest woman in the world can inspire you to go beyond them. That's what champions are for.

Sex, Lies, and Advertising

Sixteen Years Before the Mast

Goodbye to cigarette ads where poems should be.
Goodbye to celebrity covers and too little space.
Goodbye to cleaning up language so Ms. advertisers won't be boycotted by the Moral Majority.
In fact, goodbye to advertisers and the Moral Majority.
Goodbye to short articles and short thinking.
Goodbye to "post-feminism" from people who never say "post-democracy."
Goodbye to national boundaries and hello to the world.
Welcome to the magazine of the post-patriarchal age.
The turn of the century is our turn!

That was my celebratory mood in the summer of 1990 when I finished the original version of the exposé you are about to read. I felt as if I'd been released from a personal, portable Bastille. At least I'd put on paper the ad policies that had been punishing *Ms.* for all the years of its nonconforming life and still were turning more conventional media, especially (but not only) those directed at women, into a dumping ground for fluff.

Those goodbyes were part of a letter inviting readers to try a new, ad-free version of *Ms.* and were also a homage to "Goodbye to All That," a witty and lethal essay in which Robin Morgan bade farewell to the pre-feminist male Left of twenty years before.[1] It seemed the right tone for the birth of a brand-new, reader-supported, more international form of *Ms.*, which Robin was heading as editor in chief, and I was serving as consulting editor. Besides, I had a very personal kind of mantra running through my head: *I'll never have to sell another ad as long as I live.*

So I sent the letter off, watched the premiere issue containing my exposé go to press, and then began to have second thoughts: Were ad policies too much of an "inside" concern? Did women readers already know that magazines directed at them were filled with editorial extensions of ads—and not care? Had this deceptive system been in place too long for anyone to have faith in changing it? In other words: Would anybody give a damn?

After almost four years of listening to responses and watching the ripples spread out from this pebble cast upon the waters, I can tell you that, yes, readers do care; and no, most of them were not aware of advertising's control over the words and images around it. Though most people in the publishing industry think this is a practice too deeply embedded ever to be uprooted, a lot of readers are willing to give it a try—even though that's likely to mean paying more for their publications. In any case, as they point out, understanding the nitty-gritty of ad influence has two immediate uses. It strengthens healthy skepticism about what we read, and it keeps us from assuming that other women must want this glamorous, saccharine, unrealistic stuff.

Perhaps that's the worst punishment ad influence has inflicted upon us. It's made us feel contemptuous of other women. We know we don't need those endless little editorial diagrams of where to put our lipstick or blush—we don't identify with all those airbrushed photos of skeletal women with everything about them credited, *even their perfume* (can you imagine a man's photo airbrushed to perfection, with his shaving lotion credited?)—but we assume there must be women out there somewhere who *do* love it; otherwise, why would it be there?

Well, many don't. Given the sameness of women's magazines resulting from the demands made by makers of women's products that advertise in all of them, we probably don't know yet what a wide variety of women readers want. In any case, we do know it's the advertisers who are determining what women are getting now.

The first wave of response to this exposé came not from readers but from writers and editors for other women's magazines. They phoned to say the pall cast by anticipated or real advertising demands was even more widespread than rebellious *Ms.* had been allowed to know. They told me how brave I was to "burn my bridges" (no critic of advertising would ever be hired as an editor of any of the women's magazines, they said) and generally treated me as if I'd written about organized crime instead of practices that may be unethical but are perfectly legal. After making me promise not to use their names, they offered enough additional horror stories to fill a book, a movie, and maybe a television series. Here is a typical one: When the freelance author of an article on moisturizers observed in print that such products might be less necessary for young women—whose skin tends to be not dry but oily—the article's editor was called on the carpet and denounced by her bosses as "anti-moisturizer." Or how about this: The film critic for a women's magazine asked its top editor, a woman who makes millions for her parent company, whether movies could finally be reviewed critically, since she had so much clout. No, said the editor; if you can't praise a movie, just don't include it; otherwise we'll jeopardize our movie ads. This may sound like surrealism in everyday life, or like our grandmothers advising, "If you can't say something nice, don't say anything," but such are the forces that control much of our information.

I got few negative responses from insiders, but the ones I did get were bitter. Two editors at women's magazines felt I had demeaned them by writing the article. They loved their work, they said, and didn't feel restricted by ads at all. So I would like to make clear in advance that my purpose was and is to change the system, not to blame the people struggling within it. As someone who has written for most women's magazines, I know that many editors work hard to get worthwhile articles into the few pages left over after providing all the "complementary copy" (that is, articles related to and supportive of advertised products). I also know there are editors who sincerely want exactly what the advertisers want, which is why they're so good at their jobs. Nonetheless, criticizing this ad-dominant system is no different from criticizing male-dominant marriage. Both institutions make some people happy, and both seem free as long as your wishes happen to fall within their traditional boundaries. But just as making more equal marital laws alleviates the suffering of many, breaking the link between editorial and advertising will help all media become more honest and diverse.

A second wave of reaction came from advertising executives who were asked to respond by reporters. They attributed all problems to *Ms.* We must have been too controversial or otherwise inappropriate for ads. I saw no stories that asked the next questions: Why had non-women's companies from Johnson & Johnson to IBM found our "controversial" pages fine for their ads? Why did desirable and otherwise unreachable customers read something so "inappropriate"? What were ad policies doing to *other* women's media? To continue my marriage parallel, however, I should note that these executives seemed only mildly annoyed. Just as many women are more dependent than men on the institution of marriage and so are more threatened and angry when it's questioned, editors of women's magazines tended to be more upset than advertisers when questioned about their alliance.

The one exception was Leonard Lauder, scion of the Estée Lauder cosmetics empire. As you read about him later, keep in mind that he insisted to reporters—as well as in his responses to women readers who wrote letters threatening to boycott his products—that my account was "absolutely untrue." This hurt my journalistic feelings (I'd made notes and reported the conversation to my colleagues "contemporaneously," as lawyers say), but at least it was rational. After all, he and I had been the only participants in the lunch I describe. What amazed me was his further insistence that the "conversation never took place," though we had lunch at The Four Seasons, a fancy New York restaurant where we were on public display. I've included another part of our conversation there that was cut for space in the *Ms.* version of this exposé—to refresh his memory.

Then came the third wave—reader letters which were smart, thoughtful, innovative, and numbered in the hundreds. Their dominant themes were anger and relief: relief because those vast uncritical oceans of food/fashion/beauty articles in other women's magazines weren't necessarily what women wanted after all, and also relief because *Ms.* wasn't going to take ads anymore, even those that were accompanied by fewer editorial demands; anger because consumer information, diverse articles, essays, fiction, and poetry could have used the space instead of all those oceans of articles about ad categories that had taken up most of women's magazines for years. Many also reported various actions: (1) complaining directly to presidents of companies whose ads were surrounded by editorial payoffs, as well as praising those that supported worthwhile articles or any unrelated editorial; and (2) sending copies of those complaining or praising letters to corporate owners of women's magazines, with cover notes explaining that they were willing to pay more for magazines whose editorial content wasn't just an extension of ads, but nothing for catalogs. Some readers had tried such innovative techniques as returning ad-heavy issues of magazines to the publisher, postage due, with a request that advertisers pay the postage; or scrawling *Advertising* across all editorial extensions of ads in several issues, and then returning them with a request for a subscription refund. One woman said she was planning to sue for consumer fraud —on the grounds of paying for a magazine and receiving a catalog.

At a professional lunch where I was asked to address editors from a wide variety of magazines, the discussion yielded another tactic: asking one major publisher to be the leader of a long-term staged shift from mostly ad income to income mostly from readers. They identified Si Newhouse of Condé Nast as best placed to influence the industry. Not only had he allowed two of his smaller magazines, *Condé Nast Traveler* and *Allure,* to be slightly more independent of ad influence, but he was also the hereditary owner of a dozen more publications, from *Glamour* to *Vanity Fair.* By asking readers to pay a greater percentage of what magazines cost, as they do in some other countries, and by changing ad policy—that is, selling access to readers according to the usual demographic and psychographic information but not offering any particular editorial surroundings or ad placement as part of the deal—he could do a great deal to improve what we read. Of course, nobody offered to go see Newhouse —but they did suggest readers write to him. They also agreed that an impenetrable wall between advertising and editorial would benefit advertisers in the long run. Their ads' credibility would increase, with more credible surroundings, and they would be off the hot seat of haggling for ever more influence and "extras."

Last and most rewarding was the response that started in the fall. Teachers of journalism, advertising, communications, women's studies, and other contemporary courses asked permission to reprint the exposé as a supplementary text. That's another reason why I've restored cuts, updated information, and added new examples—including this introduction. Getting subversive ideas into classrooms could change the next generation running the media.

The following pages are mostly about women's magazines, but that doesn't mean other media are immune.

Take General Electric, for instance. Its happy ad jingle, "We Bring Good Things to Life," doesn't tell you that GE has been (1) a major maker of nuclear weapons parts, (2) a source of major environmental danger due to radiation and asbestos hazards from its plants as well as other toxic wastes, and according to the Environmental Protection Agency, potentially responsible for more Superfund hazardous waste sites than any other corporation in the U.S., (3) a major beneficiary of the real estate sales that resulted from the savings and loan scandals, and (4) the subject of a national consumer boycott coordinated by INFACT[2] for GE's role in the arms race. To discourage GE from making more items like guidance systems for nuclear warheads, INFACT suggested refusing to buy anything, from its smallest light bulb to its biggest piece of medical equipment. Yet the *Today* show on NBC, the network owned by GE, refused to let Todd Putnam of the *National Boycott News*[3] discuss the GE boycott, or to otherwise cover this obvious example in a report on boycotts.

That's a serious accusation. It was seriously reported by sources as diverse as the *National Catholic Reporter*[4] and FAIR (Fairness and Accuracy in Reporting), a media watchdog group, together with an NBC producer's statement that this had been "an independent news judgment."[5] If there was censorship, it's possible that everyone concerned will think twice next time. If there wasn't, both viewpoints were aired.

But if GE were a major advertiser in a woman's magazine and the situation were the same as above, it is not only unlikely that you would read about GE's nuclear weapons, radiation, asbestos, toxic wastes, savings and loan scandals, or consumer boycott. Instead, it's likely that GE light bulbs would turn up in a story about, say, new mood lighting, GE designer refrigerators would be featured in an article on remodeling kitchens, GE medical equipment would be hailed as a breast-cancer breakthrough, and fashion models would be seductively posed against a backdrop of one of GE's more questionable hazardous waste sites. Furthermore, I doubt that the rest of the media would care.

In order to get ads, women's media are not only expected to squelch criticism, but to deliver praise. That's a big difference. As the readers whose image, seriousness, and information are being distorted, it's up to us.

Suppose archaeologists of the future were to dig up women's magazines and use them to judge American women. What would they think of us—and what can we do about it?

Sex, Lies, and Advertising

Toward the end of the 1980s, when glasnost was beginning and *Ms.* magazine seemed to be ending, I was invited to a press lunch for a Soviet official. He entertained us with anecdotes about the new problems of democracy in his country; for instance, local Communist leaders who were being criticized by their own media for the first time, and were angry.

"So I'll have to ask my American friends," he finished pointedly, "how more subtly to control the press."

In the silence that followed, I said: "Advertising."

The reporters laughed, but later one of them took me aside angrily: How dare I suggest that freedom of the press was limited in this country? How dare I imply that *his* newsmagazine could be influenced by ads?

I explained that I wasn't trying to lay blame, but to point out advertising's media-wide influence. We can all recite examples of "soft" cover stories that newsmagazines use to sell ads, and self-censorship in articles that should have taken advertised products to task for, say, safety or pollution. Even television news goes "soft" in ratings wars, and other TV shows don't get on the air without advertiser support. But I really had been thinking about women's magazines. There, it isn't just a little content that's designed to attract ads; it's almost all of it. That's why advertisers—not readers—had always been the problem for *Ms.* As the only women's magazine that didn't offer what the ad world euphemistically describes as "supportive editorial atmosphere" or "complementary copy" (for instance, articles that praise food/fashion/beauty subjects in order to "support" and "complement" food/fashion/beauty ads), *Ms.* could never attract enough ads to break even.

"Oh, *women's* magazines," the journalist said with contempt. "Everybody knows they're catalogs—but who cares? They have nothing to do with journalism."

I can't tell you how many times I've had this argument since I started writing for magazines in the early 1960s, and especially since the current women's movement began. Except as moneymaking machines—"cash cows," as they are so elegantly called in the trade—women's magazines are usually placed beyond the realm of serious consideration. Though societal changes being forged by women have been called more far-reaching than the industrial revolution by such nonfeminist sources as *The Wall Street Journal*—and though women's magazine editors often try hard to reflect these changes in the few pages left after all the ad-related subjects are covered—the magazines serving the female half of this country are still far below the journalistic and ethical standards of news and general-interest counterparts. Most depressing of all, this fact is so taken for granted that it doesn't even rate an exposé.

For instance: If *Time* and *Newsweek*, in order to get automotive and GM ads, had to lavish editorial praise on cars and credit photographs in which newsmakers were driving, say, a Buick from General Motors, there would be a scandal—maybe even a criminal investigation. When women's magazines from *Seventeen* to *Lear's* publish articles lavishing praise on beauty and fashion products, and crediting in text describing cover and other supposedly editorial photographs a particular makeup from Revlon or a dress from Calvin Klein because those companies also advertise, it's just business as usual.

When *Ms.* began, we didn't consider *not* taking ads. The most important reason was to keep the price of a feminist magazine low enough for most women to afford. But the second and almost equal reason was to provide a forum where women and advertisers could talk to each other and experiment with nonstereotyped, informative, imaginative ads. After all, advertising was (and is) as potent a source of information in this country as news or TV or movies. It's where we get not only a big part of our information but also images that shape our dreams.

We decided to proceed in two stages. First, we would convince makers of "people products" that their ads should be placed in a women's magazine: cars, credit cards, insurance, sound equipment, financial services—everything that's used by both men and women but was then advertised only to men. Since those advertisers were accustomed to the division between editorial pages and ads that news and general-interest magazines at least try to maintain, such products would allow our editorial content to be free and diverse. Furthermore, if *Ms.* could prove that women were important purchasers of "people products," just as men were, those advertisers would support other women's magazines, too, and subsidize some pages for articles about something other than the hothouse worlds of food/fashion/beauty. Only in the second phase would we add examples of the best ads for whatever traditional "women's products" (clothes, shampoo, fragrance, food, and so on) that subscriber surveys showed *Ms.* readers actually used. But we would ask those advertisers to come in *without* the usual quid pro quo of editorial features praising their product area; that is, the dreaded "complementary copy."

From the beginning, we knew the second step might be even harder than the first. Clothing advertisers like to be surrounded by editorial fashion spreads (preferably ones that credit their particular labels and designers); food advertisers have always expected women's magazines to publish recipes and articles on entertaining (preferably ones that require their products); and shampoo, fragrance, and beauty products in general insist on positive editorial coverage of beauty aids—a "beauty atmosphere," as they put it—plus photo credits for particular products and nothing too depressing; no bad news. That's why women's magazines look the way they do: saccharine, smiley-faced and product-heavy, with even serious articles presented in a slick and sanitized way.

But if *Ms.* could break this link between ads and editorial content, then we should add "women's products" too. For one thing, publishing ads only for gender-neutral products would give the impression that women have to become "like men" in order to succeed (an impression that *Ms.* ad pages sometimes *did* give when we were still in the first stage). For another, presenting a full circle of products that readers actually need and use would allow us to select the best examples of each category and keep ads from being lost in a sea of similar products. By being part of this realistic but unprecedented mix, products formerly advertised only to men would reach a growth market of women, and good ads for women's products would have a new visibility.

Given the intelligence and leadership of *Ms.* readers, both kinds of products would have unique access to a universe of smart consultants whose response would help them create more effective ads for other media too. Aside from the advertisers themselves, there's nobody who cares as much about the imagery in advertising as those who find themselves stereotyped or rendered invisible by it. And they often have great suggestions for making it better.

As you can see, we had all our energy, optimism, and arguments in good working order.

I thought at the time that our main problem would be getting ads with good "creative," as the imagery and text are collectively known.

That was where the women's movement had been focusing its efforts, for instance, the National Organization for Women's awards to the best ads, and its "Barefoot and Pregnant" awards for the worst. Needless to say, there were plenty of candidates for the second group. Carmakers were still draping blondes in evening gowns over the hoods like ornaments that could be bought with the car (thus also making clear that car ads weren't directed at women). Even in ads for products that only women used, the authority figures were almost always male, and voice-overs for women's products on television were usually male too. Sadistic, he-man campaigns were winning industry praise; for example, *Advertising Age* hailed the infamous Silva Thin cigarette theme, "How to Get a Woman's Attention: Ignore Her," as "brilliant." Even in medical journals, ads for tranquilizers showed depressed housewives standing next to piles of dirty dishes and promised to get them back to work. As for women's magazines, they seemed to have few guidelines; at least none that excluded even the ads for the fraudulent breast-enlargement or thigh-thinning products for which their back pages were famous.

Obviously, *Ms.* would have to avoid such offensive imagery and seek out the best ads, but this didn't seem impossible. *The New Yorker* had been screening ads for aesthetic reasons for years, a practice that advertisers accepted at the time. *Ebony* and *Essence* were asking for ads with positive black images, and though their struggle was hard, their requests weren't seen as unreasonable.

What *Ms.* needed was a very special publisher and an ad sales staff of pioneers. I could think of only one woman with experience on the editorial side of magazines, and some on the publishing side as well—Patricia Carbine, who recently had become the vice president of *McCall's* as well as its editor in chief—and I knew her name for a reason that was also a good omen. She had been managing editor at *Look* (really *the* editor, but its owner had refused to put a female name at the top of his masthead) when I wrote a few articles and a short-lived column there. After I did an early interview with Cesar Chavez, then just emerging as a leader of migrant workers, and the publisher turned it down because he was worried about losing ads from Sunkist (their oranges were picked by migrant workers), Pat was the one who intervened. She told the publisher she would resign if the interview wasn't published. Mainly because *Look* couldn't afford to lose Pat, it *was* published (and the Sunkist ads never arrived).

Though I barely knew this woman, she had done two things I always remembered. First, she put her job on the line for a principle in a way that editors often talk about but rarely do. Second, she had been so loyal to her colleagues that she never told me or anyone outside *Look* that she had done so. Indeed, it was years before I learned why and how that Chavez interview got published—and even then, it wasn't from Pat.

Fortunately, Pat did agree to leave *McCall's,* its stock options, and its big salary behind to become publisher of *Ms.* (As the rebellious daughter in a large Catholic family, she had, as she put it, "taken the vow of poverty—but for a different reason.") Over the years, she became responsible for training and inspiring generations of young women, many of whom absorbed publishing experience at *Ms.* and went on to become "firsts" at the top of the field: Cathleen Black, the first ad director of *Ms.,* became publisher of *USA Today* and now heads the Newspaper Association of America; Valerie Salembier, our second ad director, is now vice president of The New York Times Company—and many more.

When *Ms.* first started, however, there were almost no women with experience selling magazine space to advertisers, and even women's magazines employed men. Pat and I made the rounds of ad agencies ourselves. Later, the fact that *Ms.* was asking companies to do business in a different way meant that our saleswomen had to make twice the usual number of calls—first to convince agencies and then to convince their clients, because each thought the other wouldn't agree—and also to do endless research showing that women couldn't be bought "by the ton," that they were a "segmented market," just as men were, and that some women were actually "opinion leaders." I was often brought along for a final ad presentation, or to get in to see some higher decisionmaker, or to speak to women employees so male executives could see that even the women they worked with were interested, or just to show that, if I didn't have army boots and hand grenades, maybe feminism wasn't what the media had pictured, after all. That's why, over the years, I spent more time persuading advertisers than editing or writing, which was what I had expected and wanted to do, and why I ended up with an unsentimental education in the seamy underside of publishing that few writers get.

I'm not saying that *Ms.* did everything right. We started out with a fraction of the usual investment money—the price of having an independent magazine in the first place—and we often spent time on movement events and reader concerns that didn't show up in the pages of the magazine. Though our less hierarchical style attracted and made far better use of individual talents than a traditional structure would have done, we had problems of a female cultural style: I had a hard time assuming any authority in the editorial area; on the publishing side, Pat Carbine had a hard time delegating it; having to fire anyone was such a difficult decision for all of us that it often got delayed, to no one's benefit; and none of us was good at blowing her own horn—which is why even now I can tell you our shortcomings more easily than our virtues.

But I am saying that if *Ms.* had been a magazine of comparable readership, success, editorial quality, staff talent, prizes won for writing and design, and impact on society—but by and for men instead of women—the advertising response would have been very different (and so would the media response). Let me take you through some of our experiences—greatly condensed, but just as they happened. In fact, if you poured water on any one of these, it would become a novel:

• Cheered on by early support from Volkswagen and one or two other car companies, we finally scrape together time and money to put on a major reception in Detroit. U.S. carmakers firmly believe that women choose the upholstery color, not the car, but we are armed with statistics and reader mail to prove the contrary: a car is an important purchase for women, one that is such a symbol of mobility and freedom that many women will spend a greater percentage of income for a car than will counterpart men.

But almost nobody comes. We are left with many pounds of shrimp on the table, and quite a lot of egg on our face. Assuming this near-total boycott is partly because there was a baseball pennant play-off the same day, we blame ourselves for not foreseeing the problem. Executives go out of their way to explain that they wouldn't have come anyway. It's a dramatic beginning for ten years of knocking on resistant or hostile doors, presenting endless documentation of women as car buyers, and hiring a full-time saleswoman in Detroit—all necessary before *Ms.* gets any real results.

This long saga has a semi-happy ending: foreign carmakers understood better than Detroit that women buy cars, and advertised in *Ms.;* also years of research on the women's market plus door-knocking began to pay off. Eventually, cars became one of our top sources of ad revenue. Even Detroit began to take the women's market seriously enough to put car ads in other women's magazines too, thus freeing a few more of their pages from the food/fashion/beauty hothouse.

But long after figures showed that a third, even half, of many car models were being bought by women, U.S. makers continued to be uncomfortable addressing female buyers. Unlike many foreign carmakers, Detroit never quite learned the secret of creating intelligent ads that exclude no one and then placing them in media that overcome past exclusion. Just as an African-American reader may feel more invited by a resort that placed an ad in *Ebony* or *Essence,* even though the same ad appeared in *Newsweek,* women of all races may need to see ads for cars, computers, and other historically "masculine" products in media that are clearly directed at them. Once inclusive ads are well placed, however, there's interest and even gratitude from women. *Ms.* readers were so delighted to be addressed as intelligent consumers by a routine Honda ad with text about rack-and-pinion steering, for example, that they sent fan mail. But even now, Detroit continues to ask: "Should we make special ads for women?" That's probably one reason why foreign cars still have a greater share of the women's market in the U.S. than of the men's.

• In the *Ms.* Gazette, we do a brief report on a congressional hearing into coal tar derivatives used in hair dyes that are absorbed through the skin and may be carcinogenic. This seems like news of importance: newspapers and newsmagazines are reporting it too. But Clairol, a Bristol-Myers subsidiary that makes dozens of products, a few of which have just come into our pages as ads *without* the usual quid pro quo of articles on hair and beauty, is outraged. Not at newspapers or newsmagazines, just at us. It's bad enough that *Ms.* is the only women's magazine refusing to provide "supportive editorial" praising beauty products, but to criticize one of their product categories on top of it, however generically or even accurately—well, *that* is going too far.

We offer to publish a letter from Clairol telling its side of the story. In an excess of solicitousness, we even put this letter in the Gazette, not in Letters to the Editors, where it belongs. Eventually, Clairol even changes its hair-coloring formula, apparently in response to those same hearings. But in spite of surveys that show *Ms.* readers to be active women who use more of almost everything Clairol makes than do the readers of other women's magazines, *Ms.*

gets almost no ads for those dozens of products for the rest of its natural life.

• Women of color read *Ms.* in disproportionate numbers. This is a source of pride to *Ms.* staffers, who are also more racially representative than the editors of other women's magazines (which may include some beautiful black models but almost no black decision-makers; Pat Carbine hired the first black editor at *McCall's,* but she left when Pat did). Nonetheless, the reality of *Ms.*'s staff and readership is obscured by ads filled with enough white women to make the casual reader assume *Ms.* is directed at only one part of the population, no matter what the editorial content is.

When Pat Carbine requests African-American, Latina, Asian, and other diverse images (which exist, if at all, in ads created for "special media"), she remembers mostly "astonishment." Marcia Ann Gillespie, then a *Ms.* contributing editor and previously editor in chief of *Essence,* is witnessing ad bias a second time around: Having tried for *Essence* to get white advertisers to use black images (Revlon did so eventually, but L'Oréal, Lauder, Chanel, and other companies never came through during her tenure), she now sees similar problems getting racially diverse ads for a racially diverse magazine. In an exact parallel of the fear that marketing a product to females will endanger its appeal to males, the agency response is often: "But your [white] readers won't identify."

In fact, those few ads we are able to get that feature women of color—for instance, one made by Max Factor for *Essence* and *Ebony* that Linda Wachner gives us while she is president of Max Factor—are greeted with praise and relief by white readers, too, and make us feel that more inclusive ads should win out in the long run. But there are pathetically few such images. Advertising "creative" also excludes women who are not young, not thin, not conventionally pretty, well-to-do, able-bodied, or heterosexual—which is a hell of a lot of women.

• Our intrepid saleswomen set out early to attract ads for the product category known as consumer electronics: sound equipment, computers, calculators, VCRs, and the like. We know that *Ms.* readers are determined to be part of this technological revolution, not to be left out as women have been in the past. We also know from surveys that readers are buying this kind of stuff in numbers as high as those of readers of magazines like *Playboy* and the "male 18 to 34" market, prime targets of the industry. Moreover, unlike traditional women's products that our readers buy but don't want to read articles about, these are subjects they like to see demystified in our pages. There actually *is* a supportive editorial atmosphere.

"But women don't understand technology," say ad and electronics executives at the end of our presentations. "Maybe not," we respond, "but neither do men—and we all buy it."

"If women *do* buy it," counter the decisionmakers, "it's because they're asking their husbands and boyfriends what to buy first." We produce letters from *Ms.* readers saying how turned off they are when salesmen say things like "Let me know when your husband can come in."

Then the argument turns to why there aren't more women's names sent back on warranties (those much-contested certificates promising repair or replacement if anything goes wrong). We explain that the husband's name may be on the warranty, even if the wife made the purchase. But it's also true that women are experienced enough as consumers to know that such promises are valid only if the item is returned in its original box at midnight in Hong Kong. Sure enough, when we check out hair dryers, curling irons, and other stuff women clearly buy, women don't return those warranties very often either. It isn't the women who are the problem, it's the meaningless warranties.

After several years of this, we get a few ads from companies like JVC and Pioneer for compact sound systems—on the grounds that women can understand compacts, but not sophisticated components. Harry Elias, vice president of JVC, is actually trying to convince his Japanese bosses that there is something called a woman's market. At his invitation, I find myself speaking at trade shows in Chicago and Las Vegas trying to persuade JVC dealers that electronics showrooms don't have to be locker rooms. But as becomes apparent, however, the trade shows are part of the problem. In Las Vegas, the only women working at technology displays are semi-nude models serving champagne. In Chicago, the big attraction is Marilyn Chambers, a porn star who followed Linda Lovelace of *Deep Throat* fame as Chuck Traynor's captive and/or employee, whose pornographic movies are being used to demonstrate VCRs.

In the end, we get ads for a car stereo now and then, but no VCRs; a welcome breakthrough of some IBM personal computers, but no Apple or no Japanese-made ones. Furthermore, we notice that *Working Woman* and *Savvy*, which are focused on office work, don't benefit as much as they should from ads for office equipment either.

In the mind's eye of the electronics world, females and technology don't mix, even in the designing of children's video games. Electronics is further behind than Detroit. Finally, I threaten to hire male ad reps for a magazine called *Mr.*, send them out with all the same readership statistics, and reveal only at the end of the presentation that these consumer dollars are coming from women. But I'm not sure even that would do the trick. As long as advertisers keep feeding "women" into the computer, "not our target audience" will keep coming out. The trick is to feed in "people" instead—but that isn't what happens. Even newsstands are gender segregated: *Ms.* gets placed with women's magazines—where our readers are less likely to browse and where we look odd anyway—instead of with *Time, Newsweek, Rolling Stone,* and other things our readers buy. It's still an upside-down world, with genitalia placed above heads or hearts.

• Then there is the great toy train adventure. Because *Ms.* gets letters from little girls who love toy trains and ask our help in changing ads and box-top photos that show only little boys, we try to talk to Lionel and to get their ads. It turns out that Lionel executives *have* been concerned about little girls. They made a pink train and couldn't understand why it didn't sell.

Eventually, Lionel bows to this consumer pressure by switching to a photograph of a boy *and* a girl—but only on some box tops. If trains are associated with little girls, Lionel executives believe, they will be devalued in the eyes of little boys. Needless to say, *Ms.* gets no train ads. If even 20 percent of little girls wanted trains, they would be a huge growth market, but this remains unexplored. In the many toy stores where displays are still gender divided, the "soft" stuff, even modeling clay, stays on the girls' side, while the "hard" stuff, especially rockets and trains, is displayed for boys—thus depriving both. By 1986, Lionel is put up for sale.

We don't have much luck with other kinds of toys either. A *Ms.* department, Stories for Free Children, edited by Letty Cottin Pogrebin, makes us one of the very few magazines with a regular feature for children. A larger proportion of *Ms.* readers have preschool children than do the readers of any other women's magazine. Nonetheless, the industry can't seem to believe that feminists care about children—much less have them.

• When *Ms.* began, the staff decided not to accept ads for feminine hygiene sprays and cigarettes on the same basis: they are damaging to many women's health but carry no appropriate warnings. We don't think we should tell our readers what to do—if marijuana were legal, for instance, we would carry ads for it along with those for beer and wine—but we should provide facts so readers can decide for themselves. Since we've received letters saying that feminine sprays actually kill cockroaches and take the rust off metal, we give up on those. But antismoking groups have been pressuring for health warnings on cigarette ads as well as packages, so we decide we will accept advertising if the tobacco industry complies.

Philip Morris is among the first to do so. One of its brands, Virginia Slims, is also sponsoring women's tennis tournaments and women's public opinion polls that are historic "firsts." On the other hand, the Virginia Slims theme, "You've come a long way, baby," has more than a "baby" problem. It gives the impression that for women, smoking is a sign of progress.

We explain to the Philip Morris people that this slogan won't do well in our pages. They are convinced that its success with *some* women means it will work with *all* women. No amount of saying that we, like men, are a segmented market, that we don't all think alike, does any good. Finally, we agree to publish a small ad for a Virginia Slims calendar as a test, and to abide by the response of our readers.

The letters from readers are both critical and smart. For instance: Would you show a photo of a black man picking cotton next to one of an African-American man in a Cardin suit, and symbolize progress from slavery to civil rights by smoking? Of course not. So why do it for women? But instead of honoring test results, the executives seem angry to have been proved wrong. We refuse Virginia Slims ads, thus annoying tennis players like Billie Jean King as well as incurring a new level of wrath: Philip Morris takes away ads for *all* its many products, costing *Ms.* about $250,000 in the first year. After five years, the damage is so great we can no longer keep track.

Occasionally, a new set of Philip Morris executives listens to *Ms.* saleswomen, or laughs when Pat Carbine points out that even Nixon got pardoned. I also appeal directly to the chairman of the board, who agrees it is unfair, sends me to another executive—and *he* says no. Because we won't take Virginia Slims, not one other Philip Morris product returns to our pages for the next sixteen years.

Gradually, we also realize our naïveté in thinking we could refuse all cigarette ads, with or without a health warning. They became a disproportionate source of revenue for print media the moment television banned them, and few magazines can compete or survive without them; certainly not *Ms.*, which lacks the support of so many other categories. Though cigarette ads actually inhibit editorial freedom less than ads for food, fashion, and the like—cigarette companies want only to be distant from coverage on the dangers of smoking, and don't require affirmative praise or photo credits of their product—it is still a growing source of sorrow that they are there at all. By the 1980s, when statistics show that women's rate of lung cancer is approaching men's, the necessity of taking cigarette ads has become a kind of prison.

Though I never manage to feel kindly toward groups that protest our ads and pay no attention to magazines and newspapers that can turn them down and still keep their doors open—and though *Ms.* continues to publish new facts about smoking, such as its dangers during pregnancy—I long for the demise of the whole tobacco-related industry.

• We hear that women in the (then) Soviet Union have been producing feminist samizdat (underground, self-published books) and circulating them throughout the country. Through feminists in Paris, we get one such samizdat, which has been smuggled out and translated into French: a diverse, brave, tough-minded, and lyrical collection of essays called *Mother Russia*. Soon, we also hear that four of the main organizers and writers have been exiled—given a choice between Siberia and exile, they chose with sadness to leave their country—and so are free to talk for the first time. Though *Ms.* is operating on its usual shoestring, we solicit contributions for plane fare and send Robin Morgan to interview them in Vienna.

The result is an exclusive cover story; a rare grassroots, bottom-up view of Russian life in general and the lives of Russian women in particular. The interview also includes the first news of a populist peace movement against the Soviet occupation of Afghanistan, and prediction of *glasnost* to come. From the popular media to women's studies and political science courses, the response is great. The story wins a Front Page award.

Nonetheless, this journalistic coup undermines years of hard work trying to get an ad schedule from Revlon. Why? Because the Soviet women on our cover *are not wearing makeup*.

• General Mills, Pillsbury, Carnation, Del Monte, Dole, Kraft,

Stouffer, Hormel, Nabisco: you name the food giant, we try to get its ads. But no matter how desirable the *Ms.* readership, our lack of editorial recipes and traditional homemaking articles proves lethal.

We explain that women flooding into the paid labor force have changed the way this country eats; certainly, the boom in convenience foods proves that. We also explain that placing food ads *only* next to recipes and how-to-entertain articles is actually a negative for many women. It associates food with work—in a way that says only women have to cook—or with guilt over *not* cooking and entertaining. Why not advertise food in diverse media that don't always include recipes (thus reaching more men, who have become a third of all supermarket shoppers anyway) and add the recipe interest with specialty magazines like *Gourmet* (a third of whose readers are men)?

These arguments elicit intellectual interest but no ads. No advertising executive wants to be the first to say to a powerful client, "Guess what, I *didn't* get you complementary copy." Except for an occasional hard-won ad for instant coffee, diet drinks, yogurt, or such extras as avocados and almonds, the whole category of food, a mainstay of the publishing industry, remains unavailable to us. Period.

• Traditionally, wines and liquors didn't advertise to women: their makers were convinced that even though the wife might do the buying, the husband chose the brand. After alcoholic beverages (other than beer and wine) were forbidden to advertise on television, women's magazines were at a continual disadvantage.

But with the leadership of Michel Roux of Carillon Importers (distributor of Grand Marnier, Absolut vodka, and other brands), that begins to change. With a Frenchman's assumption that food and drink have no gender, and with ads that use good artists, he begins to lead the category out of its men's club. Meanwhile, diligent *Ms.* saleswomen have carried their studies on brand choice and entertaining from one ad agency to the next, like cross-pollinating bees. By the 1980s, Drummond Bell, president of National Distillers and self-described as "to the right of Genghis Khan," has discovered that feminism is actually about fair play, something he understands as a self-made man; and Ernest Gallo, once so angry at *Ms.*'s coverage of Cesar Chavez and the United Farm Workers that he said he would put wine ads in *Ms.* "only after *Pravda*," now also comes into our pages.

As a result of countless such efforts, this category of ads supports a lot of good fiction, investigative journalism, feminist theory, humor, and art in *Ms.*

Of course, there are exceptions. Beermakers keep right on selling masculinity. Though they know college women drink beer, they assume this ends with graduation. Besides, they believe beer is "masculine," and showing women in the ads as customers, not just ornaments, will devalue it as "feminine." (Sort of like the old "Negro retainers" shown serving elegant "white" drinks on a silver tray but certainly never drinking them. The sex/race parallel rarely fails.) It takes *Ms.* eight years to get even one beer ad: Michelob Light.

But in general, liquor as a "people product" is less pushy editorially and less condescending in the creative content of its ads. When there *are* problems with an ad campaign (for instance, "After she cooks a great dinner, pay tribute to it with Grand Marnier"), there's also more willingness to change ("After a great dinner, . . ." a deletion of two words that got praise). When the "Hit Me with a Club" campaign of Heublein's Club Cocktail got letters from *Ms.* readers because it trivialized violence (it showed a smiling woman with a black eye, and some versions showed a man), the whole multimillion-dollar campaign was changed nationally, and Heublein published a letter in *Ms.* to thank readers for their responsiveness and help.

But given the underrepresentation of other categories in *Ms.*, these very facts tend to create a disproportionate number of ads for alcoholic beverages. This in turn dismays readers who are worried about women and alcoholism.

• Four years of research and presentations go into convincing airlines that women make their own travel choices and business trips. United, the first airline to advertise in *Ms.*, is so impressed with the response from our readers that one of its executives agrees to be filmed giving us a testimonial so we can use it as an ad presentation. As usual, good ads get great results.

But we have other problems. Because flight attendants for American Airlines include among their union demands a request to have their last names preceded by "Ms." on their name tags—a revolt against the standard "I am your pilot, Captain Rothgart, and this is your flight attendant, Cindy Sue"—American officials think the magazine is partly responsible for this uppity behavior. We get no ads.

At Eastern there is a different disaster. Thousands of subscriptions keep *Ms.* on hundreds of Eastern flights: part of our circulation guarantee to advertisers. Suddenly, they are canceled. Why? Because the vice president in charge of putting magazines on planes is offended by *Ms.* classified ads for lesbian poetry journals; at least, that's what he gives us as an example. As he explains to me coldly on the phone, "a family airline has to draw the line somewhere."

Obviously, *Ms.* can't exclude lesbians and serve women. That's been clear ever since our first issue, when we were warned not to include anything by or about lesbians—and so, of course, published a major article that was both. Letters from readers, both gay and straight, were appreciative: all nonconforming women can be stopped by the word "lesbian" until it becomes as honorable as any other. But Suzanne Braun Levine, our main editor, and I were lectured by such media heavy hitters as Ed Kosner, then editor of *Newsweek* (now editor of *Esquire,* and perhaps in a different state of consciousness), who insisted that *Ms.* should "position" itself as the feminist magazine *against* lesbians. In Eastern's case, the same message came with economic clout. Ad rates are based on reaching a certain number of readers, and soliciting new subscriptions to replace the canceled ones would cost $150,000 (which we don't have), plus rebating money to advertisers in the meantime.

Like most experiences with the ad world, this presents a Kafkaesque organizing problem. After days of unsuccessful searching for a sympathetic ear on the Eastern board of directors, Frank Thomas, president of the Ford Foundation, kindly offers to call Roswell Gilpatric, who is an Eastern director. I talk with Mr. Gilpatric, who kindly offers to call Frank Borman, then the president of Eastern. Frank Borman calls me to say his airline is not in the business of censoring magazines. *Ms.* will be returned to Eastern flights.

I have one more conversation with the vice president, who is angry at having been overruled—I hope he has no blunt instruments —but we're fine. Except that we've wasted three weeks of energy and ingenuity, which could have been used to move forward. Too much of our lives corresponds to the "lost-wallet" theory of life. You lose something, spend a long time finding it, and then feel grateful to be back where you started.

• Women's access to insurance and credit is vital, but with the exception of Equitable and a few other pioneers, financial ads address men. For almost a decade after the Equal Credit Opportunity Act passes in 1974, we try to convince American Express that women are a powerful growth market now that credit discrimination is against the law—but nothing works.

Finally, a former college professor named Jerry Welch becomes head of marketing and just assumes that women should be cardholders. He persuades his colleagues to feature women in an ad campaign. Thanks to this 1980s series (whose theme is "It's part of a lot of interesting lives"), the growth rate for female cardholders surpasses that for men.

Even with this success, however, problems continue. Though American Express has agreed to sponsor an award ceremony for *Ms.* Magazine's Women of the Year, its subsidy is withdrawn when Welch discovers that one of our dozen awardees is Holly Near, singer, composer, founder of a successful woman-owned record company, and pioneer of women's music. Apparently, it's her politics and sexuality that are the problem. She was once part of an anti-Vietnam entertainment troupe touring the country with Jane Fonda, and her song lyrics reflect her life as a lesbian. James Robinson, then the chairman of American Express, is a staunch Republican and a friend of Ronald and Nancy Reagan's. His wife, Linda, once worked in the Reagan White House. (Whether or not he was consulted about this, I don't know. A lot of problems come from anticipating what the boss *might* think.)

Actually, we've been around this track before. Welch refused to sponsor a *Ms.*/Louis Harris poll because women's opinions might turn out to be too critical of White House policies. This time, I decide to try humor. "Her politics and sexuality," I say, "are exactly the same as Leonard Bernstein's. Wouldn't you sponsor him?" I get a laugh—but no sponsorship.

Still, Welch's honesty is better than the usual cosmetic excuses. I was reminded of this fact when I called him at his new consulting business while researching this article. Could he explain why American Express had waited so long to address women? "Sure," he said. "They thought advertising to women would turn men off. They were afraid of having a 'pink' card."

And did it? "Just the opposite. Men were attracted by that campaign too. In the marketplace, men want to be what they think women are—smart consumers."

When I was just a writer, I thought the point of business was to make money. That was before credit cards, electronics, and other companies taught me that "masculinity" is also a bottom line. Now,

I think if you can get them to *want* to make money, you've won a battle.

• By the end of 1986, magazine production costs have skyrocketed and postal rates have increased 400 percent. Ad income is flat for the whole magazine industry. The result is more competition, with other magazines offering such "extras" as free golf trips for advertisers or programs for "sampling" their products at parties and other events arranged by the magazine for desirable consumers. We try to compete with the latter by "sampling" at what we certainly have enough of: movement benefits. Thus, little fragrance bottles turn up next to the dinner plates of California women lawyers (who are delighted), or wine samples lower the costs at a reception for political women. A good organizing tactic comes out of this. We hold feminist seminars in shopping centers. They may be to the women's movement what churches were to the civil rights movement in the South—that is, *where people are*. Anyway, shopping center seminars are a great success. Too great. We have to stop doing them in Bloomingdale's up and down the East Coast, because meeting space in the stores is too limited, and too many women are left lined up outside stores. We go on giving out fancy little liquor bottles at store openings, which makes the advertisers happy—but not us.

Mostly, however, we can't compete in this game of "value-added" (the code word for giving the advertisers extras in return for their ads). Neither can many of the other independent magazines. Deep-pocketed corporate parents can offer such extras as reduced rates for ad schedules in a group of magazines, free tie-in spots on radio stations they also own, or vacation junkets on corporate planes.

Meanwhile, higher costs and lowered income have caused the *Ms.* 60/40 preponderance of edit over ads—something we promised to readers—to become 50/50: still a lot better than most women's magazines' goal of 70/30, but not good enough. Children's stories, most poetry, and some fiction are casualties of reduced space. In order to get variety into more limited pages, the length (and sometimes the depth) of articles suffers. Though we don't solicit or accept ads that would look like a parody in our pages, we get so worn down that some slip through. Moreover, we always have the problem of working just as hard to get a single ad as another magazine might for a whole year's schedule of ads.

Still, readers keep right on performing miracles. Though we

haven't been able to afford a subscription mailing in two years, they maintain our guaranteed circulation of 450,000 by word of mouth. Some of them also help to make up the advertising deficit by giving *Ms.* a birthday present of $15 on its fifteenth anniversary, or contributing $1,000 for a lifetime subscription—even those who can ill afford it.

What's almost as angering as these struggles, however, is the way the media reports them. Our financial problems are attributed to lack of reader interest, not an advertising double standard. In the Reagan-Bush era, when "feminism-is-dead" becomes one key on the typewriter, our problems are used to prepare a grave for the whole movement. Clearly, the myth that advertisers go where the readers are—thus, if we had readers, we would have advertisers—is deeply embedded. Even industry reporters rarely mention the editorial demands made by ads for women's products, and if they do, they assume advertisers must be right and *Ms.* must be wrong; we must be too controversial, outrageous, even scatological to support. In fact, there's nothing in our pages that couldn't be published in *Time, Esquire,* or *Rolling Stone*—providing those magazines devoted major space to women—but the media myth often wins out. Though comparable magazines our size (say, *Vanity Fair* or the *Atlantic*) are losing more money in a single year than *Ms.* has lost in sixteen years, *Ms.* is held to a different standard. No matter how much never-to-be-recovered cash is poured into starting a magazine or keeping it going, appearances seem to be all that matter. (Which is why we haven't been able to explain our fragile state in public. Nothing causes ad flight like the smell of nonsuccess.)

My healthy response is anger, but my not-so-healthy one is depression, worry, and an obsession with finding one more rescue. There is hardly a night when I don't wake up with sweaty palms and pounding heart, scared that we won't be able to pay the printer or the post office; scared most of all that closing our doors will be blamed on a lack of readers and thus the movement, instead of the real cause. ("Feminism couldn't even support one magazine," I can hear them saying.)

Out of chutzpah and desperation, I spend weeks trying to schedule a lunch with Leonard Lauder, president of Estée Lauder, whose ads we've spent years pursuing. With the exception of Clinique (the brainchild of Carol Phillips, a line of skin products whose appeal is more purity than glamour), none of Lauder's brands has advertised in *Ms.* A year's schedule for just a few of his hundreds of products would make all the difference. Indeed, as the scion of a family-owned company whose ad practices influence those of the whole industry, he is one of the few people who could liberate many pages in all women's magazines just by changing his mind about "complementary copy."

Over a fancy lunch that costs more than we can pay for some articles, I explain how much we need his leadership. I also lay out the record of *Ms.:* more literary and journalistic prizes won, more new ideas introduced to the country, more new writers discovered, and more impact on society than any other magazine; more articles that became books, stories that became movies, ideas that became television series; and, most important for him, a unique place for his ads to reach women who are, to use the advertising word, "trendsetters," and just aren't reachable any other way. They don't read other women's magazines regularly or have time for television. But whether it's waiting until later to have first babies, or pioneering PABA in skin products as protection against skin cancer, *whatever* these readers are doing today, a third to half of American women will be doing three to five years from now. It's never failed. Moreover, he will be reaching a constantly "refreshed" readership, to use the advertising term, because the median age has remained in the early thirties for more than a decade, so we know younger readers are constantly arriving.

But, he says, *Ms.* readers are not *our* women. They're not interested in things like fragrance, moisturizer, and blush. If they were, *Ms.* would be writing articles about them.

On the contrary, I explain, *Ms.* readers are more likely to buy such things than are the readers of, say, *Cosmopolitan* or *Vogue*. We're out in the world more and need several sets of everything: for home, work, purse, travel, gym, and so on. But what we don't need is articles about fragrance, moisturizer, and blush. After all, would men's magazines be expected to publish monthly features on how to shave as the price of getting ads for shaving products from Aramis (his line of men's skin products)?

He concedes that beauty features are often concocted more for advertisers than for readers. But *Ms.* isn't appropriate for his ads anyway. Why? Because Estée Lauder is selling "a kept-woman mentality."

I can't quite believe this. Sixty percent of the women who use his products are salaried and greatly resemble the profile of *Ms.* readers. Besides, unlike Revlon and most others, his company has the appeal of being founded by a creative and hardworking woman, his mother, Estée Lauder.

That doesn't matter, he says. He knows his customers, and they would *like* to be kept women. That's why he will never advertise in *Ms.*

Perhaps feeling sorry for me by now, he gives me advice on getting *other* advertisers. For instance, I should borrow the apartment of a mutual friend who is rich, hold dinner parties there, and invite a lot of celebrities—plus just one advertiser. (If you invite two, he warns, each may feel demeaned by the presence of the other.) He himself often does this with department store executives and other people he needs for business. In his art-filled apartment, he hosts dinner parties, with one business target plus distinguished guests and celebrities. Why? Because if you enable executives to say in the office tomorrow, "As Henry Kissinger said to me last night . . . ," they'll do anything for you.

On my way back to the office to report this debacle to the waiting staff, I feel a terrible empathy for everybody in this crazy system— including Leonard Lauder (who, incidentally, still stoutly insists this conversation never took place). We're all being flattened by a velvet steamroller. The only difference is that at *Ms.*, we keep standing up again.

Ms. has been getting thinner and thinner and having more and more harrowing escapes from death. In November 1987, by vote of the Ms. Foundation for Education and Communication (*Ms.*'s owner and publisher, the media subsidiary of the Ms. Foundation for Women), *Ms.* is sold to Fairfax, an Australian company whose officers, Australian feminists Sandra Yates and Anne Summers, have persuaded its board to come up with the money, and who have already started *Sassy,* a U.S. version of an Australian magazine for teenage women. It's very sad—but also better than being bought for our subscription list and folded into a traditional magazine. These are two good women who want to do their best to keep *Ms.*'s feminist spirit.

In their two-year tenure, circulation goes up to 550,000 because of investment in subscription mailings, but they fall afoul of the ad world in a different way. They give in a bit to its pressures, and, to the dismay of some readers, clothes, new products, more celebrities, gardening, and other editorial features are added. Nonetheless, *Ms.* is still far from the commercial habits of other magazines, and ad pages fall below previous levels. In addition, *Sassy*, whose fresh voice and sexual frankness started out as an unprecedented success among young readers, is targeted for an ad boycott by two mothers from Indiana who began, as one of them put it, "calling every Christian organization I could think of." In response to letters from organizations like the American Family Association in Tupelo, Mississippi, at least nine major advertisers pull back. Though *Sassy* doesn't give in completely, a pre-boycott spirit that included reader letters about incest and such titles as "The Truth About Boys' Bodies" turns into a post-boycott atmosphere with such articles as "Virgins Are Cool."

This kind of link between ads and editorial was a problem in Australia, too, but to a lesser degree. "Our readers pay two times more for their magazines," Anne Summers explained, "so advertisers have less power to threaten a magazine's viability."

"I was shocked," said Sandra Yates with characteristic directness. "In Australia, we think you have freedom of the press here—but you don't."

After Fairfax gets into financial problems of its own, Anne and Sandra bravely find new investors, but they don't control their destiny as we did—which is why we could choose to keep going for so long on a shoestring. When they are unable to meet their budget's projections for ad revenue, they are forced to sell. In October 1989, *Ms.* and *Sassy* are taken over by Dale Lang, owner of *Working Mother, Working Woman,* and one of the few independent publishing companies left among the conglomerates. In response to a request from those of us on the original *Ms.* staff—as well as to reader letters urging *Ms.* to continue, plus his own belief that *Ms.*'s existence benefits his other women's magazines by blazing a trail—Lang agrees to publish *Ms.*, with the staff retaining editorial control, and to experiment with a new ad-free format supported entirely by newsstand sales and subscriptions.

The idea of having no ads at all is regarded as total folly by the magazine industry. Readers are accustomed to paying full cost of books but never magazines, readers really like the ads—there are all kinds of industry arguments against this. Nonetheless, checks come rolling in for subscriptions that cost nearly 300 percent more now that they're ad-free. Many readers even send extra money so *Ms.* can continue to be available to women who can't afford the new price, and can also continue supplying free copies to battered women's shelters and the like. Thanks also to the ingenuity of our publisher, Ruth Bowen, in finding the right mailing list and ways of distributing to bookstores, this new *Ms.* is self-supporting after only nine issues. By the end of three years, we are able to give a contribution back to the movement via the Ms. Foundation for Women. (Since it had always been our dream, we made it part of our agreement with Lang.) Moreover, the magazine is now free to be international. Overseas circulation is no longer a penalty because advertisers won't pay for it, they don't sell their products there. Robin Morgan, a past contributing editor who has set aside her own writing to become editor in chief, takes full advantage of this new freedom and uses what once were ad pages for articles of greater length and depth. So does Marcia Ann Gillespie, who takes over from Robin Morgan after three years, and brings her own gift for humor, compassion, and taking on controversial subjects by bringing disparate women together. She is also the first woman of color to head a U.S. national magazine not solely directed to women of color.

I would like to tell you that industry reporters are saying, "We were wrong, advertising was the problem all along"—but they're not. *Ms.* has found a new way of publishing by proving that readers will pay for what they really want, but we're regarded mostly as an oddity. So far, the old way is still in place—especially for publications aimed at women.

At the time of *Ms.*'s sale to Fairfax in 1987, I gave a farewell speech to the American Association of Advertising Agencies. The audience included many creative and caring people, a few of whom had gone out on a limb to help *Ms.*, and I hoped some of them would consider the possibility—I would say the fact—that insisting on "complementary" editorial actually penalizes advertisers too. For one thing, there is no research proving that an ad placed next to a similar article is more effective than the same ad next to, say, a good piece of fiction or investigative reporting. According to Joseph Smith of Oxtoby-Smith, Inc., a consumer research firm: "Broadly speaking, there is no persuasive evidence that the editorial context of an ad matters." For another thing, there is research that shows just the opposite: such links damage *everybody's* credibility. A 1987 survey by the *Journal of Advertising Research* concluded that the "higher the rating of editorial believability, the higher the rating of the advertising."

So I screw up my courage, give many examples, tap-dance my heart out, and try for a big finish. "*Ms.* won reader support and jeopardized traditional advertiser support for exactly the same reason —the editorial content wasn't dictated by the ads." In a voice shaking with sixteen years of work and emotion, I say as forcefully as I can: *"There's something wrong in a world in which women readers—and advertisers trying to reach them—don't want the same thing."*

There is polite applause. Then they all go out to play golf. The velvet steamroller goes right on.

If we're going to have diverse and free sources of information, we have to understand how deep this tradition of ad influence goes, and how wide it spreads.

Ever since *Ladies' Magazine* debuted in Boston in 1828, editorial copy directed to women has been informed by something other than their interests. There were no ads then, but in an age when married women were legal minors, with no right to their own money to pay for subscriptions, there was another controlling revenue source: husbands. "Husbands may rest assured," wrote editor Sarah Josepha Hale, "that nothing found in these pages shall cause [their wives] to be less assiduous in preparing for his reception or encourage her to 'usurp station' or encroach upon prerogatives of men."

Hale went on to become the editor of *Godey's Lady's Book,* a magazine featuring "fashion plates": engravings of dresses to be copied by one's seamstress or by readers themselves. Gradually, Hale added the "how to" articles that were to set the social tone of women's service magazines—how to write politely, how to avoid sunburn of one's ladylike skin, and, in no fewer than 1,200 words, how to maintain a goose quill pen. She also advocated women's education, but not to the point of controversy. Just as most women's magazines now praise socially approved ways of living, suggest individual solutions to what really are political problems, and avoid taking editorial stands on controversial issues like abortion (even if their own polls show that an overwhelming majority of their readers support them), Hale made sure that *Godey's* avoided the hot topics of its day: slavery, abolition, and female suffrage.

What turned women's magazines into catalogs, however, were

two events: Ellen Butterick's invention of the clothing pattern in 1863, and the mass manufacture of patent medicines that contained anything from harmless colored water to small amounts of cocaine. For the first time, readers could purchase what a magazine had encouraged them to want. As the sale of such products made these magazines more profitable and they were able to pay better salaries, they also began to attract male editors. (Indeed, men continued to be the top editors of most women's magazines until the current feminist revolt launched protests like the 1970 sit-in at *Ladies' Home Journal.*) Edward Bok, who became the *Ladies' Home Journal* editor in 1889, inadvertently discovered the power of advertisers when he rejected patent medicines as useless or worse, and other advertisers canceled their ads in retribution. By the early twentieth century, *Good Housekeeping* had started a special institute to "test and approve" products. Its Seal of Approval became the grandfather of all "value-added" programs that offer public relations and merchandising to advertisers.

Generations of suffragist struggle finally won women the vote in 1920, but women's magazines were in no position to help them use it. The magazines' main function was to create a desire for products, instruct in the use of products, and make products a crucial part of gaining social approval, catching a husband, pleasing a husband, and performing as a homemaker. A few short stories and unrelated articles might be included to persuade women to buy what otherwise would have been given away as a catalog—and some of them offered women a voice and sense of community within these pages that came into their own homes. But even those articles were rarely critical from a consumerist point of view or rebellious in other ways. Fiction, too, usually had a formula: if a woman had an affair outside marriage, she must come to a bad end. If she hadn't been chaste before marriage, she could only hope to find an unusually glamorous man who would forgive her—and to whom she would be forever grateful.

Helen Gurley Brown at *Cosmopolitan* began to change that formula in the 1960s by bringing the "sexual revolution" into a women's magazine—but in an ad-oriented way. Sex outside marriage became OK for women too, which was a major and welcome departure. Nonetheless, as the "Cosmo Girl" made clear, attracting multiple men required even more products.

In response to women who flooded the workforce in the 1970s, traditional women's magazines—that is, trade magazines for women who work at home (or, as antifeminists would say, "women who don't work")—were joined by *New Woman* (then a collection of reprints), *Savvy*, *Working Woman*, and other trade magazines for women who work outside the home (though they mostly portrayed these jobs as white-collar; since advertisers weren't interested in low-salaried blue-collar workers, or lower-salaried pink-collar ones in fields where most women work, neither were these magazines). By continuing to publish the fashion/beauty/entertaining articles necessary to get traditional ads and then adding a few career articles on top of that, these new magazines inadvertently helped to create the antifeminist stereotype of Superwoman. (They may also have contributed to their own demise in some cases, for Superwoman made women tired just to read about her.) This male-imitative, dress-for-success woman carrying a briefcase—as well as raising perfect children, cooking gourmet meals, having multiple orgasms, and entertaining beautifully—became the media image of a woman worker. Though women at a real briefcase-carrying level are statistically rare and the glorified secretarial jobs that occupy most women in offices pay less than blue-collar women often earn, advertisers continued to believe that a prime female target must be like her male executive counterpart—only cook, have children, and be sexy besides. Needless to say, dress-for-success women were also thin, white, and beautiful. The majority of women in the workforce might see their family work in traditional women's magazines, but they rarely see their paid work as secretaries, salesclerks, teachers, and nurses.

Do you think, as I once did, that advertisers make decisions based on rational and uniform criteria? Well, think again. There is clearly a double standard. The same food companies that insist on recipes in women's magazines place ads in *People* where there are no recipes. Cosmetics companies support *The New Yorker*, which has no regular beauty columns, and newspaper pages that have no "beauty atmosphere."

Meanwhile, advertisers' control over the editorial content of women's magazines has become so institutionalized that it is sometimes written into "insertion orders" or dictated to ad salespeople as official policy—whether by the agency, the client, or both. The following are orders given to women's magazines effective in 1990. Try to imagine them being applied to *Time* or *Newsweek*.

• Dow's Cleaning Products stipulated that ads for its Vivid and

Spray 'n Wash products should be adjacent to "children or fashion editorial"; ads for Bathroom Cleaner should be next to "home furnishing/family" features; with similar requirements for other brands. "If a magazine fails for ½ the brands or more," the Dow order warned, "it will be omitted from further consideration."

• Bristol-Myers, the parent of Clairol, Windex, Drano, Bufferin, and much more, stipulated that ads be placed next to "a full page of compatible editorial."

• S. C. Johnson & Son, makers of Johnson Wax, lawn and laundry products, insect sprays, hair sprays, and so on, insisted that its ads *"should not be opposite extremely controversial features or material antithetical to the nature/copy of the advertised product."* (Italics theirs.)

• Maidenform, manufacturer of bras and other women's apparel, left a blank for the particular product and stated in its instructions: "The creative concept of the _____ campaign, and the very nature of the product itself appeal to the positive emotions of the reader/ consumer. Therefore, it is imperative that all editorial adjacencies reflect that same positive tone. The editorial must not be negative in content or lend itself contrary to the _____ product imagery/message (e.g., *editorial relating to illness, disillusionment, large size fashion, etc.*)." (Italics mine.)

• The De Beers diamond company, a big seller of engagement rings, prohibited magazines from placing its ads with "adjacencies to hard news or anti-love/romance themed editorial."

• Procter & Gamble, one of this country's most powerful and diversified advertisers, stood out in the memory of Anne Summers and Sandra Yates (no mean feat in this context) because its products were not to be placed in *any* issue that included *any* material on gun control, abortion, the occult, cults, or the disparagement of religion. Caution was also demanded in any issue that included articles on sex or drugs, even for educational purposes.

When I went back to see if these orders were still in effect, my ad agency source said that giving out such information would "breach our contract" with clients, so you'll have to make your own judgment by looking at those ads and their surroundings in current magazines. But here are three insertion orders given to a national women's magazine in 1993.

• Kraft/General Foods, a giant with many brands, sent this message with an Instant Pudding ad: "urgently request upbeat parent/ child activity editorial, mandatory positioning requirements—opposite full page of positive editorial—right hand page essential for creative—minimum 6 page competitive separation (i.e. all sugar based or sugar free gelatins, puddings, mousses, creames [sic] and pie filling)—Do not back with clippable material. Avoid: controversial/negative topics and any narrow targeted subjects."

• An American Tobacco Company order for a Misty Slims ad noted that the U.S. government warning must be included, but also that there must be: "no adjacency to editorial relating to health, medicine, religion or death."

• Lorillard's Newport cigarette ad came with similar instructions, plus: "Please be aware that the Nicotine Patch products are competitors. The minimum six page separation is required."

Quite apart from anything else, you can imagine the logistical nightmare this creates when putting a women's magazine together, but the greatest casualty is editorial freedom. Though the ratio of advertising to editorial pages in women's magazines is only about 5 percent more than in *Time* or *Newsweek,* that nothing-to-read feeling comes from all the supposedly editorial pages that are extensions of ads. To find out what we're really getting when we pay our money, I picked up a variety of women's magazines for February 1994, and counted the number of pages in each one (even including table of contents, letters to the editors, horoscopes, and the like) that were not ads and/or copy complementary to ads. Then I compared that number to the total pages. Out of 184 pages, *McCall's* had 49 that were non–ad or ad-related. Of 202, *Elle* gave readers 48. *Seventeen* provided its young readers with only 51 non–ad or ad-related pages out of 226. *Vogue* had 62 out of 292. *Mirabella* offered readers 45 pages out of a total of 158. *Good Housekeeping* came out on top, though only at about a third, with 60 out of 176 pages. *Martha Stewart Living* offered the least. Even counting her letter to readers, a page devoted to her personal calendar, and another one to a turnip, only seven out of 136 pages had no ads, products, or product mentions.

Those are only the most obvious chains around women's magazines. There are also rules so understood that they don't have to be written down: for instance, an overall "look" compatible with beauty and fashion ads; no fat, grubby, or otherwise unacceptable women (except perhaps if she is a "before" in a beauty makeover, or someone very famous); a minimum of bad news, war, violence, illustrations of unsuccessful plastic surgery, or other insults to an illusion of a marzipan world. Even "real," nonmodel women photographed for a woman's magazine are usually made up, dressed in credited clothes, and their photos are retouched. When conscientious editors do include articles on less-than-cheerful subjects (for instance, domestic violence or surviving breast cancer), they often have to keep them short and unillustrated, or use photogenic, upscale examples. (Grace Mirabella, in the magazine that bears her last name, often profiles achieving women, and sponsored a 1993 Washington conference and fund-raiser for breast cancer. But as it appeared in the August issue, you would have thought only beautiful women got breast cancer, and the Armani public relations director was in a model-esque photo at the conference—a couple of pages away from an Armani ad.) The point is to be "upbeat." Just as women in the street are asked, "Why don't you smile, honey?" women's magazines are expected to have an institutional smile.

Within the supposedly editorial text itself, praise for advertisers' products has become so ritualized that fields like "beauty writing" have been invented. One of its practitioners explained to me seriously that "It's a difficult art. How many new adjectives can you find? How much greater can you make a lipstick sound? The FDA restricts what companies can say on labels, but we create illusion. And ad agencies are on the phone all the time pushing you to get their product in. A lot of them keep the business based on how many editorial clippings they produce every month. The worst are products [whose manufacturers have] their own name involved. It's all ego."

Often, editorial becomes one giant ad. An issue of *Lear's* featured an elegant woman executive on the cover. On the contents page, we learn she is wearing Guerlain makeup and Samsara, a new fragrance by Guerlain. Inside, there just happen to be full-page ads for Samsara, plus a Guerlain antiwrinkle skin cream. In the article about the cover subject, we discover she is Guerlain's director of public relations and is responsible for launching, you guessed it, the new Samsara.

When the *Columbia Journalism Review* cited this example in one of the few articles to include women's magazines in a critique of ad influence, Frances Lear, editor of *Lear's,* was quoted at first saying this was a mistake, and then shifting to the defense that "this kind of thing is done all the time."[6]

She's right. Here's an example with a few more turns of the screw.

Martha Stewart, *Family Circle*'s contributing editor, was also "life-style and entertaining consultant" for Kmart, the retail chain, which helped to underwrite the renovation of Stewart's country house, using Kmart products; *Family Circle* covered the process in three articles not marked as ads; Kmart bought $4 million worth of ad pages in *Family Circle,* including "advertorials" to introduce a line of Martha Stewart products to be distributed by Kmart; and finally, the "advertorials," which at least are marked and only *look* like editorial pages, were reproduced and distributed in Kmart stores, thus publicizing *Family Circle* (owned by the New York Times Company, which would be unlikely to do this kind of thing in its own news pages) to Kmart customers.[7] This was so lucrative that Martha Stewart now has her own magazine, *Martha Stewart Living* (owned by Time Warner) complete with a television version. Both offer a happy world of cooking, entertaining, and decorating in which nothing critical or negative ever seems to happen.

I don't mean to be a spoilsport, but there are many articles we're very unlikely to get from that or any other women's magazine dependent on food ads. According to Senator Howard Metzenbaum of Ohio, more than half of the chickens we eat (from ConAgra, Tyson, Perdue, and other companies) are contaminated with dangerous bacteria; yet labels haven't yet begun to tell us to scrub the meat and everything it touches—which is our best chance of not getting sick. Nor are we likely to learn about the frequent working conditions of this mostly female work force, standing in water, cutting chickens apart with such repetitive speed that carpal tunnel syndrome is an occupational hazard. Then there's Dole Food, often cited as a company that keeps women in low-level jobs and a target of a lawsuit by Costa Rican workers who were sterilized by contact with pesticides used by Dole—even though Dole must have known these pesticides had been banned in the U.S.

The consumerist reporting we're missing sometimes sounds familiar. Remember the *Ms.* episode with Clairol and the article about potential carcinogens in hair dye? Well, a similar saga took place with L'Oréal and *Mademoiselle* in 1992, according to an editor at Condé Nast. Now, editors there are supposed to warn publishers of any criticism in advance, a requirement that might well have a chilling effect.

Other penalties are increasing. As older readers will remember, women's magazines used to be a place where new young poets and short story writers could be published. Now, that's very rare. It isn't that advertisers of women's products dislike poetry or fiction, it's just that they pay to be adjacent to articles and features more directly compatible with their products.

Sometimes, advertisers invade editorial pages—literally—by plunging odd-shaped ads into the text, no matter how that increases the difficulty of reading. When Ellen Levine was editor of *Woman's Day,* for instance, a magazine originally founded by a supermarket chain, she admitted, "The day the copy had to rag around a chicken leg was not a happy one."

The question of ad positioning is also decided by important advertisers, a rule that's ignored at a magazine's peril. When Revlon wasn't given the place of the first beauty ad in one Hearst magazine, for instance, it pulled its ads from *all* Hearst magazines. In 1990 Ruth Whitney, editor in chief of *Glamour,* attributed some of this pushiness to "ad agencies wanting to prove to a client that they've squeezed the last drop of blood out of a magazine." She was also "sick and tired of hearing that women's magazines are controlled by cigarette ads." Relatively speaking, she was right. To be as controlling as most advertisers of women's products, tobacco companies would have to demand articles in flat-out praise of smoking, and editorial photos of models smoking a credited brand. As it is, they ask only to be forewarned so they don't advertise in the same issue with an article about the dangers of smoking. But for a magazine like *Essence,* the only national magazine for African American women, even taking them out of one issue may be financially difficult, because other advertisers might neglect its readers. In 1993, a group called Women and Girls Against Tobacco, funded by the California Department of Health Services, prepared an ad headlined "Cigarettes Made Them History." It pictured three black singers— Mary Wells, Eddie Kendricks, and Sarah Vaughan—who died of tobacco-related diseases. *Essence* president Clarence Smith didn't turn the ad down, but he didn't accept it either. When I talked with him in 1994, he said with pain, "the black female market just isn't considered at parity with the white female market; there are too many other categories we don't get." That's in spite of the fact that *Essence* does all the traditional food-fashion-beauty editorial expected by advertisers. According to California statistics, African American women are more addicted to smoking than the female population at large, with all the attendant health problems.[8]

Alexandra Penney, editor of *Self* magazine, feels she has been able to include smoking facts in health articles by warning cigarette advertisers in advance (though smoking is still being advertised in this fitness magazine). On the other hand, up to this writing in 1994, no advertiser has been willing to appear opposite a single-page feature called "Outrage," which is reserved for important controversies, and is very popular with readers. Another women's magazine publisher told me that to this day Campbell's Soup refuses to advertise because of an article that unfavorably compared the nutritional value of canned food to that of fresh food—fifteen years ago.

I don't mean to imply that the editors I quote here share my objections to ad demands and/or expectations. Many assume that the women's magazines at which they work have to be the way they are. Others are justifiably proud of getting an independent article in under the advertising radar, for instance, articles on family violence in *Family Circle* or a series on child sexual abuse and the family courts in *McCall's*. A few insist they would publish exactly the same editorial, even if there were no ads. But it's also true that it's hard to be honest while you're still in the job. "Most of the pressure came in the form of direct product mentions," explained Sey Chassler, who was editor in chief of *Redbook* from the sixties to the eighties and is now out of the game. "We got threats from the big guys, the Revlons, blackmail threats. They wouldn't run ads unless we credited them.

"But it's not fair to single out the beauty advertisers, because these pressures came from everybody. Advertisers want to know two things: What are you going to charge me? What *else* are you going to do for me? It's a holdup. For instance, management felt that fiction took up too much space. They couldn't put any advertising in that. Over the last years, the number of fiction entries into the National Magazine Awards has declined.

"And pressures are getting worse. More magazines are more bottom-line oriented, because they have been taken over by companies with no interest in publishing.

"I also think advertisers do this to women's magazines specially," he concluded, "because of the general disrespect they have for women."

Even media experts who don't give a damn about women's magazines are alarmed by the spread of this ad-edit linkage to other media. As *The Wall Street Journal* headlined: "Hurt by Ad Downturn, More

Magazines Use Favorable Articles to Woo Sponsors."[9] Women's products are increasingly able to take their practices with them wherever they go. For instance, newsweeklies publish uncritical stories on fashion and fitness to court ads. *Vanity Fair* published a profile of Ralph Lauren, a major advertiser, illustrated by the same photographer who does his ads, and turned the lifestyle of another, Calvin Klein, into a cover story. At *Longevity,* the editor-in-chief quit because publisher Bob Guccione (who invented *Penthouse*) insisted on running a Nuprin ad featuring tennis star Jimmy Connors right next to a Connors interview, with a photo a lot like the ad.[10] Even the outrageous *Spy* has got tamer since it began to seek fashion ads.

Newspapers seem to give in more often, too. *The New York Times Magazine* recently ran an article on "firming creams," complete with mentions of advertisers. Toward the end of 1993, it ran an eight-page article and fashion spread photographed in Vietnam—the same crowded streets and poor countryside we remember from the war. Only now, the Vietnamese were modeling $3,000 Chanel dresses, or clothes from Ralph Lauren, Armani, and other advertisers, all available in New York department stores. ("Eastern dress is subtly sexy," we are told, "Indo-chic" clothes and "frog closures are like erotic flash points.")[11] As for women's pages in general, now often called the "Style" or "Living" section, they were originally invented to report on social events given by wives of prominent citizens, often the president of the local supermarket chain or other advertisers. Even now, the commercialism on some of those pages might cause a scandal if transferred to the front page.

Some advertisers of "people products" are also feeling emboldened even when dealing with serious media. Columbia Pictures (part of the Sony empire) recently threatened to withhold ads from the Los Angeles *Times* as punishment for a scathing review of a Schwarzenegger movie (though it's rumored that the *Times* got even by reporting a prostitution scandal involving Columbia executives). Graef Crystal, a former columnist for *Financial World* who did investigative reporting that helped make excessive corporate salaries a national issue, feels he was fired because of pressure from corporate advertisers; and NBC offered to feature advertisers in a sports program if they would purchase commercials during its breaks.[12] "Many journalists, who are paid to see trends," reported *The Wall Street Journal,* "think they see an alarming one in their own industry. With newspapers facing tough times financially, they see an increase in the tendency of newspapers to cater to advertisers or pull their punches when it comes to criticizing advertisers in print."[13]

And just to make us really worry, films and books, the last media to go directly to the public without having to pass through the minds of advertisers first, are seeing some inroads, too. Producers are beginning to depend on fees paid for displaying products in movies. Books, the chief refuge of in-depth investigative reporting, have been commissioned by companies like Federal Express.

But women's products—in or out of women's magazines—have never been the subjects of much serious reporting anyway. Even news and general-interest publications write about food and clothing as "cooking" and "fashion," though male-oriented banking and financial services wouldn't be reported with such a cheerful and uncritical eye. Food products are almost never evaluated by brand name, and rarely by category. Though chemical additives, pesticides, and animal fats are major health risks in the United States (for instance, as contributors to the one-in-eight incidence of breast cancer, and one-in-three rate for all cancers combined), they don't get a fraction of the investigative attention lavished on one political campaign. Clothes take up more of our consumer dollars than cars, but their shoddiness, sweatshop production, and durability are mostly ignored in favor of uncritical fashion stories that would be a Ralph Nader–level scandal if applied to Detroit. The ingredients in beauty products are usually overlooked, too, though they're absorbed into our bodies through our skins, and also have profit margins that would make a loan shark blush.

The truth is that individuals are fair game for the media and corporations are not—individuals don't advertise.

W hat could women's magazines be like if they were as editorially free as good books? as realistic as the best newspaper articles? as creative as poetry and films? as diverse as women's lives? What if we as women—who are psychic immigrants in a public world rarely constructed by or for us—had the same kind of watchful, smart, supportive publications on our side that other immigrant groups have often had?

We'll find out only if we take the media directed at us seriously. If readers were to act in concert in large numbers for a few years to change the traditional practices of *all* women's magazines and the marketing of *all* women's products, we could do it. After all, they depend on our consumer dollars—money we now are more likely to control. If we include all the shopping we do for families and spouses, women make 85 percent of purchases at point of sale. You and I could:

• refuse to buy products whose ads have clearly dictated their surroundings, and write to tell the manufacturers why;

• write to editors and publishers (with copies to advertisers) to tell them that we're willing to pay *more* for magazines with editorial independence, but will *not* continue to pay for those that are editorial extensions of ads;

• write to advertisers (with copies to editors and publishers) to tell them that we want fiction, political reporting, consumer reporting, strong opinion, humor, and health coverage that doesn't pull punches, praising them when their ads support this, and criticizing them when they don't;

• put as much energy and protest into breaking advertising's control over what's around it as we put into changing the images within it or protesting harmful products like cigarettes;

• support only those women's magazines and products that take us seriously as readers and consumers;

• investigate new laws and regulations to support freedom from advertising influence. The Center for the Study of Commercialism, a group founded in 1990 to educate and advocate against "ubiquitous product marketing," recommends whistle-blower laws that protect any members of the media who disclose advertiser and other commercial conflicts of interest, laws that require advertiser influence to be disclosed, Federal Trade Commission involvement, and denial of income tax exemptions for advertising that isn't clearly identified—as well as conferences, citizen watchdog groups, and a national clearinghouse where examples of private censorship can be reported.[14]

Those of us in the magazine world can also use this carrot-and-stick technique. The stick: If magazines were a regulated medium like television, the editorial quid pro quo demanded by advertising would be against the rules of the FCC, and payola and extortion would be penalized. As it is, there are potential illegalities to pursue. For example: A magazine's postal rates are determined by the ratio of ad pages to editorial pages, with the ads being charged at a higher rate than the editorial. Counting up all the pages that are *really* ads could make an interesting legal action. There could be consumer fraud cases lurking in subscriptions that are solicited for a magazine but deliver a catalog.

The carrot is just as important. In twenty years, for instance, I've found no independent, nonproprietary research showing that an ad for, say, fragrance is any more effective placed next to an article about fragrance than it would be when placed next to a good piece of fiction or reporting. As we've seen, there are studies showing that the greatest factor in determining an ad's effectiveness is the credibility and independence of its surroundings. An airtight wall between ads and edit would also shield corporations and agencies from pressures from both ends of the political spectrum and from dozens of pressure groups. Editors would be the only ones responsible for editorial content—which is exactly as it should be.

Unfortunately, few agencies or clients hear such arguments. Editors often maintain the artificial purity of refusing to talk to the people who actually control their lives. Instead, advertisers see salespeople who know little about editorial, are trained in business as usual, and are usually paid on commission. To take on special controversy editors might also band together. That happened once when all the major women's magazines did articles in the same month on the Equal Rights Amendment. It could happen again—and regularly.

Meanwhile, we seem to have a system in which everybody is losing. The reader loses diversity, strong opinion, honest information, access to the arts, and much more. The editor loses pride of work, independence, and freedom from worry about what brand names or other critical words some sincere freelancer is going to come up with. The advertiser loses credibility right along with the ad's surroundings, and gets more and more lost in a sea of similar ads and interchangeable media.

But that's also the good news. Because where there is mutual interest, there is the beginning of change.

If you need one more motive for making it, consider the impact of U.S. media on the rest of the world. The ad policies we tolerate here are invading the lives of women in other cultures—through both the content of U.S. media and the ad practices of multinational corporations imposed on other countries. Look at our women's magazines. Is this what we want to export?

. . .

After sixteen years between the grindstones of advertising pressures and readers' needs, it took me a while to realize that a few edges got smoothed down, in spite of all our resistance.

I remember feeling put-upon when I changed "Porsche" to "car" in a piece about Nazi imagery in German pornography by Andrea Dworkin, feeling sure she would understand that Volkswagen—the distributor of Porsche and one of our few supportive advertisers—was asking only to be far away from Nazi subjects. It's taken me all this time to realize that Andrea was the one with a right to feel put-upon.

I remember the craziness of publishing a pioneering package on women's health and then describing it on the cover as "The Beauty of Health," hoping that our readers would see the "health" and the advertisers would see the "beauty." I don't have to tell you that we got few ads for moisturizers and shampoos, but a lot of smart letters from readers.

I remember varied responses to hundreds of full-dress presentations to advertisers and agencies: an agency head going out on a limb to recommend us to clients; young women trying to convince their superiors that some women, like some men, were worth a higher page rate in a serious magazine; an executive who actually spat on an issue when a *Ms.* saleswoman put it on his desk; another who finished an expensive dinner we could ill afford, and then announced to the restaurant at large that he wouldn't advertise in *Ms.* if it were the last magazine on earth.

I also realize that for a long time, women's collective edges have been worn down by blaming each other—whether as readers or editors—for wanting what was in women's magazines. In 1963, *The Feminine Mystique,* based partly on a twenty-year study of *McCall's* and other mass-circulation women's magazines, saved women's sanity by exposing the narrowing of editorial content to "feminine" images, but the word "advertising" didn't appear in its index. Women were being assigned the role of full-time, stay-at-home consumers to replace the economic engine of the war, and magazines addressed to us were the recruiting stations for that suburban economic army. Yet we rarely looked behind the "feminine" curtain to see the economic Wizard of Oz.

Now we're blaming one another and even feminism for the cruel

Superwoman hoax, though it came from adding work-oriented articles to an ad-oriented beauty/fashion mix—and even that much newness is economically risky. *Savvy* has bitten the dust, as has everything from *New Dawn* to *New York Woman*. *Lear's* started out bravely as a magazine for older women, but advertising pressures have made sure those older women look very young and glamorous. *Mirabella* does its best to provide good articles under the slickness, but like *Lear's,* it has needed deep pockets to stay alive. *Working Woman* and *Working Mother*—titles derived from advertising categories that at first spawned protest buttons like *"Every* woman is a working woman," and *"Every* mother is a working mother"*—*are having to scrap for ads to support articles on how to earn money, not just how to spend it. I notice that *Working Woman,* a business magazine, has trouble being regarded as one in an advertising world where only men mean business.

Should *Ms.* have started out with no advertising in the first place? The odd thing is that, in retrospect, I think the struggle was worth it. For all those years, dozens of feminist organizers disguised as *Ms.* ad saleswomen took their courage, research, slide shows, humor, ingenuity, and fresh point of view into every advertising agency, client office, and lion's den in cities where advertising is sold. Not only were sixteen years of *Ms.* sustained in this way, with all the changeful words on those thousands of pages, but some of the advertising industry was affected in its imagery, its practices, and its understanding of the female half of the country. Those dozens of women themselves were affected, for they learned the art of changing a structure from both within and without, and are now rising in crucial publishing positions where women have never been. *Ms.* also helped to open nontraditional categories of ads for women's magazines, thus giving them a little more freedom—not to mention making their changes look reasonable by comparison.

But the world of advertising has a way of reminding us how far there is to go.

Three years ago, as I was finishing this exposé in its first version, I got a call from a writer for *Elle*. She was doing an article on where women parted their hair: Why, she wanted to know, did I part mine in the middle?

It was all so familiar. I could imagine this writer trying to make something out of a nothing assignment. A long-suffering editor laboring to think of new ways to attract ads for shampoo, conditioner, hairdryers, and the like. Readers assuming that other women must want this stuff.

As I was working on this version, I got a letter from Revlon of the sort we disregarded when we took ads. Now, I could appreciate it as a reminder of how much we had to disregard:

> We are delighted to confirm that Lauren Hutton is now under contract to Revlon.
>
> We are very much in favor of her appearing in as much editorial as possible, but it's important that your publication avoid any mention of competitive color cosmetics, beauty treatment, hair care or sun care products in editorial or editorial credits in which she appears.
>
> We would be very appreciative if all concerned are made aware of this.

I could imagine the whole chain of women—Lauren Hutton, preferring to be in the Africa that is her passion; the ad executive who signed the letter, only doing her job; the millions of women readers who would see the resulting artificial images; all of us missing sources of information, insight, creativity, humor, anger, investigation, poetry, confession, outrage, learning, and perhaps most important, a sense of connection to each other; and a gloriously diverse world being flattened by a velvet steamroller.

I ask you: Can't we do better than this?

The Masculinization of Wealth

A Question of Class

A pedestal is as much a prison as any other small space.
ANONYMOUS [1]

Above the desk where I write, there is a framed letter from Victoria Woodhull, the most controversial suffragist of them all. People who see her big scrawled signature assume I must be looking for inspiration in her life as the first woman to address Congress, the first to run for President, the first to originate and run her own weekly newspaper, and one of the few women to live out in public the principles of female emancipation and sexual freedom that were not only unusual in her day but illegal. All of that is true, but hiding within her spidery script is a lesson I think I and many other women need even more: how *not* to be ladylike about money.

"My Dear Mr. Wilson," she begins this letter to a man who must have refused her lecture fee and offered her a percentage of the house instead. "I have propositions from several places in the far east, which makes it possible for me to amend my proposition to you. I will speak for you at some agreed night for ($100) one hundred dollars. I do not like to arrange for any part of net proceeds. Hoping this may meet your views, I remain—Yours truly, Victoria C. Woodhull."

I don't know about you, but I would have added apologies and explanations to such a request, and probably gone off in a corner to give myself a pep talk first. Women have had centuries of training to consider money impure, undeserved, mysterious, not our worry, or, as this mind-set is sometimes reflected even inside current feminism, a male-imitative and politically incorrect concern. Yet Victoria Woodhull seemed free of all that. Though she was writing in 1873, when husbands and fathers could claim any wages their wives and daughters earned, she was negotiating for herself. She wasn't trusting this Mr. Wilson by relying on proceeds, knowing from experience that promoters didn't always count them honestly. Furthermore, she was demanding a large fee for public speaking, an act that was still illegal for women in some states. True, she was obviously coming back with a lower offer, but even that she couched in terms of being in demand in the New England area.

This was just the tip of the iceberg. A few years earlier, she had opened a Wall Street brokerage house with her younger sister, Tennessee Claflin, which made them the first women stockbrokers. It was backed by Cornelius Vanderbilt, whose proposal of marriage Tennessee had refused (she seemed to understand the power difference between wife/chattel and mistress/stockbroker, and probably remained his mistress), but the sisters did surprisingly well on their own. When the press ridiculed them as "The Bewitching Brokers" and worse, they attracted crowds by arriving each morning in an open carriage pulled by white horses, and displayed a large book of their clippings, good and bad, to customers. Instead of denying their checkered past as spiritualists they suggested that stock tips came to them in a trance—Vanderbilt himself touted this as his reason for following them—but they also made headlines with such unexpected street smarts as detecting a forged payment for gold.

At the same time that Victoria Woodhull was becoming an exception within the economic and social system, however, she was preaching its overthrow. Her popular weekly published the first American edition of Marx's *Communist Manifesto,* and her speeches advocated the one thing more shocking than Marx or suffrage: Free Love, a serious movement against marriage law and the double standard. (Even Frederick Douglass, a former slave and great suffragist as well as abolitionist, declined to note in his autobiography that he had been nominated as vice president to run on the ticket with this scandalous woman.) "I have an inalienable, constitutional, and natural right," she declared in "The Principles of Social Freedom," "to love whom I may, to love as long or as short a period as I can, to change that love every day I please!"[2] She regretted that speeches on sexual matters got more publicity than those attacking the rich and hypocritical, but she gave both. In "The Impending Revolution," she said: "An Astor may sit in his sumptuous apartments and watch the property bequeathed to him rise in value from one to fifty millions. . . . But if a tenant of his, whose employer had discharged him because he did not vote the Republican ticket, fails to pay his month's rent to Mr. Astor, the law sets him and his family into the street."[3]

Where did this outrageous strength come from? One source was her combination of a quick mind, charisma, and physical beauty, but there were other women who possessed those qualities in greater degree and still remained too fearful to speak up for themselves, much less to stand up to the powerful. I think it was something else: a question of class—in reverse. Victoria Woodhull was a rare woman who had escaped all training to be a lady—whether in school, family, or church. Because she and Tennessee were the main attractions of a traveling spiritualist and medicine show that supported their big, brawling family, they had the power of breadwinners. Though Victoria married at fourteen, her doctor husband turned out to be an alcoholic and a philanderer, whom she was also to support for most of her life. By the time she became a national figure in New York, her household included many siblings and their spouses and children, her parents, her own two children, the doctor she had divorced plus a freethinking second husband, various friends, lovers, and traveling radicals who often stayed for months—all supported by her newspaper, stockbrokerage, and charismatic speeches. With only three years of formal education, she became an intellectual influence of her age. Her name is found in the history of suffrage, socialism, and Wall Street, and in the pantheon of spellbinding orators.

But that framed letter is also a reminder of something else. Even Victoria Woodhull fell victim to the lady trap once she entered into its most powerful stronghold—the world of inherited wealth. This began with a growing vulnerability. She was arrested, imprisoned, and her newspaper was shunned for exposing the hypocrisy of one powerful and respected man too many; in this case, the famous preacher Henry Ward Beecher, whose well-known habit of taking mistresses from his congregation, while condemning sexual freedom for others, she had put into print. Forced to choose between a scandalous female accuser and a respectable male accused, society made a choice that would be familiar today. In the aftermath of this scandal that was described as the biggest story since the assassination of Lincoln, she took her sister, parents, and grown children, and escaped first to Paris and then to London. Tired of fighting, with a household that included a brain-damaged son requiring constant care, she must have looked upon the life of the English upper classes as safe and enviable. She and Tennessee began to trim their sails to attract rich and respectable husbands. Tennessee married a lord with a castle in Spain, Victoria found a wealthy banker, whom she had to wait years to marry (his mother disapproved), and the sisters settled into a life of expurgating and simply lying about their colorful past.

Victoria even concocted and published a royal lineage for their parents—in reality the illiterate daughter of a German immigrant and a handyman often on the wrong side of the law—but society never really accepted them.

From a chaotic childhood and a painful early marriage, to public censure and a financial burden far beyond that imagined by most men, no force had been able to tame Victoria Woodhull—until she decided to become a lady. The woman who had become a public legend when a lady's name was supposed to appear in the papers only twice—when she was married, and when she died—now insisted she had never espoused Free Love, never believed in radical causes; it was all a misunderstanding due to articles written by others under her name. Her days devolved into lawsuits against authors who published accounts of her past, no matter how well documented, blaming her still-devoted second ex-husband for everything, and a few disastrous trips to New York to "clear my name." Only after her English husband's death did some of the old Victoria come back—driving full speed around her estate in a sports car, opening a progressive kindergarten for children of the town, and becoming a benefactor to the poor in the surrounding countryside. Nonetheless, she denied her past to the end.

I think of this outrageous woman when I talk with the wives and daughters in families of inherited wealth who are beginning so bravely to rebel. To me, she symbolizes the strength they've often been denied and the seductive power of the ladylike training against which they must struggle. More dramatically than any other example I know of, Victoria Woodhull went from the bottom to the top of the class system. She found her strength at the bottom, used it to pioneer and triumph—but when the fruits of her own work were taken away, she lost her freedom by seeking refuge in an envied place.

This essay is my own journey of learning about class. I don't know if anyone's experience can counter the power of myth and make us rethink our assumptions that women are the same class as husbands or fathers, and that proximity to money is the same as its control. After an earlier version was published, I got skeptical, give-me-a-break letters from readers whose need for child care, housing, health care, and other basics was so painful that looking past them to different kinds of deprivation was impossible. Which is as it should be: survival takes priority. But there are important ways in which class works in reverse for women. Inherited wealth and power enforce patriarchy pure, and envy of this ladylike trap makes the rest of us behave against our own best interests. That will continue until women have a feminist class analysis of our own. We need to honor the strength and knowledge of women at the bottom, as well as the experience and access to resources of women at the top—and combine them to achieve power for females as a caste.

So as you read the next pages, ask yourself this question: What would happen if the women through whose wombs pass the concentrated power of this and other nations were to catch the spirit of the real Victoria Woodhull—not the other way around?[4]

The Masculinization of Wealth

Upper class men . . . are no more likely to be shaken in their positions as heads of their families than they are to be shaken in their positions as heads of society's economic institutions.

SUSAN OSTRANDER[5]

Marx and Engels acknowledged that women's labor—in producing the labor force itself (reproduction) and in maintaining it (housewifery and motherhood)—was the underpinning of all economic activity. Having noted that, they went on to ignore it . . . otherwise, they would have wound up with a very different vision of the proletariat.

ROBIN MORGAN[6]

When I was growing up, the world seemed to be divided into rich people and the rest of us.

The rich were magical families who went to country clubs and showed up in society columns; men who owned the factories in our industrial midwestern city and women who gave dinner parties with real linen napkins; sons who played at college and tennis before joining their fathers, and daughters who always seemed to marry someone a little older, a little taller, a little richer than they, or, if they had no brothers, perhaps a son-in-law to join their father's business.

We were ordinary families whose names got in the newspapers only as part of an athletic team or an accident; men who worked in factories as long as they were able and women who cooked and cleaned for their own families if they were lucky, and for other families, too, if they were not; sons whose high school years were a last fling before the assembly line, and daughters who got pregnant and married in that order or, if they were very ambitious, worked at the gas company until the first baby came.

It was a world of difference marked by possessions. Between Saturday night movies and winter vacations; weekly pay envelopes and checking accounts; Easter outfits bought on the layaway plan and designer clothes ordered a season ahead; social security checks and stock dividends; kids who slept on sofa beds and children with nannies; in short, between an envious life and an enviable one. Because these symbols of class changed visibly from top to bottom, they seemed unnatural, perhaps unjust, and we resented them. Because male-female roles changed very little from their elegant dinner parties to our kitchen tables, they seemed natural, and very just indeed.

Were wives and daughters in these rich families the ultimate possession? We wouldn't have understood the question, much less asked it. As members of enviable families, they lived in the same pretty houses and drove in the same fancy cars, and that was enough to make us resent them.

In retrospect, I remember only one clue that such women might be less powerful, even a different class from their fathers and husbands, and so a little more like us. In my high school, girls dreamed out loud of marrying into this world of country clubs and fur coats. Of course this didn't happen, but in theory, a girl didn't need any special education or skills to be the wife of a powerful man. All she needed was the magic moment of being chosen. On the other hand, boys didn't dream out loud about becoming one of the factory owners. That would have been a betrayal of their fathers. Like enlisted men who would never think of becoming officers, they both envied and hated their superiors who ordered them into daily battle on the

production line from the safety of their desks, fought against paying
workers' compensation when one of them got mangled by a machine, and handed out layoffs with a callousness that only an equally
tough union could handle. Besides, real men didn't wear suits and
shuffle papers; they worked with their hands and used their strength
—a bit of bluster that was also an admission that being a boss took
a kind of training they didn't have.

After I became one of the very few from my high school to go to
college—an exception that was due more to my mother's sacrifice
and foresight than to my own—I noted but just accepted the differences between the rich young men and rich young women I was
now seeing up close for the first time. At the women's college where
I was, my wealthy classmates seemed a little apologetic for having
"daddyships" instead of the scholarships that marked achievers in
this intellectual school; for having money they couldn't have earned
and didn't control; for living a lifestyle they were likely to continue
by marrying a man from the same circles, since fear that a poor man
might marry them for their money was like a cold wind on their
hearts; and generally for carrying by accident of birth something as
unfeminine as power.

On the other hand, rich young men seemed quite comfortable
with the thought of dating and marrying women who were not as
rich as they were. It was a power difference that only enhanced their
male role. If the women's motives included something other than
pure love, so what? These men, unlike their sisters, were not dependent on love for their sense of themselves, and buying a suitable wife
wasn't that different from acquiring other things appropriate to their
station. They drove expensive cars, spoke easily of assured futures,
and—with a few exceptions born of social conscience or rebellion
against their fathers—seemed comfortable with the idea that their
family's power was just another attribute of their own. Indeed, even
their rebellions took the form of choosing an unacceptable profession or political stance, not giving up or giving away their inheritance. If they married into a family of equal or greater wealth in a
kind of corporate merger, that was OK too. I remember a young
man who joked about the Securities and Exchange Commission
giving permission for his wedding, such was the wealth that his
fiancée was about to bring under his family's control. Neither he nor
those of us listening gave a thought to the idea that she could be
anything other than a conduit.

Some of the rich young women rebelled too, but in a very different way. One eloped with a mechanic, fled her family's efforts to have him arrested for abducting a minor, and proved her love by being disinherited. Another scandalized the campus by going to a local nightclub, wearing a mink coat with nothing underneath, and dancing on a tabletop each Saturday night until the college finally expelled her. A third married a socially acceptable man, but one so much older that she could expect few sexual demands in the present and early widowhood in the future. ("It's a way of getting out of the house," she explained, "and after he dies, I'll be free.") In short, these rebels punished their families, but only in the most tradition-ally "feminine" way. They punished themselves.

Most of my wealthy classmates conformed in the style of the day —by marrying men who had the profession we wanted but assumed we couldn't have on our own. One intelligent, Candice Bergen–looking heiress from a literary family married the heir and executive of a major publishing house. After much publicity for a country wedding that featured shampooed lambs in pink ribbons—like the perfect toy farm created for Marie Antoinette—this talented young woman was never heard from again. Several young women who had no brothers to take over the family business were encouraged to marry proper sons-in-law who could play this dynastic role. Even the very few women who were politically radical and had control of their own money didn't seem to have the confidence to give it away themselves. They married ambitious young radicals who published obscure magazines, contributed to political causes and candidates, started intellectual communities that pioneered everything except justice for women, or otherwise used their wives' family money to pursue goals of their own. Oddly, those men seemed to be accepted by their still poor radical colleagues—it was almost as if they had sacrificed themselves for the cause by marrying a rich woman. Mean-while, the wives not only relinquished their power but seemed so guilty at ever having had it in the first place that they often lived and raised children under very difficult conditions of pretended poverty. They had paid for entry into an idealistic world that promised power to everyone except them.

The civil rights and antiwar movements of the 1960s did little to change or even challenge this pattern. If anything, those important political events reinforced a kind of populist socialism that counted women as exactly the same class as their husbands or fathers, whether or not the women had any of the same power. Since rich wives and daughters were made to seem even more frivolous and less produc- tive than rich men—by masculine standards that didn't include child rearing and homemaking as work—the 1960s increased resentment of women in rich families for the majority of us who were not among them, and increased the isolation and guilt of those few who were. Besides, rich women could be ridiculed and condemned with far less fear of retribution than came from opposing men with real power. It was OK for male writers and revolutionaries, from Norman Mailer in *An American Dream* to Eldridge Cleaver in *Soul on Ice,* to portray raping women from powerful families as a legitimate and manly way of fighting against the male adversaries they "belonged" to.

Certainly, many activist women went along with all this. Those who had grown up poor could take pride in it at last, and perhaps those from well-to-do families felt they had to cheer most of all. Being accepted in a male-led movement was still the measure of political seriousness, and going along with ridicule or even hatred of one's own group was the admission price for some middle- or upper- class men too—but especially for women. Since feminist insight and mutual support were still a few years off—and since many white women identified with other powerless groups without knowing why, and many women of color were asked to fight racism as if only male suffering mattered—supporting these "masculine" rebellions seemed to be the only game in town. I'm sure there were many women feeling hollow inside as they listened to antiwar Vietnam vets telling stories about rapes and bar girls, or to sex jokes about women that made us laugh in order to separate ourselves from the victim. Only in retrospect did I realize that women born to certain families had been made to feel shame twice over, not only by jokes and stories but by hostile rhetoric based on birth, not deed.

Though the violent writings of Cleaver, Mailer, and many others who seemed intent on imitating their adversaries made me su- premely uncomfortable, I, too, tried not to admit this in public. In a world that still seemed class divided between rich and poor—but offered the same place to women in both—I always chose the poor. At least I could find one reliable piece of empathy. Besides, I was still fighting my own demons. If you've grown up in a house so ramshackle and unheated that you're ashamed to invite your friends over, it takes a long time to understand that your privileged friends may be ashamed to invite you home for the opposite reason. In college, I had a hint of my rich classmates' isolation when they asked

me to teach them how to iron and mend their clothes (an autonomy
so satisfying that they helped me with French grammar in return).
But I still couldn't get past the fact that, unlike them, I had to earn
money during the summer and would soon be completely on my
own, a prospect that tapped into both my class and my female fears
of being unable to do this. I hadn't yet learned that small sums
earned were more empowering than large sums given, and so I
continued to envy them.

Even in the 1970s when many women began to realize that, if
idealistic movements like those against the Vietnam war and for civil
rights weren't allowing women equal power, we needed women's
liberation too, I didn't understand why women who earned a little
money were more likely to use it in support of their sisters than were
those who had inherited a lot. As a fund-raiser, I was being referred
almost totally to women for the first time—especially by radical men,
who assumed that, unlike any other social justice movement, this
one should fund itself—and I was mystified to find that many of
these women hadn't been approached as donors on their own before,
or had only given to the same causes as their families, or didn't know
how much money they had, or if they had enough control to write
a check. To be honest, I didn't try to understand. It seemed more
important to disprove the media's mischaracterization of feminism
as a white-middle-class movement, and thus to phrase issues in a way
that was least likely to touch the lives of the very women I was
asking. So I talked about child care (in ways that excluded women
who had been raised too little by parents and too much by servants),
or about reproductive rights for poor women (even if that meant
disparaging women who could pay for illegal abortions but had
risked their safety and health nonetheless), or about battered women
(as if violence weren't just as frequent in well-to-do families, where
women have money to flee, but society is even less likely to punish
the batterer), or about equal pay (with little thought to women who
were maintained on allowances in the midst of power and plenty
and resented if they tried to get a paid job like everybody else).
Obviously, all the issues being supported were crucial, but my exclusion, disparagement, and lack of empathy were not. I realize now
that I was still seeking approval from my radical male friends who
behaved as if women's issues were frivolous and middle class—even
though, statistically speaking, the women's movement was far more
multiclass and multiracial than the anti-Vietnam, environmental, and
most other movements had been.

In fact, I'm not sure that if a woman from a powerful family had been present at one of those feminist meetings of the 1970s, she would have felt more welcome than many of us had in the unfeminist, male-led groups of the 1960s.

Nonetheless, the lack of textbooks or reporting that explained our own experiences eventually forced us to turn to each other's lives as textbooks. The more I traveled during the 1970s and 1980s and listened to women's stories, the more I learned about the problems of those who were supposed to have none. For instance:

• From the small towns of Alabama to the suburbs of Long Island, I met with women, especially the wives of powerful men, who had no work of their own (other than the job of homemaking, child rearing, and hostessing, which wasn't honored as work) and identified emotionally with two other groups: prostitutes and domestics. In a glorified, socially approved way, that was the work those women felt they were doing. Their self-esteem was sometimes as low as or lower than those counterparts. Because it was harder for them to change employers, their feelings of dependence were higher, and so was their sense of being out of control of their lives; yet they were more likely to be envied than supported by other women. Given all that free-floating envy and resentment, they were also more likely than those at the bottom of the economic pile to assume that any problems must be their own fault, thus turning healthy anger into depression.

• Most of the wealthy widows I'd heard so much about—the basis of the belief that "women control the economy"—turned out to be conduits for passing power to children, especially to sons and sons-in-law. These widows had comfortable homes, good dental care, trips to exotic places, and other enviable benefits (though lifetimes of childrearing and homemaking, if properly valued, could have earned some of these pleasures anyway), but the real money and decisionmaking powers were consigned to unbreakable trusts and to family trustees who were generally paternalistic, often condescending, and occasionally corrupt. I met only one widow who was in control of her own financial life, and she had spent several hard years getting there—though the money in question had come from her family, and her husband had taken over as a son-in-law. Generally, these widows had been left uninformed, untrained, and scared to ask questions, much less mount challenges. "If General Motors is going to pass through your womb," as a more typical widow explained to me in one of those unforgettable "clicks" of changing consciousness, "they make damn sure you can't grab it on the way through."

• While speaking at a national convention of the Young Presidents Organization, a group of executives who had become heads of large businesses before turning forty, I mentioned that, though inheritance in general was certainly more destructive for the country than a meritocracy, its restriction to male relatives cut even that talent pool in half and thus made it twice as limiting. It was a minor point in a general speech about feminism, but it turned out to be the major controversy with that YPO audience, most of whom, I was surprised to discover, were the heads of family-owned companies. (One turned to a male friend of mine sitting next to him and, wrongly assuming him to be a YPO member, said only half in jest, "You get the cross, I'll get the hood.") On the other hand, raising this subject also brought me invitations to private, late-night conversations with many YPO wives, especially those who would have inherited family businesses if their own fathers had not assumed only sons or sons-in-law could run them. They explained to me that:

Because so few women were YPO members on their own (indeed, it had been de facto segregated for years, and I had been refusing to speak unless they called themselves the Young White Male Presidents, but a handful of women and black men had just been admitted), you could always tell the status of women in general at these meetings by their decreasing average age. Old wives were being traded in for new ones. "Pretty soon," as one explained, "the wives will be younger than the Scotch."

If the business was in your family, not your husband's, your marriage would last longer, mainly because the phrase "till death do us part" took on a new meaning. Sons-in-law tended to get a divorce only *after* their powerful fathers-in-law died, and could no longer fire or disinherit them. Even after divorce, the ex-husband remained more likely to control the business than the woman to whose family it had belonged. "It isn't women who sleep their way to power," said one woman. "It's sons-in-law."

If you got divorced from a man who wasn't rich on his own or who didn't stay in a family business, he was likely to get a settlement: a lump-sum payment that wasn't conditional on good behavior (for instance, it couldn't be withdrawn if he remarried), unlike the controlling monthly payments given to ex-wives. According to one of the wives who was a student of economics, the national total of these large settlements given to sons-in-law was greater in any given year than the total amount paid to women in the much-resented and publicized form of alimony. "Besides, men can start their own businesses or live off the interest from a lump sum," she explained. "Women can't do that with alimony."

• We've read about rich girls who were victims of incestuous relationships, from the fictional Nicole Diver in Fitzgerald's *Tender Is the Night* to the real Edie Sedgwick as revealed in the 1970s or the son and daughter of J. Seward Johnson as made known in the 1980s —and innumerable others. Yet pre-feminism, a Freudian bias, eroticized incest as a fantasy of the victim, while class bias depicted it as an immorality of the poor. In fact, part of Freud's reason for abandoning his interest in the sexual abuse of children was society's hostility to the idea that so many abusers were solid patriarchs of the middle and upper classes, not to mention the possibility of Freud's reluctance to believe it of his own childhood. Though I know of no abuse study that has pinpointed families of inherited wealth and power—which may be one more way in which privileged children are assumed not to need attention, an overview of a variety of studies tells us that about one in three women (and one in seven men) have been sexually abused before the age of eighteen by someone with access to their households, and that 90 percent of the abusers of both girls and boys are males. We also know that the greater the imbalance of power—between genders as elsewhere—the greater the abuse. In families where men are captains of industry and finance in the outside world, the internal power differences between men and women are extreme, and men's sense of being able to do no wrong is often greater than elsewhere. So is the reluctance of authorities to intervene. Furthermore, children are more likely to be isolated, cared for by servants who may be passing on their own abuse or acting out a resentment of wealth itself. Many observers believe that sexual abuse is *more* prevalent among families of inherited wealth and power than in the population at large—and I agree. In the 1980s, when the Ms. Foundation for Women started a group for women managing wealth, for instance, it was one of the first subjects discussed. Violence against women in general and sexual abuse in particular remain the issues women from wealthy families are most likely to single out when they contribute.

• Even in the absence of any inequity or wrongdoing—and even with the best will in the world—there are still the problems of socialization and self-confidence that come from ladylike training in the upper classes. What happens, for instance, to a forty-five-year-old woman who has been shut out of self-sufficiency, has no training or experience at supporting herself by paid work, and feels dependent on a money source she doesn't control or understand? I never forgot going back to see women from my high school neighborhood who were about that age, and then going to my twenty-fifth college reunion. The contrast was startling. Most of the first group had supported themselves or helped to support their families—they had no choice. As a result, most had found professions, gone back to school, even run for local office, and generally discovered they could be self-sufficient and affect the world around them. In the second group, some of the most privileged—the same rich young women of whom I had once been so envious—were self-deprecating, lost, and fearful of losing their looks or their husbands. They might have taken courses or acquired advanced degrees, but more as an end than a means. Generally, they seemed uncertain that they could be independent, much less have their own impact on the world. It echoed what I had seen in years of fundraising.

By the mid 1980s, I had come to a conclusion I wasn't sure I should state out loud: _There are many ways in which class doesn't work for women—and some in which it's actually reversed._

Once I'd begun to look beneath the myth of class for women in families of inherited wealth, I noticed that it wasn't an unmitigated advantage for middle-class and upper-class women either. Take higher education and advanced degrees, for instance. They were simply expected to go to college, whether it was related to their own interest and career or not. There were times when I listened to privileged young women on campus, and heard stories about lack of choice that sounded remarkably like my high school classmates who had felt forced into clerical jobs or factories. Yet being told on all sides they were fortunate had left them less prepared than my classmates to fight for themselves, or even to see the necessity. A study that followed a multiracial group of high school valedictorians through college was released in 1987. It found that intellectual self-esteem was about equal among females and males when they entered, but after four years, the number of young men who considered themselves "far above average" had grown, while the number of women who did so had dropped to zero.[7] This was not related to grades, in which the women were equal or better, but apparently to the frequent invisibility of women in what they were studying, the rarity of women in authority in classroom or campus, more "masculine" competition than "feminine" cooperation in the academic atmosphere, and the approaching conflict between gender role and career role. One hopes that this disempowerment of women will change with a mainstreaming of women's studies and other reforms, but many women on campus are still left feeling there's something wrong with them.

There was also the lens of eating disorders through which to look at class. Anorexia and bulimia are almost unknown among the poor in this country, just as they are in the populations of poor countries. As Joan Brumberg reported in *Fasting Girls:*

> Ninety to 95 percent of anorectics are young and female, and they are disproportionately white and from middle-class and upper-class families. . . . The rare anorexic male exhibits a greater degree of psychopathology, tends to be massively obese before becoming emaciated, and has a poorer treatment prognosis. Moreover, the male anorexic is less likely to be affluent. Anorexia nervosa is not a problem among contemporary American blacks or Chicanos; neither was it a conspicuous problem among first-generation and second-generation ethnic immigrants such as Eastern European Jews. As these groups move up the social ladder, however, their vulnerability to the disorder increases. In fact, the so-called epidemic seems to be consistently restrained by age and gender but promoted by social mobility.[8]

In other words, those eating disorders that literally starve females out of all sexual characteristics—from breasts to menstruation—are almost totally restricted to social groups in which the "feminine" role itself is the most restrictive, and to that time of life in which young girls are entering it. It's as if young women look at the dependent, decorative, lesser, ladylike role that awaits them, and unconsciously starve themselves out of it. Young women born into African-American or white working-class families see less male/ female power difference around them and behave accordingly. In the midst of the economic plenty of class, eating disorders are a political protest against the increased restriction of sexual caste.

Though this questioning of class was (and still is) an unpopular endeavor, it's evident the moment we look at women's individual experience instead of group myth. Here are an African-American and a Hispanic woman interviewed by Linda Sanford and Mary Ellen Donovan for their classic *Women and Self-Esteem:*

> We lived in a very stable black neighborhood, and year after year my mother's friends would come over to talk, and as long as I sat quietly, I could listen. They sometimes talked about sex and orgasms and how you had to ask for what you wanted sexually. They also talked about their work when I grew up, too—not because I would *have to* but because it was a good experience. And moreover, it was wonderful to have your own money. My white, upper-class women friends told me they had a totally different experience. Although it was always assumed they would go to college, it wasn't assumed that they would work. Instead, their security was in getting a man to support them—even though they had skills to do it for themselves. I can't imagine being raised like that—so unsure of my future, putting time and energy into being prepared for something I wasn't expected to do.[9]

> I didn't particularly like growing up in Harlem, but the one thing it did is teach me survival skills and I see that as a big advantage. I teach self-defense now and there is a world of difference between the urban Hispanic kids I teach and my classes that have some middle-class white women in them. I try to get them to make a fist and hit the punching bag, pretending it's an attacker, and most of them say, "Oh, I could never do that."[10]

Those educational, physical and social underminings are probably familiar to many women, but the very rich add more safeguards against woman's gaining control of real power. Most of them relate to depth training within the family—and nothing is more effective. At a 1990 conference of women managing wealth, I heard anthropologist Terry Odendahl, author of *Charity Begins at Home,* sum up her six years of research and interviews:

> The lives of most wealthy women are defined by family relationships, especially their roles as wives and mothers, but also as daughters and sisters and widows of rich men. Gender roles are much more rigid in the upper classes than they are in the wider society. . . . Wealth is *not* a

guarantee of authority. Women have less control over their assets. . . . Much of the money is in trusts and they just receive the income. Male attorneys and accountants are viewed as the culprits—keeping the money out of the hands of women. Usually, however, it is male family members who established the original trusts that limit the female beneficiaries' control over assets. . . . The modern women's movement affected most wealthy American women at least ten years later than it did women of the middle class.[11]

Even at that, more than a third of her interviewees had married into families of great wealth, and thus had escaped some of the training of those born into such families. But whether it was General Motors passing through one's womb, in the memorable phrase of my early informant, or a daughter who hears secrets of the establishment passed around the dinner table; whether it's an old-fashioned need to control women as the means of reproduction in order to keep the ruling class inheritance system in order—usually the task of first wives—or a modern need for what *Fortune* magazine called media-star hostesses or "trophy wives"—usually second wives—the general truth is this: *The closer women are to power, the weaker those women have to be kept.*

This is not the same as the poor-little-rich-girl myth that is so much a part of our popular culture. That story is half of a double fantasy that the rich are unhappy and the poor are a jolly lot; a fantasy still well represented by such television staples as the *Dynasty* genre of melodramas about rich white families, and the various comedies about white ethnic and African-American families of the poor or middle class. The political purpose is to convince us that the burdens of power are too great to seek, and the happiness of powerlessness is too great to leave—thus preserving the status quo. Looking at the lack of strength and power among women in families of inherited wealth has a purpose that is quite the opposite: upsetting the status quo—increasing those women's strength to seize power and redistribute it.

This rethinking of sexual caste versus social class is also not—repeat: *not*—intended to diminish the importance of everything money brings for women of wealth, from good health care and housing, to travel, the arts, and time to enjoy them. A weakened body, a mind obsessed with survival, children who can't develop their intellectual capacity because of poor diets and violent schools:

all these are tragedies of poverty that must never be minimized. They cause a person to suffer more—and millions more to suffer—than do such tragedies of dependency as unused strength, atrophied talents, and a circumscribed knowledge of the world.

Nonetheless, there is a clear continuum from the feminization of poverty to the masculinization of wealth. It's no accident that women and their dependent children are 92 percent of those on welfare, and female-headed families make up most of the working poor, while the gender of those who control this country's great concentrations of wealth is even more uniformly male. It's simply not possible to attack one ghetto without also attacking the other. The concentration of wealth is extreme. According to a 1987 report of *Forbes* magazine, for example, the total net worth of the four hundred richest people and/or families in the United States—about half of whom have inherited wealth and almost all of whom are likely to pass it on to descendants—was $220 billion, more than enough to pay off the entire U.S. budget deficit accumulated to that point. To get an idea of how disproportionate this distribution is, a minuscule top 0.5 percent of the country owns between 20 and 25 percent of the wealth—a figure derived from taxes on estates worth $60,000 or more, and one that has remained relatively unchanged throughout this century.[12] One clear but undiscussed way of breaking up these hereditary concentrations is to seize and disperse them from within—a process that at least some women would be ready for, and a handful have begun. Therefore, it's in the interest of women at both ends of the spectrum to consider the class system *as women experience it,* not as women have been taught it—to see the ways it disguises and preserves a deeper system of sexual caste, and to explore how we might pool strengths and support one another for mutual benefit.

To do this, the range of women from poor to middle class have to go against class myth by trading envy of those above us for a recognition of our strengths. We are more likely to have the experience of supporting ourselves, and thus to discover our abilities and learn about the world. We may underrate the fact that we also have had to learn to run a household and navigate the shoals of daily life on our own. The men we live with are not accustomed to great power in the world, and they probably know we can earn at least half as much as they do. In other words, the imbalance of power between us and them may be painful, but it's not as extreme as at society's upper reaches. We need to look realistically at rich women, who have no excuse of necessity, the most common reason for anybody's discovery of confidence and capabilities, not even a responsibility for managing the family portfolio. A wealthy wife or daughter who tries to learn self-sufficiency by entering the daily work world may be resented, ridiculed, or forced to conceal her background. The men she deals with intimately are accustomed to command, including female service, and their egos may be overblown by women who treat them like the pot of gold at the end of a marital rainbow, as well as by men in their sphere of power. Meanwhile, the dependent woman knows she could not earn a fraction of the family income if she were on her own, may worry about female competition for this gold-plated meal ticket, and often witnesses adulation of a man she knows to be very human indeed. Though she may start out loving her husband—or her father or her brothers—it's more difficult for love to survive years of such imbalance of power without the worm of resentment eating it away. Nor is it easy for a daughter who has seen what dependency has done to her mother.

But women in such families do have an intimacy and access to power. Otherwise, their rebellion would not be so dangerous that all the weaponry of gender roles and a patriarchal legal structure are brought into play. At the upper levels, it's patriarchy pure.

Our suffragist foremothers had a better understanding of these anomalies of economic class. For one thing, the laws about marriage and property were more obviously oppressive in their day, and there was less need for psychological seduction to keep women in line. When men could drink up their paychecks with no obligation to save even subsistence money for families, take children away from mothers without bothering to accuse them of anything, and legally beat their wives, providing they used a rod no bigger than a thumb (hence, "rule of thumb"), there was less need for the sugar coating of gender persuasion. Even Victoria Woodhull got considerable support for announcing: "They say I have come to break up the family. I say amen to that with all my heart." Susan B. Anthony shocked and alienated even abolitionists by offering shelter to the runaway wives of violent men, just as she did to runaway slaves. About the pain of dependency, with or without violence, she wrote: "There is not a woman born who desires to eat the bread of dependence, no matter whether it be from the hand of father, husband, or brother, for anyone who does so eat her bread places herself in the power of the person from whom she takes it." There were also the constant reminders from black women in or newly out of slavery, with all the parallels that had made seventeenth-century slaveholders adopt the legal status of wives as the "nearest and most natural analogy" for that of slaves, as Gunnar Myrdal wrote in *An American Dilemma*. The seduction of being a lady was the subject of Sojourner Truth's famous speech: "That man over there says that women need to be helped into carriages. . . . Nobody ever helps me into carriages. . . . I could work as much and eat as much as a man—when I could get it—and bear the lash as well." As Elizabeth Cady Stanton wrote: "The Negro's skin and the woman's sex are both [used as] *prima facie* evidence that they were intended to be in subjection to the white saxon man."

With all the parallels between sex and race to bind the abolitionist and suffragist movements into one drive for universal adult suffrage —until this unity was fractured by white liberal males who helped to get the vote for black males fifty years before women of all races, plus white women who then used racist arguments for their own "educated" vote—there was a long and activist period in which consciousness of caste exceeded that of class. It was also the peak of European immigration, and thus a greater belief in class mobility. Women could see similarities in their female status across chasms of class and make alliances and be less seduced by a conventional, male-centered sense of class as a result. Only a handful of women had control over money, usually as widows or because of tolerant men in their family, but some acted on the unselfconscious connections with shop and factory girls, prostitutes and domestics, that I was to hear upper-class wives discussing privately a century later.

The most famous was Alva Belmont, a Southerner who had divorced a Vanderbilt, then married and been widowed by Oliver Belmont, a man of almost equal wealth. She paid many of the operating expenses of NAWSA (the National American Woman Suffrage Association), of which Elizabeth Cady Stanton and Susan B. Anthony were the first two presidents. In 1909, even before the Triangle fire had forced the country to face the truth of immigrant women's working conditions, she endorsed a strike of women shirtwaist workers and hired the Hippodrome in New York for a rally of eight thousand to support them. At the podium with her were Clara Lemlich and Rose Schneidermann, radical trade unionists who were Belmont's enemies by class. A shirtwaist manufacturer sued Alva

Belmont and other suffragists for triple damages under the Sherman Act, accusing them of organizing an illegal boycott, but his action only created more publicity for this cross-class alliance. As an officer of the Women's Party during World War I, Belmont also opposed President Wilson's hypocrisy in saying that the nation was fighting for democracy, when the female half had none. It was a radical act in wartime, and one that supported workers' groups who were then saying that only an international ruling class would benefit from workers fighting each other.[13]

Though there were many tensions on the basis of class, some of these women's coalitions would be hard to match today. To organize working women's suffrage clubs in Connecticut, for instance, NAWSA hired the well-known socialist Ella Reeve Bloor, later known as "Mother Bloor" of the Communist Party. The meetings she organized were held in halls rented and paid for by a niece of J. P. Morgan, a financier who headed the list of socialism's enemies.[14]

In fact, suffrage might not have been put over the top had there not been a bequest of $2 million from a woman known as Mrs. Frank Leslie (she had taken the name of her third husband after his death, for it was also the name of his publishing empire). It was money she had made by saving the failing magazines she had inherited. In the words of her will, this sum was left "to Carrie Chapman Catt, leader of the cause of woman suffrage, to further that cause, so that all the women of this country will be able to live women's rights and shoulder women's responsibilities, so that for the women of the future all things will be possible."[15] However, even a woman of her business acumen wasn't able to conquer the rich woman's bane of condescending lawyers and corrupt trustees. After her death in 1914, her lawyer, William Nelson Cromwell (the founder of the still famous law firm of Sullivan and Cromwell), spent two years contesting the purpose of her will, and thus cut the bequest in half by collecting $1 million in lawyers' fees from her estate. Nevertheless, the remaining half was finally used as she intended.

Of course, both Alva Belmont and Mrs. Frank Leslie had lived relatively independent lives before marrying into wealth, and so had missed some upper-class conditioning. There were a few women born into powerful families who may have had less control over family wealth, but who lived in settlement houses with immigrant women, taught the knowledge of contraception they themselves had once been denied, established shelters where prostitutes could flee from pimps and corrupt police, and provided homes for newly arrived young working women who might otherwise have been forced onto the streets—just as teenage runaways are now.

In this modern wave of feminism, however, there are fewer places for women to come together across class boundaries, and no obvious institutions like the settlement houses where women lived together while doing feminist work. Though feminist groups often share an American denial of some of the deep effects of class, it's also true that a Marxist class analysis has entered the popular culture since the suffragist wave. Some of that insight has been especially valuable to women in helping us separate nature from nurture and appreciate the unlimited human diversity among us. In its absence, our suffragist foremothers often fell back into the biological determinism of arguing that women were more moral "by nature." But now we need a whole fresh look at what class means to women, and at the way caste and class intersect.

Anne Hess, an effective and compassionate activist, grew up with a stronger tradition of philanthropy, handed down by her great-grandfather Julius Rosenwald, of the Sears fortune, and by women within her family, than most women of wealth; yet she still remembers sitting silently in antiwar, women's liberation, and black power meetings of the 1970s. "We were the enemy," she said, "even though we were there as friends. More women than men are in the closet about their wealth, partly because they're drawn to other powerless groups, by their own experience as women—and then shunned by them." Shad Reinstein, a woman from a family of relative wealth in her upstate New York community, remembers hearing a line from an antiwar song of the 1970s—"We're going to rape the daughters of bankers." "It was harder to come out as a wealthy person, even though I was doing constructive things with my land and resources," she said, "than it was to come out as a lesbian." When she moved to a different part of the country, she didn't use her given name or share her background until she had established herself as a working part of that community. These are the exceptions. Even though there are now a few groups of women of wealth around the country who are supporting each other in taking control of their money, breaking trusts, and initiating a new kind of philanthropy to empower women,[16] it's still not easy to overcome the sexual caste system of families in which, for generations, only men have been socialized to power. Jenny Warburg, the forty-one-year-old daughter of the Ger-man-Jewish banking family, was trained as a social worker and a photographer, but she didn't go on a retreat with women peers struggling with the same issues of wealthy families until five years ago. "I was terrified of talking about money," she explained. "I didn't want to admit to myself that I had it, much less talk about it with anyone else. Growing up, I was embarrassed to have friends over to the house because of things like finger bowls." None of this seemed to be as difficult for her brothers, who had very different expecta-tions set for them and who were automatically given more power and credibility on the family foundation board. "It took many years to be taken seriously on that board—even though I am the most politically active member and chaired a community foundation board for four years." While she lobbies hard for the support of issues she cares about within her family foundation, emotional and economic ties to her family still make it difficult to seek out indepen-dent investment or legal advice.

The point is not to romanticize connections among women or to ignore class differences, but to figure out why many women in to-day's powerful families seem even less able than their foremothers to work on their own behalf, and to support other women who are doing so. Their giving and volunteering are more likely to support socially approved causes and organizations that do little to change women's lives; for example, statistics show that most widows keep on donating to their dead husbands' colleges while ignoring or giv-ing less support to their own. When giving to their family's charita-ble priority of a local symphony, they rarely make that gift conditional on employing more women and people of color as mu-sicians; or to an art museum while challenging the absence of a diversity of women artists; or to a drug treatment program while insisting there be more programs for female addicts and addicted babies; or to political candidates according to their positions on issues of special importance to the female half of the country; or to Israel and other group causes while making sure that at least half of those dollars are going to women. In spite of the one-in-nine breast cancer rate that affects us all, fundraisers for major cancer organiza-tions say confidentially they are surprised that women donors—including those giving very large gifts—rarely earmark their gifts for breast and other reproductive cancers, or even ask tough questions about where organizational resources are going.

Tracy Gary, a San Francisco activist who has used her own inheritance experience to become a pioneer organizer among women trying to gain control of family money for the empowerment of women, has done research showing that poor women actually give away a slightly larger percentage of their incomes than do women with incomes of $50,000 and more. Looking at the human truth behind those statistics often reveals women of wealth who lack control of their own money, the self-confidence and knowledge to use it, or support from other women in gaining that confidence and control.

The first step as the support groups of women in wealthy families that are now spreading (and are listed in the endnotes), but we also need to develop more women's communities that are welcoming across class lines. The integration of some women into the mainstream—for which our foremothers fought and we continue the battle—has meant that we can buy entry and approval into male provinces; all the more so if we are willing to ignore our own interests. A woman with a checkbook is welcome in many places, but if she wants to be welcome *as herself,* with or without money, she needs to use that checkbook to attack the system of sexual caste. Yet if she wants to do this, how many feminist groups offer her understanding of her situation?

The vast majority of us who are not in powerful families must admit that we have not been very open to those who are. And I mean really open—not with preconceived ideas or envy or an effort to create guilt, but with honest questions and answers, and an understanding that we each bring a part of the mix that the other may need. Those of us who have the confidence and well-developed muscles that come from survival must recognize our worth and stop thinking that money would solve whatever problems we may have. In a way, we treat problems of women in rich families like those of the famous. It's the rare listener who isn't thinking: "Oh, come off it, you really love it—how about trading places?" Yet fame is democratic enough to give some women, athletes, rock stars, and other members of "out" groups a power they could have in no other way, while the internal workings of powerful families are often hierarchy in its most intimate form. It takes strength to challenge family traditions, powerful trustees, and investment advisers, plus relatives who are also the country's rulers—or even to roll over in the morning and say to your husband that from now on, half of the family's charitable gifts are going to be distributed by you—and women in those situations need support.

What we all need, as adults or children, is at least one person who has confidence in us, so we can have confidence in ourselves. We also need community. Women can become that for each other.

The good news is that, even with less encouragement than almost any other group, some women in powerful families are rebelling. In addition to those groups of women managing wealth who meet to support each other in many cities, there are individuals like Sallie Bingham, a sort of matron saint for rebellious women born into wealthy families. A playwright, short-story writer, and novelist, she asked questions and raised challenges which eventually led to the sale in 1986 of the media properties that the Bingham family of Kentucky had owned for two generations, a conscious political rebellion against their patriarchal control as well as what she considered their mismanagement. Now she has started the Kentucky Foundation for Women to aid women in her area, and she also redistributes on her own about half a million dollars each year. ("I give out of rage," she writes, "rage that there is never an end to giving . . . rage that I didn't use to believe what I gave was mine.") Some of the women in such famous families as the Rockefellers have become active—in a setting where there was definitely no Rockefeller *Sisters* Fund—and are giving in new ways designed to empower the powerless. There is also Peg Yorkin, a longtime activist and theater producer, who emerged from a thirty-year marriage to a television producer—which both had entered without inherited money—with enough to give a $10 million endowment in 1991 to the Fund for the Feminist Majority, a multi-issue action organization that she started with Eleanor Smeal, former president of the National Organization for Women. It is the largest grant to be given by a woman for advocacy on behalf of women as a group since Mrs. Frank Leslie. Like her, she has become an inspiration to women whose marriages, and their own work within those partnerships, have given them resources to use on women's behalf.

They and many others have rebelled with very little support from their sisters. Imagine what could be done with that support. As I sit in meetings of the Ms. Foundation for Women and see brave women donors helping other women who are survivors of violence, especially sexual abuse in childhood—and yet are themselves still silenced about their own experiences by the powerful families from which they come—I realize how far we have to go. It is often a struggle to bring up the forbidden and unladylike subject of money in those families, much less subjects still more forbidden.

I think it will be women from the bottom of the class structure—with strength and a literal knowledge that "money isn't everything"—who may be more able than middle class women to welcome this personal and political connection to women at the top. I realized this again in 1990 while listening to the generosity of spirit in which Byllye Avery, founder and director of the National Black Women's Health Project, addressed a few women of inherited wealth. "Women with wealth and women without wealth share a sense of isolation, alienation, and powerlessness," said this woman who had every reason to feel bitter and estranged. "We feel this way no matter where we are . . . people like me need people like you, and people like you need people like me. Together, we make a wonderful whole. . . . We must look inside ourselves, take the risk to learn who we are and acknowledge all the pieces."

Is the world of women so neatly divided into the rich and the rest of us? I no longer think so. Like art, revolutions come from combining what exists into what has never existed before.

Revaluing Economics

Revaluing Economics

I've lived in cities for many months broke, without help, too timid to get in the bread line. I've known many women to live like this until they simply faint on the street from privation, without saying a word to anyone. A woman [without children or other dependents] will shut herself up in a room until it is taken away from her, and eat a cracker a day and be as quiet as a mouse so there are no social statistics concerning her.

MERIDEL LE SUEUR [1]

If public opinion polls are any measure, "economics" is a boring word that clouds our brains and makes us feel we've hit a blank wall. Economics anxiety may be even more common than the often identified "math anxiety," [2] for unlike math, which has its personal uses, economics is seen as a mysterious set of forces manipulated from above.

At first, I escaped this ailment by the accident of approaching economics through the biographies of great economists. As an extension of reading about the Bloomsbury group, I got hooked on the life and theories of John Maynard Keynes, its most famous nonliterary member, who made money each morning before breakfast by calling the international money market from his bed, wrote brilliant and controversial economic treatises that included ideas of human behavior as well as numbers, was the first to predict the disaster to come from imposing crushing reparations on Germany after World War I, and hung out with Virginia Woolf, E. M. Forster, his own ballerina wife, Lydia Lopokova, and other Bloomsburyites. It was this diversity of interests—this idea that an economist should be "as aloof and incorruptible as an artist, yet sometimes as near the earth as a politician" [3]—that produced his advice to the Roosevelt administration on ending the downward spiral of the Depression by the simple human means of "priming the pump"— that is, increasing "relief" spending on everything from road building and forestry to producing plays and painting murals, thus creating employment, buying power, and more employment. If Keynes had spent his time with other economists instead, he might have been more influenced by their belief that the free market would create employment on its own and the suffering of joblessness just had to be waited out; such is the human element of economics.

After reading about John Kenneth Galbraith's spartan farm-boy upbringing in Canada, I could imagine the source of his ability to criticize the hyperconsumption of this affluent society, and even to name its conversion of "housewives" (or homemakers, as many women prefer, since they are not married to houses) into the first educated, full-time consumers in history. (After all, who else could have time to buy all that stuff we don't need, not to mention waiting for its delivery and repair?) As Galbraith wrote with elegant sarcasm, "The decisive economic contribution of women in the developed industrial society is . . . overwhelmingly, to make possible a continuing and more or less unlimited increase in the sale and use of consumer goods. . . . If population is relatively stable, as in our case, this must be increased per-capita consumption. . . . The higher the standard of living, that is to say, the greater the consumption, the more demanding is this management. . . . The family of higher income, in turn, sets the consumption patterns to which others aspire. That such families be supplied with intelligent, well-educated women of exceptional managerial competence is thus of further importance . . . for its demonstration effect for families of lesser income."[4]

Galbraith's insight remains true even now that the presence of two thirds of all mothers in the paid labor force, plus male avoidance of housework and child care, have combined to produce the marketing stereotype of Superwoman, a new "housewife" who is sold everything on the pretext of saving time.[5] I notice busy women are now being persuaded through advertising to rebuy their kitchen ranges one function at a time—from egg boilers and potato bakers to the ultimate capitalist *chutzpah* of a machine to make tea—even though there is no evidence that such gimmickry decreases time demands, and quite a lot that it increases them. To the extent that time spent doing housework has decreased in the last fifty years, for instance, it's because of a lowered birth rate, not because of any labor-saving device, including husbands.[6]

But in my academic life, such intriguing insights into economics as human behavior were soon obscured by courses that substituted flow charts for ideas, and phrases like "the marginal propensity to consume" for narrative. Soon I had become convinced that if I studied very hard, I might one day understand what was being done to me—but never how to change it.

Over the years, I noticed that even activists I otherwise loved to read seemed to behave as if there were a prize for coming up with the most paralyzing news when it came to economics. Here, for instance, is Noam Chomsky, the author and radical social critic:

> The U.S. (like other states) will continue to defend U.S.-based corporate and financial interests while seeking to maintain a global environment in which they can flourish. That requires, in particular, that the Third World be kept in its service role. Meanwhile at home, state power will continue to be employed to dissolve popular structures (unions, etc.) that might serve the needs of the general public and enable them to interfere illegitimately in the management of public affairs. It will also be necessary to find ways to control the growing "Third World at home," no small problem. The Clinton Mandate for Change promises no change.[7]

Sort of takes the heart right out of you, doesn't it? Not because he's wrong—he's probably right about the economic forces we have to deal with—but because he places all power in the depersonalized state, other-izes the entire "third world" into the role of victim, and does the same with people of color and/or the poor here. Even this might be useful if his purpose were to forge a coalition of "out" groups, but that isn't stated, and if it's implied, he neglected to include women, the largest part of any such coalition.* In fact, women might be described as a kind of free-floating "third world" wherever we live: low on capital, low on technology, and labor intensive—not to mention the world's biggest source of free or cheap labor, plus its means of reproduction.

But I'm getting ahead of myself.

My first empowering "click" in the still ongoing process of de-

---

* I hope the myth that "women control the U.S. economy" has disappeared. Perhaps it came from women's longer life expectancy and the myth of rich widows, though the few who exist rarely control the wealth that is passed through them. The facts are these: female-headed households and women over sixty are the single poorest demographic groups in the nation, women and children are 78 percent of the poor and 92 percent of those on welfare, and one in five mothers in the paid labor force is the sole support of her family. Worldwide, women and children are not only a disproportionate number of the poor but also more than 90 percent of all refugee populations. In the U.S., adult women are 62 percent of illiterates, and worldwide, at least two thirds.

mystifying economics came in the aftermath of the Houston Women's Conference in 1977. You may remember this event as a sort of belated Constitutional Convention for women. Inspired by the United Nations' International Women's Year in 1975, it was funded by congressional legislation written by Congresswomen Bella Abzug and Patsy Mink, and was made up of conferences in each state and territory, some with as many as twenty thousand participants each. Out of those deliberations came proposals for a National Plan of Action, a list of core issues and actions crucial to equality for women, as well as two thousand delegates who were elected to decide on its final form in Houston. That final three-day conference turned out to be the most economically, racially, and geographically representative nationwide gathering this country had ever seen.

It's worth going back to look at the twenty-six-plank plan of action that resulted.[8] In economic rights, homemakers were included as workers; a "minority women's plank" was hammered out by women of color, from many tribes of Native Americans to new arrivals from South Asia and Mexico, who outlined steps necessary to end double discrimination, from programs to address the high unemployment rate among black teenage women to ending the deportation to Mexico of mothers of U.S.-born children, and the removal of Native American children from their families; a "sexual preference" plank made discrimination against lesbians a women's issue for the first time at a national level; and a call for a "national health security program," which was to become a national priority a dozen years later. Those are just a few of the points in a plan that crystallized a majority consensus among U.S. women and helped to create a gender gap in favor of candidates of either party who represented its issues.

Much of the hard work of translating these issues into reality after Houston was taken on by coalitions in each state,[9] but a National Advisory Committee for Women was also created by President Carter to advise on implementing the plan from Washington. With forty members, co-chaired by Bella Abzug and Carmen Delgado Votaw of the National Conference of Puerto Rican Women, the committee's first task was to analyze the federal budget for its differential impact on the female half of the country.

Unfortunately, the President didn't seem to realize this meant the *whole* budget. When the committee took on military spending, not just child care, welfare, and other traditionally female concerns, Carter and his aides were reported to be angry. How dare these women, whose support Carter felt he should have, be so critical, especially of areas that were none of their business? Since aides were urging Carter to toughen his image in response to declining public approval ratings, the idea of firing an outspoken woman like Bella Abzug came up as a way of disciplining the committee and making Carter look stronger at the same time.

Those who remember this "Friday night massacre" will also remember how badly the White House miscalculated. For one thing, Carter's aides underestimated popular support for Bella Abzug. A Harris poll showed that the public disapproved of her firing by almost two to one.[10] For another, they hadn't fired Carmen Delgado Votaw on the assumption that she couldn't have been as responsible for the committee's actions as her co-chair, but she resigned anyway. So did the majority of the committee. As they explained: "The President's response was not to the issues we brought to him, but rather to use our co-chair, Bella Abzug, as a scapegoat in an effort to suppress our independence. . . . We believe that all women and men of like mind will refuse to participate in an advisory committee in which disagreement with the President and legitimate criticism are not acceptable." [11]

Though some committee members remained and a few others came back on the promise of access to the President, they soon found themselves operating under a new executive order, with a limited mandate that prevented them from advocating the plan in Congress. As Carolyn Reed of the Household Technicians of America said when she resigned, "As a household worker, I've learned never to confuse access with influence."

During this brief but heated controversy, I and others who had worked on the Houston Conference were being called by the press. I heard myself explaining over and over again that a national budget was really the only statement of values a country ever makes—thus, we as citizens have the right and the responsibility to criticize the *whole* budget for its relative values.

Somewhere in those repetitions, the idea of values began to sink in as the basis of any budget. I realized that if this was true of the federal book-size variety, it was true of my small budget too. If the nation revealed values by allocating big money to nuclear weaponry and superhighways, but peanuts to increasing literacy and lowering infant mortality, then my values as a citizen were revealed not only by my response to that public budget but by the relative spending in my own—and this was true for any of us with even a few dollars left over after subsistence. I began to wonder: Suppose I were hit by a Mack truck tomorrow; how would my checkbook stubs reflect what I cared about?

I liked to think I put my money where my beliefs were, but when I looked at those stubs, I wasn't pleased. Not only were some of my relative expenditures out of kilter, but I was also treating money as if it were a passive thing to be needed or demanded, not an opportunity to initiate, give, and pursue change.

From that day forward, I found myself balancing my checkbook in a different way and thinking about economics as at least partly a form of expression. Even when I tried to forget this sometimes uncomfortable idea of a statement of values when paying my bills—and even though I knew that buying flowers, dinner for friends, or a new dance record were important values too—that insight began to change my economic behavior. In budgets large and small, I'd begun to see the best-kept secret of economists: Economic systems are not value-free columns of numbers based on rules of reason, but ways of expressing what varying societies believe is important.

Soon, I was speaking of my committee and checkbook experience on those many occasions when I engaged in what I'd come to think of as the world's second-oldest occupation: fund-raising. The budget-as-values insight seemed to be a "click" of understanding for other people too: a practical guide to looking at the way our federal and state tax dollars were spent, and also at the way we as individuals calculated and used our dollars. I began to feel more comfortable about asking for contributions for projects designed to redress an imbalance of power, a major occupation in any social justice movement. Instead of begging or relying on guilt, a resentment-producing emotion I wouldn't wish on anybody, I realized I was offering a way for the donor to invest in what she or he cared about. If the investment paid off, it would create *in*dependence, not dependence, which is what women-run projects do so well—nobody knows the price of dependency, or the kind of support it takes to get out of it, better than women. Donors would have a satisfying bottom line, and recipients could see themselves as a good investment, thus avoiding women's cultural disease of terminal gratitude. Besides, with the idea of balancing one's checkbook for values every month, even a big goal like equality became a simple part of paying the bills.

I also found this concept of values helpful in sorting out what *shouldn't* be supported. If the return on a charitable investment was more social cachet than social change, the cause probably was acceptable enough to have been funded by tax dollars in the first place. Supporting already famous artists in order to rub shoulders with them, funding mainstream medical research, and creating organizations that relieved government agencies of an obligation to provide services—all were common examples. Of course, one could give to, say, cancer research *and* pressure for its support by future tax dollars, but that kind of activism was (and is) rare in charitable giving. As the only industrialized democracy that doesn't routinely support free higher education, national health care, a national system of child care, and institutions of the arts, this country still seems to specialize in giving tax deductions for charitable contributions that let the government off the hook and allow tax dollars to go right on paying for corporate welfare, agribusiness subsidies, grandiose Pentagon purchases, big bureaucracies, and other values that the majority doesn't share—thus creating disillusionment with government, resentment of what is actually a low rate of taxation, and a continuation of this alienating spiral.

As for values within the world of charitable giving, I discovered when I began fund-raising for women's projects almost twenty-five years ago that of the total charitable dollars given in the United States each year by corporations, foundations, and individuals, less than one percent went to projects that were specifically for women or girls, or had an identified goal of improving their status. Within what were supposed to be general grants—for instance, on health research—females were often specifically excluded on the grounds that menstrual cycles skewed the research (though one might say that men's lack of menstrual cycles did the same), and in public fund drives, even the Boy Scouts got a bigger share than the Girl Scouts. I could find no foundation that had a category for women of all races. In 1975, Mary Jean Tully, the first active president of the National Organization for Women's Legal Defense and Education Fund, released a study documenting the real figure of charitable dollars going to women and girls at less than one half of one percent. In 1977, Women and Foundations/Corporate Philanthropy was founded and began doing regular studies, so we know that years of pressure and initiatives from the women's movement did increase that proportion to a high of 5.2 percent in 1989. Then it settled down to 4.1 percent in 1990. Now national and local women's foundations have joined in the battle for a fair half of all philanthropic dollars instead of only pressuring existing foundations and giving programs.[12] But it will take all donors insisting that half of their charitable dollars go to women and girls—or more than half, for temporary remedial purposes—to right the balance.

To cite just one result of this gender bias that runs through most government and private funding, many drug programs were designed for male addicts. Our stereotype of an addict is male; we fear men who become destructive to pay for drugs more than women who become self-destructive as prostitutes to pay for them; and in a male-dominant culture even male suffering dominates. Yet according to some urban surveys, at least half of addicts are women, and many are not only destroying themselves but giving birth to drug-addicted, perhaps AIDS-infected babies besides. Moreover, if a female addict does recover, she probably has a tougher time being accepted into society than her male counterpart, especially if she bears a double stigma as an ex-prostitute. I point out this example as one way that biased values underlying our social welfare budgets, both public and private, punish not only those directly involved but the rest of society too.

That's an example of the problem seen up close, but there is also the larger problem that we see only from standing back and looking at the whole. Because we don't demystify economics by understanding it as a system of human values, we leave it in the hands of the experts. That leaves us among those who are economics-impaired— in more ways than one.

Let's take math anxiety as a model. The first part of its cure is realizing that there is no more a math mind than there is a history or an English mind; there are only people who learn math or history or English at different paces and in different ways. In the same way, it's helpful to realize there is no such thing as an economics mind. Some people might love numbers and abstract theory, but that doesn't mean they're better suited to this messy, emotional, and idea-driven field than those who love sociology or politics. To pursue the parallel with math anxiety, U.S. girls have been so much more afflicted with it than boys that some experts hypothesized a male "math gene" or a link with testosterone—which only increased girls' paralyzing conviction of having the "wrong" kind of mind. Yet in Japan, where women are usually responsible for household budgets, major purchases, savings, and even family investments in the stock market, males are often the ones with math anxiety. As students, they are at least as likely as girls to go to the special *juku* courses for coaching in math, are often tutored by their sisters, and sometimes are judged by lower math standards in universities. ("If there weren't lower math standards for boys than girls," teacher Cathy Davidson was told, and recorded in *36 Views of Mount Fuji*, her memoir of teaching in Japan, "our best universities would be filled with women.") The Japanese belief that managing money is "women's work" dates back to an ancient samurai tradition, when no self-respecting, supermasculine samurai warrior would deign to carry money, and wore clothes with no pockets as a point of pride. So much for testosterone.[13]

What we need to do as a society is to develop an array of teaching methods that make no assumptions about the right way, or the right group, for learning math, economics, or anything else. What we need to do as individuals is to keep looking until we find the path into a subject that works for us—which was exactly what a values-driven approach was for me.

Once into this demystification, I actually found myself contemplating numbers with interest and even playfulness for the first time: a big step for someone so afflicted with economics anxiety that budget figures were the most feared part of any political argument, I had a hard time remembering to look at the amount before I paid a bill, and I also feared ending up as a bag lady. If the ability to have fun with a subject is a good indication of making it one's own, then amusing myself by devising "money reviews"—alternative ways of assessing books, movies, music, museums, or anything else with a price—was a good sign that my years of economics aversion were passing. After all, even a few dollars offer more units of value than do all but the most resourceful use of adjectives. For instance: Why not take the national average movie ticket price of $5.00 and distribute it accordingly? An economic review of a classic like *The Godfather* might list the script at $4.00, tot up all the good acting performances as another $4.50, credit the film's realistic look at $3.00 and its historically accurate linkage of pre-Castro Cuba and organized crime at $2.50—and then recommend the movie as worth $9.00 *more* than its admission price. On the other hand, a typical Woody Allen film might have a script worth 50 cents, a portrayal of women so neurotic that a viewer should be paid $5.00 to sit through it, another $2.50

debit for the inevitable Allenesque character who wants to win and still get the sympathy due a victim, and several fine performances by good actors adding up to a positive $3.50. Thus, an economics review would recommend it—but only if a ticket buyer got a rebate of $3.50. Similarly, a novel could have one scene that was worth the hardcover price, a pleasure of learning that balanced the clunky writing but only at paperback cost, or a poetry of language that made up for the poverty of plot at both prices. A museum's entry fee might be cut in half to make up for the exclusion of women artists of all races; a music tape might have a balance sheet for each "cut"; and a television show could help to amortize the price of a TV set—or not. It's easy to get carried away.

But the more I pursued serious and not-so-serious ways of exploring economics as values, and the more I read about federal and other budgetary dilemmas, the more I began to notice the great lacunae in the accounting systems that government, business, and we ourselves used. Thanks to my values insight, plus the good luck of being asked to write an introduction for a book by New Zealand's Marilyn Waring, one of a new international wave of feminist thinkers about economics, I began to see that big chunks of life were simply missing or underplayed.

First, labor costs didn't always reflect the country's values—as imperfect as they might be. Child care attendants were paid less than parking lot attendants, and nurses' aides often got less than the men who picked up garbage at their hospitals—not because we were consciously valuing our children less than our cars, or patients less than garbage. The truth was (and still is) that in the United States as in almost every country, categories of work are less likely to be paid by the expertise they require—or even by importance to the community or to the often mythical free market—than by the sex, race, and class of most of their workers. This becomes clear when similar work by different groups of workers is compared *within* countries. Women in the United States might be poorly paid "office-cleaning women" who do the same job that men do as better-paid "janitors" or even "maintenance engineers," and men who wouldn't dream of being typists might now be "keyboard literate" information processors of the computer age, who are paid more than secretaries doing the same task. It is also evident when the same categories of work are compared *among* countries. Road building might be well paid here and in Canada, where it's done by men, but poorly paid in other countries, from vast Russia to tiny Nepal, where women do it. In Japan, electronics assembly is done primarily by men and is decently paid, while in Hungary and Mexico, it's the province of women who get poor pay and working conditions. In Turkey, tobacco processing is low-status "women's work," but in the United States, it's romanticized by cigarette ads and tradition as "men's work"—and is better paid.[14] A cheap labor force cheapens whatever it does—until it rebels.

This wage fixing by cultural caste system is at least as effective as any conspiratorial price fixing for which businesses are legally prosecuted, and sometimes as conscious—as when 9to5, the clerical workers' union, discovered that insurance companies in Boston were fixing the range of clerical salaries in the guise of information sharing. The free market has little to do with it. There is no shortage of nurses in this country, for instance, only a shortage of wages and respect that drives nurses into other professions. Instead of raised salaries, this dilemma has often been met with attempts to change training requirements and import nurse from other countries. When nurses' unions fight lowered salaries on everyone's behalf, they are said to be opposing immigrant women. Imagine the response if car makers lowered salaries and standards for the much less skilled but mostly white male work on assembly lines, and tried to import workers from other countries.

Though the first few women in a male field may benefit from its higher pay and status, it's as temporary as the values in a white neighborhood where the first "minority" families buy houses at prices at least as high as white families, but may lose investment value as white families leave. Indeed, even for female tokens in prestigious male fields, the salaries aren't yet equal. According to the January 1994 salary survey of *Working Woman* magazine, male engineers get $11,000 a year more than female engineers, and women corporate vice presidents get only about 57 percent of the salary level of their male counterparts. Once any field includes "too many" women (usually when females become about a third of the whole), it is devalued, just as is the neighborhood into which "too many" families of the "wrong" race have moved, and for the same reasons —exclusivity and bias. Thus, bookkeeping in this country was fairly well paid while it was a male occupation but became devalued once women gained entry in large numbers. Men invented "certified public accountant," and moved on due to a certification process that first excluded women of all races (the American Institute of Certified Public Accountants had a "no women" policy into the 1950s), and then required experience at public accounting firms that rarely hired other than white males. That remained true until recent social justice movements forced the issue. In managerial and professional jobs in general, an Urban League study from the late 1980s predicted that the percentage of blacks and whites is unlikely to narrow significantly before the year 2039, and even if that happened, salary parity for black and white men wouldn't arrive before 2058; such is the depth of workplace racial segregation.[15]

Whether in the United States or in the international economy, it's a rule with few exceptions: Work is valued by the social value of the worker. A category of work is paid least when women do it, somewhat more when almost any variety of men do it, and much more when men of the "right" race or class do it.

In a way, the ultimate proof of this rule is its reversibility. When men enter a mostly female, "pink-collar" field, rare though that might be, they tend to *raise* the status of the occupation and to be treated better than their counterpart females (including by those very counterparts), even though they may be looked at as odd for being there. Thus, males were nurses until the Civil War created a shortage and the influx of women lowered the status of the profession, but military medics and a few other men who re-entered after Vietnam were often called "physicians' assistants" and paid better than their female counterparts. Males integrated into the overwhelmingly female job of telephone operator fared far better with their coworkers than did females who entered the overwhelmingly male field of telephone installation and repair. The first male flight attendants were more likely to be given special perks and status, and addressed by their last names, than were females who had been "stewardesses" all along. Areas go up or down as the favored group enters or leaves.

Sometimes an increase of salary precedes an influx of the favored group. Males went from 10 percent to 50 percent of coaches of women's teams within a decade after Title IX of the Civil Rights Act required schools to increase their spending on female athletic programs, for example, thus increasing coaches' salaries.[16] Sometimes, integration of the favored group pushes the less favored one out. The percentage of black teachers and especially black principals plummeted after public school integration in the South, not only because of job competition but because blacks would have been in positions of authority over whites. When sex-segregated private schools or colleges merged, the same thing happened to many female staff and faculty, especially in positions that would have given women authority over men.

Even male and female prostitutes seem to abide by the rule of valuing work by the value of the worker. Based on ads for "escort services" in the yellow pages of various cities, plus interviews with street prostitutes in San Francisco, male prostitutes are paid more than female prostitutes for their sexual services, regardless of whether their customers are male or female.

It was this problem of the way work is valued—if not all its applications—that inspired U.S. and Canadian feminists to supplement the first "equal pay for equal work" concept with the standard of "comparable worth," also known as "equal pay for work of equal value" or "pay equity." It had been around since World War II when the National War Labor Board used it to compare dissimilar jobs within a plant to see if pay inequities existed (but then it was discarded along with child care centers and other inducements to work in the war effort). The idea was to compare the salary range in a mostly female profession (say, registered nurse) to that in a mostly male profession requiring similar training and skill (say, pharmacist), and set women's long-term salary and benefit goals accordingly.

It will take many years of organized pressure to adjust all the mostly female jobs upward to the level of mostly white male areas— almost as many as to reach the ultimate goal of an integrated workplace. Though there have been some victories for "comparable worth," especially among government employees from Minnesota to California, secretaries are still 99 percent female nationwide (in spite of all the men who came out of the military trained as clerk-typists and could have used such jobs). They are usually paid much less than the construction trades, which are still 98 percent male (in spite of all the women who have trained in nontraditional jobs in the last twenty years).[17] Any attempt to revalue work according to the job itself, not the social identity of the worker, amounts to not only a redistribution of wealth, but a reconfiguration of professional egos. Even some mostly male unions have sided with management in resisting comparable-worth standards.[18] Though some unions are supportive and see pink-collar organizing as the future of unions (for instance, the Service Employees' International Union, SEIU, which backs the clerical organizing of 9to5), the protection of workplace territory is also signaled by responses like that of the International Typographers' Union to a new Linotype machine. Because it was easily operated by anyone who could type, the union pressured employers to hire only those with other printing skills, kept closed off the apprenticeships that taught them, and so preserved a workplace as white male turf.[19]

We have to be clear about the values here. Education isn't one of them. Degrees don't compensate for sex or race; at least, not without a powerful social justice movement to accompany them. In fact, the female unemployed and underemployed are acquiring more degrees every year, and the female cheap labor force is getting better educated. For example, about 28 percent of all clerical workers had some college in 1976, according to the U.S. Bureau of Labor Statistics, but by 1987, 40 percent did—at the same time that many clerical jobs were being de-skilled (for instance, by replacing shorthand with dictating machines, or spelling skills with computer spell-checks). Surveys show women in clerical jobs often feel depressed because they know they could do much more.[20] Meanwhile, the average male manager continues to be less well educated than the average female clerical worker. Though craft skills should be valued along with academic ones, you can bet that truckdrivers would no longer be paid more than social workers—as is now the case—if truckdrivers were mostly women and social workers were mostly men with MSW degrees. Though women are encouraged to see degrees as a path to higher incomes—especially now that lowered birth rates have made many campuses recruit older students for economic reasons—they might learn more about the life ahead from the realities of faculty employment than from their textbooks. According to 1992–93 surveys, academic women at every level, from lecturer to full professor, were still making less than their male counterparts.[21]

Whether it's the sticky floor of the pink-collar ghetto or the glass ceiling of the executive suite, degrees won't help—not without an attack on the sexual caste system.

To change these surrealistic values embedded in labor costs—often the biggest item in government and business budgets, certainly the first to affect our lives, and, as Keynes knew, the fastest way to affect the economy—we need to innovate through everything from union contracts and lawsuits to comparable-worth standards and a civilian job corps to combat a Depression that, for many, is still going on. But we must also remember to change what we control.

Since I'd learned so much from my own checkbook stubs, I decided to look at the occasional sums I'd been paying for by-the-hour help with research, cleaning, or fund-raising events. Sure enough, I discovered that I'd sometimes paid less for the mostly female job of fact checking than for the comparable but mostly male one of computer tutoring; more for an all-male window-cleaning service than for a woman *or* man who did the "women's work" of cleaning the same room; and more to a man who delivered rented chairs to a benefit than to a woman who served food. I also realized I'd been comparing my lecture fees to those of other feminists and feeling guilty if I was paid more, instead of looking at counterpart male speakers in social justice movements and objecting when I was paid less. Moreover, I hadn't been taking into account the huge fees paid to Henry Kissinger for a view of foreign policy long past, or to Oliver North for talking about illegal Iran-contra arms deals, or to General Schwarzkopf for rehashing the Gulf war. I hope it's not true everywhere, but it seems that lecturers on war get higher fees than those on peace, consumption experts are paid more than those on the environmental cost of overconsuming, and women do better when they say what men want to hear (as on the campus of Ohio's Miami University in 1991, when Christie Hefner of *Playboy* got almost twice as big a fee for defending pornography as author Andrea Dworkin did for opposing it).[22] Lecture fees could give us a multilevel insight into our values.

Once we stop accepting the idea that any economic system is objective and value-free, however, at least we have an Ariadne's thread of values to follow through the economic maze. My own lack of a comparable-worth standard had been penalizing more than myself. Because I was helping to establish speaking fees for other feminists and was giving away some of what I earned, I had become part of the problem. It was an intimate lesson in how we internalize economic values, even when we know better. From that moment forward, I tried to use a kind of do-it-yourself comparability standard, whether I was the worker, the employer, or asking for a fee on someone else's behalf.

I'm not suggesting that such personal acts are a substitute for organized pressure, or for systemic remedies like legislation and a 1930s-size wave of unionizing to give pink-collar ghettos a powerful voice—with unions like 9to5 as a model.[23] Even individual efforts may need organizing; for instance, the Household Employment

Pledge asking each employer not to give less than spelled-out basics of pay and working conditions—and each employee not to accept less.[24] But neither do such larger efforts substitute for individual acts. Each of us is an indispensable piece of an economic quilt that only lasts and warms everyone if it's assembled from the bottom, not woven from above, no matter what the economists say. Moreover, we do what we see, not what we're told. As Gandhi said: "We must be the change we wish to see in the world." As the civil rights movement put it: "Walk like you talk."

In addition to degree of value, however, there are productive areas that aren't valued at all. Take the economic vacuum called "women who don't work." It's a form of semantic slavery that industrialized countries reserve for homemakers (in spite of the fact that homemakers in the United States work longer hours for less pay, and have more likelihood of being replaced by a younger worker, than any other category). Agricultural countries reserve it for women who are productive in nonmonetary ways, or are not considered "primary producers" (even though they grow most or all of the food their families eat). If I had internalized the lower economic value of my own work, and even underpaid some "women's work" myself, how much deeper did it cut to be economically nonexistent?

The truth is that almost every woman knows this economic invisibility in some part of her life. Whether or not she is in the paid labor force, a major part of her energy is probably devoted to productive work within the family and household, work that isn't counted as work at all. It's a reality of patriarchal economic systems, both in capitalist countries like the United States, where the invisibility of homemaking leads to employed women having two jobs, and in the socialist past or hybrid present of countries in East Europe and Russia, where so-called emancipation meant the right to do two jobs, one visible and one not.

To get a fix on how big this invisible part of the economy might be, I went back to look at Galbraith's calculations: The U.S. gross national product—the total value of the nation's annual output of goods and services—would go up by 26 percent if homemakers' labor were included at replacement cost. In Canada, with a population only one tenth as large, Statistics Canada, the national information-gathering body, estimated the cost of replacing one year of homemakers' work at $200 billion, almost 40 percent of Canada's gross domestic product (which is the GNP minus income from a country's resources that are owned by nonresidents).* In both cases, such pink-collar jobs as cook (not the predominantly male one of chef) and child care worker had been used to calculate homemakers' pay. When the Canadian Human Rights Commission used "equal pay for work of equal value" tables instead, homemakers' worth turned out to be comparable to that of middle-level supervisors, senior specialists, and such nonsupervisory professions as therapist and social worker; jobs that paid better because they were also done by men. Homemakers' worth was raised by 200 to 300 percent.[25] Even so, neither method calculated double and triple time for home-makers who work a sixteen-hour day—or more.

The same economic nonexistence is a problem in agricultural countries where fewer women work in the marketplace as defined. A 1993 World Bank conference of seventy nongovernmental organizations from around the globe concluded that 50 percent of the world's food is produced by women's labors, and that women are "the chief organizers of community efforts to combat poverty and hunger."[26] Yet their work frequently doesn't show up in economic figures at all, and thus is less likely to be part of economic planning —nor are they themselves consulted or included in the usual decision-making process of agricultural policy. Hazel Henderson, political economist and futurist, estimates that even in industrial countries, about 50 percent of all production is unpaid—"i.e., do-it-yourself home construction and repairs, food growing, household maintenance, parenting children and volunteering"—and that "in developing countries, up to 75 percent of all production can comprise such unpaid work, particularly in subsistence-based agricultural societies."[27]

* I'll use GDP/GNP for the concept of a nation's gross product here, unless one applies specifically. Countries tend to choose the one that puts a better spin on their situation. A developing country where multinational and other foreign investments make the GNP much bigger might prefer it. On the other hand, the U.S. switched to GDP in 1992, perhaps to make the trade deficit look smaller. Are you beginning to see economics as a very subjective process? Well, here's another problem. One of those figures divided by the adult population yields per capita income, even if the reality consists of a hundred billionaires plus the poor. There has yet to be a widely accepted poverty gap measure to prevent this masking. According to current economic values, there is often a big distance between what you see and what you get.

Thanks to our new ability to measure worldwide suffering with computers, the United Nations has come up with conclusions like this often cited one: Women do a third of all the paid work in the world, and two thirds of all work, paid and unpaid, yet receive only 10 percent of the world's salaries, and own only one percent of its property.

In order to keep from being paralyzed by the sheer magnitude of that U.N. statement—and also to get good and angry—we should look at the forms those statistics take in everyday life:

• Water carried through pipes has an economic value, but water carried for miles in jars on women's heads is usually given no value at all.*

• What a homemaker buys has value because it has been produced for wages, but the hours she spends waiting in line and shopping to buy it—for instance, a whole day in line to buy cooking gas in Bolivia, several hours a day for food in Russia, and eight hours of shopping per family each week in European countries—have no value.

• Purchased, processed, and shipped food contributes to the GDP/GNP—the more processed the food and the greater the distance it's shipped, the greater its value to the gross national product—but food fresh from a kitchen garden or a home-tended field does not.

• A woman taking care of her own children is a person who is "not working"—which is why welfare, initially conceived as a widowed mothers' allowance, is treated as a handout, but unemployment compensation, which involves doing nothing at all, is not—though a person or an institution raising the same children if that mother died or deserted would be "working" and getting much more than a welfare-level payment.

• Fuel gathered by hand—a major occupation of women, whether it's brush on the African veld or cow dung patties in an Indian village—has no value within the GDP/GNP, but the same fuel bought in a market would be counted.

• Bills and taxes paid by an accountant have a double economic life—one for the transactions themselves and one for the job of paying them—but bills paid by a household manager have only one.

* Of seventy developing countries, Derek Blades, a statistician for the Organization for Economic Cooperation and Development, found only six that included water carrying as productive work in their national accounts—one of which, Kenya, included it only when carried by a man.

• Feeding formula to a baby increases the GDP/GNP—though it's less nutritious and immunizing than breast milk and dangerous where contaminated water sources must be used to mix it, not to mention having no contraceptive value for the mother—but breast-feeding, which is usually healthier for the baby and perhaps the mother, has no value at all. Indeed, taking a sick baby to the doctor enriches the GDP/GNP, but having a well baby does not.

• A woman taking care of an aging relative at home (or a man doing this "women's work") is not counted in the GDP/GNP, yet in a nursing home, the same relative and her (or his) caretaker would become a job-creating asset.

• Charitable donations of cash or other assets are deductible according to U.S. tax law, as in many countries, but time given to charitable work is not. In 1980 alone, the GNP failed to include $18 billion in volunteer hours worked by 52.7 million women.[28] Is it an accident that the monetary form of contribution preferred by males is deductible but the 90-percent-female one of giving time is not?

• A "primary producer" (the agricultural version of "head of household") may have the value of nonmonetary acts imputed into the GDP/GNP (e.g., the estimated value of farm animals butchered to feed the family), while his wife, the "secondary producer," does not (e.g., the plantains and yams she grows as family staples). Indeed, a wife may grow, cook, process, and preserve food, carry water, gather fuel, make pots and weave baskets, repair the home, raise domestic animals, weave cloth, make clothing, nurse the sick, and bury the dead—not to mention reproducing and socializing the next generation of workers—and still be called "unproductive."

Such is the power of classical monetary thinking that I, like many others, assumed for years the only way to value the universe of work rendered invisible under the homemaking umbrella was to arrive at some system for paying homemakers wages. That raised the troubling prospect of depersonalizing and devaluing this most personal of work by counting only its replacement value, extending current wage inequities into the home by calculating a homemaker's worth in pink-collar wages, increasing the husband's power by turning him into a pseudo employer, or following the example of authoritarian governments that pay "hero mothers" subsistence wages to stay home and produce more workers and soldiers. Perhaps there could be the choice of collecting wages if the homemaker wished, but it's not the only way. In fact, there are many other areas in which value is imputed, even if no cash changes hands, and standards of comparable worth could be applied to the tasks of homemaking in a new way, as we've seen from Statistics Canada's calculations. That allows unpaid productive work in the home to be valued at the same rates, whether done by women or men, and gives policy planners a more realistic sense of the work that contributes to the life of a country. It also increases choice, for both men and women, by taking away the economic penalty. (Who knows, giving the imputed value of a middle-level manager to a homemaker might encourage more men to take on or equally share this work.) Furthermore, many economists say the process of imputing value is possible and desirable, especially those who live in parts of the world where the habit of "disappearing" agricultural and other productive work done largely by women has even more disastrous results for economic planning than it does for industrial countries that leave out homemakers and other unpaid producers. As Raj Krishna, a distinguished Indian economist, has written:

> Every bit of quasi-productive work can be valued. . . . The part of the net output of tangible goods collected or produced (fuel, fish, meat, clothes, fruits, vegetables, milk and milk products, etc.) which is not already included in the national product, can also be valued at their market prices. . . . Many components of the national product are currently imputed by national accounts statisticians with similar or worse procedures. . . . Therefore, there should be no objections to another exercise in imputation to assess women's economic contribution more appropriately.[29]

In fact, many nations even impute the worth of such nonmonetary, off-the-books, hidden, or illegal parts of their economies as bartered goods and services, child labor and other work in the subsistence-level agricultural or indigenous economy, the goods and services supplied by charitable institutions, and even the huge underground economy of black-market goods, illegal drugs, prostitution, and other criminal transactions. Whether or not they're included within the sacred confines of the GDP/GNP, these bodies of information are available to be used as the bases of informed policy decisions. It's not an overstatement to say that many industrialized countries, including the United States, know more about the worth of the illegal drug trade than the legal homemaking trade —and accordingly, make more informed policy decisions about the

former than the latter. For example, no government agency calculated how many homemakers or others were at home to take care of
those who were deinstitutionalized when a particular mental institution, home for the aged, or program for the disabled was closed
in a community—which was one of the many reasons why this
society was blindsided by what is lumped together as "the homeless
problem." Other disastrous decisions are constantly being made in
this information vacuum. As Berit Ås, former member of Parliament
in Norway and representative to the United Nations, reported:

> Women researchers are concerned about the fact that growth in many
> sectors of the economy takes place by adding more work to the existing
> unpaid work performed by women. For instance, all over the Western
> world, supermarkets replace small retailers. This requires housewives to
> increase the time needed for shopping. A Swedish study revealed that a
> majority of women customers had no car at their disposal. Either they
> had to shop every day and walk longer distances or they had to carry
> heavier burdens and use bus transportation when it was available. Re-
> ducing the number of sales personnel in the supermarkets and hiring
> unqualified people make it necessary for housewives to inform them-
> selves more thoroughly by reading labels and comparing products. . . .
> American studies of consumerism have shown that the average shopping
> time per family amounts to eight hours weekly compared to about two
> hours per week only a few decades ago.[30]

Obscuring the visibility of women's work are the absent or very
poor records of it, census categories that simply don't fit or that
perpetuate invisibility by focusing on the "head of household" or
"productive worker," and even census takers who ask male heads of
households about their wives' economic contribution, thus getting
prideful but inaccurate replies. Patriarchal cultures steeped in the
semantic slavery of "women who don't work" won't easily make the
necessary changes. As far as I can tell in the United States, for instance, the value of a homemaker's productive work has been imputed mostly when she was maimed or killed and insurance
companies and/or the courts had to calculate the amount to pay her
family in damages. Even at that, the rates were mostly pink collar,
and the big number was attributed to the husband's pain and suffering.

Personally, I like the option of treating the full-time homemaker
and her or his wage-earning spouse as partners at least as equal as a
business partnership—as we are so often assured marriage is—and

crediting the homemaker with half of her (or his) spouse's total income. Especially at middle and upper levels, this could help compensate for the fact that, as Galbraith has pointed out, consumption increases and elaborates as income goes up, thus demanding a "consumption manager" with more time and expertise.[31] Anything less than an economic partnership enforces a very intimate inequality: Do we really want a family in which a megabucks entrepreneur has a spouse valued as, say, a social director? On the other hand, the tax meaning of this partnership principle would create tax breaks for families with high incomes and nothing at all for the poor—unless combined with income maintenance programs.

But the truth is: Almost anything would be better than what we have right now. A homemaker in an ongoing marriage has the legal right to only room and board, even if "full-time" means "all the time." That right disappears if her husband loses his job.* A one-in-two divorce rate makes her not only most likely to be replaced by a younger worker, but also least likely to get unemployment benefits, job retraining, a pension, or even the dignity of recognition as a displaced homemaker. A few much-publicized, atypically big divorce settlements may be used for antiwoman jokes. (Q: "Why is it so expensive to divorce a wife?" A: "Because it's worth it.") But in reality, only about 10 percent of divorced women are awarded "temporary maintenance," as alimony is now called, and one study found that the average such payment was only $4,000 a year.[32] Furthermore, the average child support awarded by the courts is less than half the amount necessary to support a child, and only half of these court-ordered or otherwise agreed upon payments are actually paid.

All this was summed up in Lenore Weitzman's famous statistic from *The Divorce Revolution:* Women with dependent children experience a 73 percent drop in standard of living after a divorce, while their ex-husbands' living standard goes up by 42 percent.[33] The colloquial summing up is simpler: If women have young children, they are only one man away from welfare.

Yet if two homemakers were to cross the street and work for each

* As Gail Koff, a founder of the populist law firm Jacoby & Myers, explained in *Love and the Law,* "Generally speaking there is a legal obligation to provide necessities for one's spouse. These necessities include food, clothing, and a roof over one's head. This obligation to support is dependent, of course, on there being money to do so. If there is no money, the wife would not be able to take him to court to force him to provide for his family. . . . All the law actually demands is that either spouse prevent the other from becoming a public charge."

other's husbands, they would be entitled to an eight-hour day and a forty-hour week, Social Security, disability pay, and unemployment compensation—and perhaps paid vacations, transferrable health benefits, and a retirement plan (not to mention a better legal safeguard against violence, which also has economic value). Something is very wrong here.

Furthermore, whether in agricultural or industrial countries, none of the above calculations include pregnancy, birth, lactation, and the reality of women's share in reproducing and nurturing the next generation. (Only Hazel Henderson included parenting.) Reproductive labor is not imputed positively, though millennia of wet nurses and, more recently, surrogate mothers have given reproduction a monetary value—if only out of desperation and lack of economic alternatives. Nor is it valued negatively, though in other circumstances, at least an "opportunity cost" might be used to put a number on salaried work lost. Only those few women who receive paid pregnancy leave—less than 4 percent of U.S. women working full-time for large companies, and an even lower percentage of those working part-time or in small concerns—are given the negative value of a "disability" for childbearing.[34] As feminist theorist Christine Littleton has pointed out: "what makes pregnancy a *dis*ability rather than, say, an additional ability, is the structure of work, not reproduction."[35] The truth is that a salaried worker with a sports injury probably has a better chance of being counted in the GDP/GNP than a woman giving birth to the next generation. The reproduction of farm animals has an economic value, but the reproduction of human beings does not.

Sociologist Maria Mies explains the invisibility of reproductive labor this way: "All the labour that goes into the production of life, including the labour of giving birth to a child, is not seen as the conscious interaction of a human being *with* nature, that is, a truly human activity, but rather as an activity *of* nature."[36] In other words, women are assumed to be in the grip of forces beyond our control, even though we are expected to be individually responsible for the consequences of our reproductive acts—the worst of both worlds. It's one more motive for women to control our own bodies. Only the ability to say "no" forces others (as well as ourselves) to experience "yes" as a conscious act.

This is the deep economics of patriarchy: the valuing of male-style "production" but not female-style "*re*production." Women aren't supposed to be free agents who can bargain with our reproductive cartel. That's something patriarchal politicians recognize every time they vote against their own monetary self-interest by refusing to spend a small sum on contraception and abortion as part of the health care system in the U.S., knowing that unwanted births will cost hundreds of times more in the long run. For women to have the power of choice, the power to decide if our bodies will repro-duce, would mean that we had taken control of the means of repro-duction—and this control is the bottom line of patriarchy.

Even the supposedly sacred and priceless bodily products that men possess—say, blood or sperm—can be sold with little social disapproval, but women are routinely condemned for trying to con-trol our bodies through abortion or even contraception, much less to profit from what they can uniquely do.* Whether or not one thinks these transactions should be legal, the growing reality of birth technology, according to the Glover Report to the European Com-mission, is that "Some hospitals and sperm banks pay semen donors, while egg donors are rarely paid"[37]—a truly stunning fact, since the collection process for the former involves masturbation and for the latter, body-invading semisurgery. In addition, one of the most fre-quent arguments of antiabortion groups opposed to the use of fetal tissue for research, even tissue from spontaneous abortions, is that women might get pregnant and have abortions for that purpose—a lack of empathy for the reality of the experience of pregnancy and abortion, as well as a lack of trust in women as ethical beings. From right to left of patriarchal economics, the common thread seems to be the fear of women's power to control and profit from our natural monopolies and thus to achieve a balance of power with men.

It's no wonder that many women especially feel bored, mystified, or generally turned off by economics. In her landmark 1988 book, *If Women Counted*, Marilyn Waring, former member of Parliament in New Zealand and international advocate of attributing economic

---

* As law professor Patricia Williams reports in *The Alchemy of Race and Rights:* "On the bulletin board just outside my office, there hangs a notice from the department of obstetrics and gynecology of the University of Wisconsin. It offers fifty dollars for every semen specimen 'we are able to use' in an artificial insemination program. Donors must be under thirty-five years old and have a college degree. I wonder every time I enter my office at this market of selling sperm . . . [of] probably-blond college graduates." In addition to a difference of value by race, what would happen if women students were benefiting from selling their ova to be introduced into other wombs or scientific petri dishes? Would they be treated with the same casual approval?

value to unpaid productive and reproductive work as well as to the environment, explained this as a rational judgment: " 'economics anxiety' . . . is also evidence of a quite sane alienation from the subject matter. This occurs when I tell any housewife that she is unoccupied, economically inactive, and doesn't work. If a system treats you like that, you don't spend much time examining it." [38]

Galbraith explained why women can study economics and emerge brainwashed instead of radicalized:

> That many women are coming to sense that they are instruments of the economic system is not in doubt. But their feeling finds no support in economic writing and teaching. On the contrary, it is concealed, and on the whole with great success, by modern neoclassical economics—the everyday economics of the textbook and classroom. This concealment is neither conspiratorial nor deliberate. It reflects the natural and very strong instinct of economics for what is convenient to influential economic interest—for what I have called the convenient social virtue. . . . First, there is the orthodox identification of an increasing consumption of goods and services with increasing happiness. . . . Second, the tasks associated with the consumption of goods are, for all practical purposes ignored. . . . The third requisite for the concealment of women's economic role is the avoidance of any accounting for the value of household work. . . . To keep these matters out of the realm of statistics is also to help keep them innocuously within the sacred domain of the family and the soul. . . . The separate identities of men and women are merged into the concept of the household. The inner conflicts and compromises of the household are not explored; by nearly universal consent, they are not the province of economics. . . . One notices, at this point, an interesting convergence of economics with politics. It has long been recognized that women are kept on a political leash primarily by urging their higher commitment to the family. Their economic role is also concealed and protected by submerging them in the family or household. . . . Once women see that they serve purposes which are *not* their own, they will see that they can serve purposes which *are* their own. [39]

It also helps if women realize that we are experiencing a larger problem, and thus have allies. The process by which monetary values have been used to render women's productive and reproductive work invisible is very like the colonial process by which the productive work of indigenous economies has been rendered invisible. In South Africa, for instance, taxes were imposed on land, livestock, even owning a dog. With no way to get cash in a largely agricultural, non-cash economy, formerly self-sufficient groups were forced to go to work for wages—whether as domestics or in factories and mines. An underpaid labor force was created—just by imposing a monetary system and deciding what it would value. Similarly, women's productive and reproductive work in the home is given no monetary value, and in a cash economy she either becomes dependent on her husband, who works for wages, or she herself must do two jobs, one paid and one unpaid. The household that was a unit of production, even in agricultural patriarchies, becomes a unit only of consumption—at least, in limited economic terms. It's another reason why the analogy between many or most females and countries recovering from colonial economic systems makes such political sense. It's also why women in those parts of the world—like racial and other groups that have been colonized within this and other countries—usually must struggle up through a double layer of forces rendering their actions undervalued or invisible—an indigenous patriarchy and also an imported one.

In spite of major differences in degree, the kinds of economic problems from which women suffer are amazingly similar across national boundaries. Whether it's Kenya or Kansas, for instance, the (mostly male) workers who grow crops for sale are the ones who get government help with agricultural methods, irrigation, labor-saving equipment, low-interest loans, and the like—even if their crops are the wrong ones and have to be stockpiled or destroyed—while the (mostly female) workers whose food growing, processing, and preserving may be just as important to the family, and whose diverse skills, bartered goods, piecework, and "egg money" keep it going, get no such help. Especially in Africa and other agricultural areas where men have been forced off the land and into faraway salaried jobs, "unproductive" women may be the sole family support for most of the year, yet they are left with the most labor-intensive methods. Whether it's Nairobi or New York, the processed food, relatives in nursing homes, and salaried hours in a woman's day go right on getting slender economic recognition, while the subsistence gardens, home caretaking of relatives, and unsalaried human maintenance in a woman's day get none at all.

There's a certain clarity and relief to putting women's position in economic terms—to looking at the economic world as if women mattered. There is less self-blame and more energizing anger once we realize that patriarchal systems "disappear" or undervalue women's labor in order to have an unpaid or underpaid means of production, and "disappear" reproduction so it doesn't yield power as a female cartel.

Looking at international economic life brings to mind the ancient image of the world riding on the back of a turtle—only in reality, the turtle is a woman. She inches along, laboring just beneath the level of economic visibility, often blaming herself for not being able to bear more weight. Occasionally, she retreats into her shell, as if withdrawal were the only form of rebellion. But only when she upsets its balance will the world roll off her back.

In my own cloud of economics anxiety, I never would have thought I could get excited about two such dry and numerical entities as a census and an accounting system. Certainly, I didn't imagine there were two semiconsistent sets of values being imposed on all the diverse cultures and corners of the globe. But that's exactly what has been happening with the census that each country conducts every five or ten years, and with the United Nations' System of National Accounts (UNSNA), a Western-invented accounting system that has been imposed worldwide. They sit at the heart of obscurantist economics like twin minotaurs at the heart of a maze. The path to them may be tortuous, academic, and mysterious, but once you get there, you're confronted with two forces that are all-powerful but also simple. The census decides what is visible. The national system of accounts decides what is valuable. Anyone who is concerned about where the world is being led by current values, whether it's rendering unimportant some groups of people or rendering invisible the entire environment, will have to convert these guardians.

In the United States, the once-a-decade national census was a way of apportioning electoral representation. That was the purpose for which it was originally mandated by the Constitution. By the mid-nineteenth century, however, its questions had grown from six to seventy, and the answers had become the main source of information for legislation, economic planning, educational systems, and social services. Because it purposefully started out to include only a percentage of slaves as property and to exclude Native Americans, its greatest controversies have centered not around what kinds of questions it asked about work, but whether it even included everyone in the country. Most recently, the question has been whether its methods undercount racial minorities, migrants, immigrants, the homeless, and other groups, whose census invisibility deprives them of economic, social, and political power.

In the 1970s, the modern women's movement waged its first battle against sexist census categories and information-gathering methods, mainly the "head of household" category, which imposed a hierarchy on families and meant that men were more likely to answer the questions on everyone's behalf. Now, one "reference person" may answer questions for the household in the United States, as in Canada and other countries; a great improvement, but still a problem. Until the census is focused on individuals, not households, the situation of women and children may continue to be distorted—just as it might be if there were only one vote per household. There is such a wide range of constituencies with an interest in Census Bureau policies that journalists have coined the phrase "census politics." But social justice movements haven't yet focused on the fact that census categories also determine what is counted as work, who is defined as a worker, how we conceptualize the health and progress of the country, how class is measured, what is counted as social mobility—and much more. In fact, the census is the one populist instrument that feeds almost every other defining and decisionmaking process in the country. What doesn't get included may continue to exist, but it exists in the dark.

In the 1980s, when the United Nations' Decade for Women exerted its educational force on both governments and women's groups, women in many countries began to stage a not-so-quiet revolt against census definitions of what was and wasn't productive work. Sometimes they worked within the government, changing definitions to include what they themselves knew to be productive. In Burkina Faso, the West African nation known as Upper Volta when it was a French colony, the economic activity of women hadn't been counted at all unless they could be categorized as *functionnaires* —rare in a 92-percent agricultural country. But the end of colonialism, a progressive government, and more women in government jobs (partly because many men had been forced to find better-paid work in other countries) combined to produce a new determination to count all productive work, whether it was "paid" in a Western sense or not. Everyone over ten was asked how most of their time (principal occupation) as well as the next largest time share (secondary occupation) was spent. The result was stunning. Only in cities where jobs were salaried were women more likely to be more economically inactive than men. One result was a 1991 resolution to restore the women's land and irrigation system rights that had been taken away by Western, patriarchal land registry systems.* In other African and Asian countries, sophisticated women's groups campaigned outside the government to change the census takers as well as their questions, and used the work of specialized United Nations agencies such as the U.N. Statistical Commission and the International Research and Training Institute for the Advancement of Women (INSTRAW) to buttress their arguments. In India, women's organizations successfully agitated for more women to be hired as census takers and for the training of all census takers, male or female, in "special efforts for capturing women's work by asking probing questions," as its census instructions now say. The parameters of productive work still don't include "producing or making something *only* for the domestic consumption of the household," which is more likely to be done by women, and do include "persons who cultivate land to produce for domestic consumption only," who are more likely to be men. Nonetheless, the inclusion of a wide variety of unpaid productive work has made women more economically visible in India than ever before, and thus increased the possibility of accurate economic planning. Just by switching from a more Western-influenced, monetary definition of productive work to the 1982 International Labor Organization's criteria,† for example, the

* The imposition of patriarchal and individualized ownership has been a major cause of land loss in parts of the world where land was passed through the woman's family or owned communally. In the U.S. even jointly worked family farms were considered to be the property of the husband. If he died first, the wife was required to pay inheritance taxes, and her inability to do so often caused her to lose her land. If the wife died first, there were no such taxes, since the farm was considered his. It was for this reason that rural women's groups supported the Equal Rights Amendment, which would have eliminated the basis for these laws and the need for fighting them one by one. These and many other stories lie behind the United Nations statistic that women own only one percent of the world's property.

† In the ILO definition, "the economically active population includes all persons of either sex who provide labour for the production of economic goods and services. All work for pay or in anticipation of profit is included. In addition, the standard specifies that the production of economic goods and services includes all production and processing of primary products, whether for the market, for barter or for home consumption." The ILO acknowledges that this still does not capture the domestic service work that occupies 63 hours a week for rural women in Pakistan and 56 hours a week for women in advanced technological societies, but

estimated proportion of economically active women in India went from 13 percent to 88 percent.

In more industrial and technological countries where the exclusion of homemaking and other unpaid work carries less penalty for government planning than the exclusion of female food producers in agricultural countries, census methods have changed much less. Protests have to be more forceful. From postcard campaigns to demonstrations and even refusing to answer census questions as a form of civil disobedience, protests have been getting more informed and spirited in the last few years. In Canada, for instance, Carol Lees, a homemaker in Saskatoon, looked at a 1991 census question about "number of hours worked in the past week," realized she would have to answer "zero" by census definitions, and decided to celebrate March 8, International Women's Day, by writing the following letter to the minister in charge of the census that Canada takes every five years:

> I am attempting to initiate a national campaign that would be very troublesome for you. It has come to my attention that in the upcoming census there is no classification recognizing labour performed in the home as work. Since I have worked full-time within the home for the past 13 years raising three children, I take exception to the fact that my labour is not defined as productive. As a result of the exclusion of women's labour from information gathering and dissemination, we are denied proper access to programs and policy at every level of government in every country.
>
> I am aware of the penalties I may face for my actions, and will have no trouble in dealing with them. It is my understanding that I face either a $500 fine or three months in jail for refusing to provide information for the census. I could not pay such a fine as my income as a home manager is so limited. The government will not show well if it levies a fine on a mother of three with no income because she is refused recognition for her labours in raising her children. Removing the mother from the home to send her to jail will not go down well either.
>
> This is a very interesting issue to be resolved and a challenge to both of us. I wish us well in finding an amicable solution.[40]

Though Lees and thousands of other grassroots census resisters did not succeed in changing work definitions, the government did

---

compared with most current practices, enacting this definition in all countries would be a great leap forward.

admit defeat by levying no charges against them, though their post-card campaign made their civil disobedience very clear. When Statistics Canada proposed sampling the population on homemaking work instead (Canada is already ahead of the United States in its ability to do this, as well as in its understanding of comparability standards), Lees and others made clear that wasn't good enough. "No other sector of the labor pool would consent to be 'sampled' rather than fully included," as she explained to me, "so why should homemakers? I'm good and damn mad." Her activism had come about as a result of the distance between what she experienced as the reality of productive work and what the census and the economic structure admitted as work. "I'd just been meeting with a group of other homemakers," she explained, "and we talked about how to answer when someone says, 'What do you do?' Then I got the census question telling me I did nothing—and it was just too much. I'm an ordinary person who wants to be counted, as everyone deserves to be. There's a lot of sentiment and support on our side."

In anticipation of the 1996 census, she and other Canadian women have organized a group called Work Is Work Is Work and are circulating test questions for inclusion in the census. As she says, "A lot of us are never going to give up until we're counted."[41]

The Beti women of southern Cameroon have more in common with Carol Lees and her colleagues than economic institutions would like to admit. They, too, have been rendered invisible. Their plight has been recognized in this United Nations description: "Beti women labour for 11 hours a day. Five hours are spent on food production . . . they devote three or four hours a day to food processing and cooking and two or more hours to water and firewood collection, washing, child care and tending the sick. In addition to their family specific duties, women are often involved in community projects, such as the installation of pumps, wells, schools, and health care centres." Beti men work about seven and a half hours on their cocoa plots, palm wine production, and house building or repair, yet as the U.N. report points out: "most conventional studies would count the male as the active labourer and the wife as simply a helper to her husband. Moreover, as tangible evidence of their status, the men would be credited with decision-making power."[42]

This international revolt against patriarchal definitions of work is growing. Since the late 1980s, women's international pressures on their national census and the UNSNA (United Nations System of

National Accounts) categories have taken the form of petitioning their governments, boycotting the census, or writing in what women really do, whether there were categories or not. Imputing value to homemakers' productive work has focused on everything from social security and disability benefits to the still losing battle to define women on welfare who care for young children as working. There has yet to be much focus on "the second shift," that is, valuing the second job of homemaking done by women (and a few men) who are also in the paid labor force. Except for a few U.N. studies on the economic importance of breast-feeding, there has been no emphasis on valuing reproductive work. But now, there is also a growing cadre of women who crisscross the globe, carrying economic organizing advice from one country to the next.*

In New Zealand, Marilyn Waring wrote about the objections of "conceptual difficulties" and "problems of data collection" that were raised against including unpaid work in the 1986 census; difficulties that arose because *too many women did too much work.*" But she and others were successful in adding the question: "What is your main work or activity?" Possible answers included "home duties" and "looking after children," as well as such alternatives as "unpaid work in a family business." As Waring wrote: "The women of New Zealand have shown how to challenge the system, at least in regard to unpaid productive work. But a woman still has no way of informing the census about her reproductive work."[43]

"The combination that works," said Waring in 1994 after a decade of such efforts, "is grassroots women organizing in a forceful way, plus feminist experts inside the system—someone like Joann Vanek, in the U.N. Statistical Office in New York, and a few other hardy souls—who can have enormous impact if they have international women's efforts to back them up and keep them informed. Changing a phrase or adding a concept to a social instrument like the census has leverage like nothing else. Individual women just have

---

* And who are part of a fund of expertise that has grown over the last twenty-five years, from a few pioneers trying to make the overdeveloped world listen—for instance, Swedish economist Ester Boserup in her 1970 book, *Women's Role in Economic Development*, which added a new gender analysis to neoclassical economic assumptions—to networks of feminists from developing countries who are changing those assumptions in research, analysis, policy making, and activism—for instance, DAWN (Developing Alternatives with Women for a New Era) with leaders like Devaki Jain from India and Peggy Antrobus from the Caribbean. For information, write DAWN, School of Continuing Education, University of the West Indies, Barbados, West Indies. Fax 809-426-3006. For suggested reading, see endnotes.

to pressure their governments, refuse to cooperate in their own in-visibility, and insist on reporting the work they really do, whether it fits the census categories or not."[44]

What would happen if the women of the world answered questions like those in the Burkina Faso census about the work really done and the time really spent? I always knew Muriel Rukeyser was right when she said:

> What would happen if one woman told the truth about her life?
> The world would split open.[45]

I just didn't know her poetry applied to the census.

If the census is the first minotaur at the heart of the maze, deciding what raw data are gathered and in what categories, the United Nations System of National Accounts is the second mino-taur. It chooses from this data, as well as from a river of ongoing economic estimates and transactions, to calculate the gross domestic or gross national product. An accounting system based on the as-sumption that monetary exchanges are pretty much the whole ball game, the UNSNA was universalized for worldwide application in the 1950s by a U.N. task force headed by a British economist, Sir Richard Stone. This accounting system gained the authority of use by the World Bank and other financial institutions that are lending agencies, investors, and aid-givers: the "haves" in a world of "have-nots." Its guidelines became the general accounting principles deter-mining what is and is not included in a country's GDP/GNP, a function whose importance is hard to overemphasize. To turn to Galbraith again: "The test of success in a modern economic society, as we all know, is the annual rate of increase in the Gross National Product. At least until recent times this test was unquestioned; a successful society was one with a large annual increase in output, and the most successful society was the one with the largest increase. Even when the social validity of this measure is challenged, as on occasion it now is, those who do so are only thought to be raising an interesting question. They are not imagined to be practical."[46]

Information not included in the GDP/GNP, even if available as what is often called a satellite account—for example, the computations of the replacement value of homemakers, or the cost of air or water pollution in a particular year or area—is not part of the bottom line and is much less likely to be taken seriously. Even to break the information out of its computer nest may require a payment, thus restricting information to those who can afford it. Like the so-called "social audits" now done by some companies in response to questions on the diversity of their work force or impact on the environment, satellite accounts are a step forward, but they still don't show up in the stock market pages, or within the accounting system that determines GDP/GNP.

This powerful UNSNA didn't evolve entirely from the minds of Stone and his colleagues. In order to properly disrespect what we have been taught to respect, we might look at its origins. Understanding how narrowly and haphazardly it began shows how replaceable it is.

Economic theorists had been squabbling over how to estimate the income of "the People," not just the government, since the seventeenth century when only agriculture was calculated, on the theory that it was the only enterprise that produced a net product after costs. There followed a century or so of debate over whether any services at all should be included or, as Adam Smith and Karl Marx argued, only those services directly related to the production, distribution, and repair of goods. As Smith wrote in *The Wealth of Nations:* "the labour of a manufacturer adds, generally, to the materials which he works upon, that of his own maintenance, and of his master's profit. The labour of a menial servant, on the contrary, adds to the value of nothing."[47] You can imagine what he would have said about homemakers.

By the 1920s, governments had taken over from private scholars and theorists this function of measuring national income, with all the conflicts of interest that this implied. Even the most market-oriented monetarist countries included some items whose value had to be imputed (for instance, dweller-owned housing), thus proving they were able to value nonmonetary transactions when they wanted to. But neither the value of the natural resources being used nor the unpaid productive work done mostly by women made it into the mainstream discussion. By the 1930s, the Depression had so sobered this country that the U.S. Senate decided to find out what the national income really was, and gave the job to a brilliant statistician named Simon Kuznets. The report that resulted acknowledged its male staff members by name but thanked its equally experienced female staff in a nameless clump, a good indication of how women's work fared within its pages.

To be fair, Kuznets later criticized the government's refusal to measure such things as subsistence farming as a cheaper source of nutrition, but as a statistician, he, too, was spurned by some of the academic economists. He later won a Nobel Prize for opening an era of measurement, not just theory, and he remained critical of an accounting system that told so much about where the money was and so little about how people were actually living. Nonetheless, his idea of "devising a single yardstick (of nutrition, warmth, health, shelter, etc.)"[48] remained a dream. Other valuable lessons learned during the Depression—for instance, people's survival through subsistence farming and a barter economy—didn't show up in the Senate's figures at all. Neither did the fact that bank loans made on character and past performance were more likely to be repaid than those based on collateral.

In the late 1930s, Richard Stone entered the picture as a coauthor with John Maynard Keynes of a paper entitled "The National Income and Expenditure of the United Kingdom, and How to Pay for the War." The uniform accounting system Stone eventually advanced in the 1950s had its roots in these limited definitions, and in the wartime system of paying for the huge costs of arming England during World War II. There was thought only of winning, not of accounting for the human or ecological costs of war, or the cost to the civilian population of diverting raw materials and productive capacity into the war effort. These are the crumbling pillars on which our complex system is built—and it is complex. While still in the U.S. Senate, Vice President Gore persuaded the Joint Economic Committee to hold hearings on cataloging all the economic formulas that would have to be changed to include environmental and natural resource costs in our calculations. (Needless to say, the human resources of unpaid productive labor weren't included in this effort.) At a minimum, however, the principles Stone universalized are being recognized as limited, fallible, destructive, and out-of-date—even if they are still the only game in town.

It is the rising consciousness of environmental danger that has brought the values embedded in UNSNA into increasing question in the last decade, not the exclusion of a third to three quarters of all productive labor (depending on the country)—always overwhelmingly female labor. Like female production and reproduction, the environment has been regarded as conquered, unlimited, and free. Thus, the environment has no value in this worldwide accounting system. It doesn't appear on the balance sheet at all. Consider these examples:

• A tree standing there giving us oxygen has no economic value —as an environmental asset for us or a home for other species— but the minute a paid ax strikes its bark, it acquires economic worth.

• Forests or other newly extracted raw materials aren't being deducted from national assets, which is why recycled paper and environmentally smarter materials may seem to be *more* expensive. The true cost of new paper isn't recorded.

• Water acquires a value if it is "employed" in production (for instance, if it arrives through a meter to sustain cattle, or over a water wheel to create electricity), but otherwise it has none—though the World Health Organization estimates 25 million deaths per year from waterborne diseases, and lives lost by lack of water are incalculable.

• The cleanup costs of polluting a river, injecting pesticides into the groundwater, or putting noxious gases into the air have not been figured into the cost of the manufacturing or agribusiness that put them there in the first place. Historically, the economic incentive has been to pollute.

• Current toxic waste sites will cost $400 billion to clean up over the next thirty years, according to a 1993 estimate by the Departments of Energy and Defense. Since the GDP/GNP will include that amount on the positive side, and environmental damage doesn't turn up the debit side, this will actually come out as an economic boon.

• Clearing, selling off, and building roads into the Amazon rain forest was counted as "development" and financed by the World Bank and its agencies*—with no resource depletion on the other side of the ledger and no value attributed to one of the world's last

---

* The biggest single source of loans for international development, and the main link between the world's overdeveloped countries (where most of the top 20 percent of the world population lives and receives 82.7 percent of its income) and its underdeveloped countries (where most of the bottom 20 percent lives and gets 1.4 percent of the world's income). Created at the Bretton Woods Conference in 1944 as part of the post–World War II economic order, the World Bank has always been headed and headquartered by the U.S. and dominated by the U.S., Japan, Germany, France, and the United Kingdom.

rain forests as an asset for climate and pollution control, medicinal plants, species diversity, and much more.

When environmental costs are deducted from the GDP/GNP, there is a whole different picture of progress. For example, in Costa Rica, the World Resources Institute calculated that in the past twenty years, natural resources worth one entire year's GDP have been lost.[49]

But the old economic values grind on. The air you're breathing and the grass outside your door have no value, but the concrete and asphalt do; safe driving has no economic value, but a car crash enriches the GDP/GNP; the work generated by an oil spill makes the GDP/GNP grow, as do the claims the oil company may pay out, but the damage done to the sea and its species, and therefore to a balance crucial to us, is economically invisible.

Mind you, fixing any of the above isn't impossible. If you can imagine a world in which value is attributed to natural resources, it can be created. If it sounds logical that a television manufacturer should take back your old set and recycle its materials, then it can be done. If environmentally skilled engineers and architects can now create modern buildings with materials that are entirely biodegradable, then it's been possible for a long time. (And it is possible, you know. As environmentalists say now and indigenous cultures have always said, the waste of this generation must contribute to the food of future generations.) If we figure out the real cost of what we buy, its damage will begin to be self-limiting. According to the World Resources Institute in Washington, for instance, a gallon of gas would cost 400 percent more if pollution, waste disposal, health impact, and the costs of defending foreign oil fields were figured in. A study of the University of California at San Francisco showed that each resident of the state was paying another $3.63 in hidden health care costs per pack of cigarettes. If women control reproduction, the cost to our health and bodies causes us to limit and space births—as cross-cultural experience shows—and to replace, not exponentially increase, the voyagers on this spaceship Earth.

A different world can be created or re-created—but not until we stop enshrining the economic values of invisible labor, infinite and obsessive growth, and a slow environmental suicide.

There have been rhetorical steps forward. Change has to be imagined first. At the 1992 Earth Summit in Brazil, 178 countries supported Agenda 21, thus agreeing to include environmental costs and benefits in their GDP/GNP measurements; a statement of great importance for its intent, though there is still little research and less agreement on how to go about it. Thanks to fervent lobbying by international women's groups, a limited but important pledge of women's role in environmental decisions, and of counting women's work, was also included.* On Earth Day, 1993, President Clinton ordered the agencies of the U.S. government that calculate the GDP to begin this process of including the environmental costs and benefits. Growing up like grass around the old concrete of the GDP/GNP values, there are also alternative measures. Guidelines for calculating environmentally adjusted and sustainable national income have been given in the 1993 *Handbook of National Accounts* issued by the U.N. Statistical Office. There are also the Physical Quality of Life Index and the Measure of Economic Welfare, both of which have been around as extra indicators for two decades. In the wake of the Amazon rain forest damage, even the World Bank has been under such pressure from environmental groups that it began in the late 1980s to include an environmental assessment unit within each of its regional offices.

But so far, as homemaker Carol Lees pointed out when she was offered an alternative process to "sample" homemaking work in Canada, those are still optional satellite events, not transformations of the main system. Right now in the United States, systemic values still count education as an expenditure, not an investment; don't make the connection between prenatal care or inoculations for children and economic development; and are generally far more likely to reward investment in *things* than in *people*. The term "infrastructure" is taken seriously because it applies to highways and sewer systems, but it could also be applied to prenatal care and child care, the educational and health care systems. When public education benefits by comparing it to highways—but not vice versa—that in itself reveals values.

Yet our system of national accounts is so limited to a profit psy-

---

* Among the goals stated by Agenda 21:

"Countries should take urgent measures to avert the ongoing rapid environmental and economic degradation in developing countries that generally affects the lives of women and children in rural areas . . . women should be fully involved in decision-making and in the implementation of sustainable development activities. . . .

"The integration of the value of unpaid work, including work that is currently designated 'domestic,' in resource accounting mechanisms in order better to represent the true value of the contribution of women to the economy using revised guidelines for the United Nations System of National Accounts, to be issued in 1993."

chology that even the physical infrastructure isn't counted as an asset. This in turn has discouraged maintenance, and left it in bad shape, not to mention leaving our national budget askew. As futurist Hazel Henderson wrote, with her gift for making the complex understandable: "we need to account for our country's infrastructure on the books, so as to have a national 'net worth' statement, just as companies do. As we try to cut the deficit, we need to be sure that we have a correct account of it. If our infrastructure is not included as an asset, we may actually cut too deeply."[50]

Most pressures are still on the side of accepting the values of the UNSNA—especially because old Cold War tensions are being translated into fear of international economic competition whose very language is like an alternate form of warfare. There is no such effort toward saving the environment. In overdeveloped countries where current values and accounting systems originated, many of us have been persuaded that they're the most advanced or even the only ones. In developing or more agricultural countries where such systems have been imposed—for instance, formerly colonized countries left without the industrial capacity to process their own raw materials, or indigenous cultures that are isolated inside industrial nations —loans and investments are dependent on earning the cash to repay with substantial interest, instead of creating satisfying, balanced, sustainable ways of living.

Fatima Mernissi, a feminist and sociologist from Morocco, writes about the view from outside this system:

> The new imperialism that dominates us, the non-Westerners, no longer appears as physical occupation. . . . It is more insidious—it is a way of reckoning, of calculating, of evaluation . . . of consuming, of buying. The multinational corporation forces us to make diagnoses, prognostications, and programs according to its models. The vocabulary that we use for our national budget is its language. . . . The West, "drugged with growth," projects its present into the future and forces us to realize that, in order to take up its challenge, we must fight on the grounds that it has chosen: the present.[51]

Women haven't been sitting around all these years, allowing our work to be counted out or military and consumerist values to go uncriticized. There were such economic thinkers in the suffragist era as Charlotte Perkins Gilman, a largely self-educated theorist who wrote *Women and Economics,* a still relevant exposé of androcentric values,[52] and Olive Schreiner, whose *Women and Labour* assumed that equality in work and sexual life went hand in hand.[53] There were also pioneers of a then progressive new field called "domestic science" or "home economics," and others of the late nineteenth and early twentieth centuries who were trying to redefine productive work. They wanted to include any activity ending in a product or service that another person could be hired to perform: a definition that would have included most of women's productive work, though not reproduction, as well as large parts of men's unsalaried labor. They also protested the limited and joyless characterization of work by patriarchal economists—for example, Adam Smith's assumption that work itself must require the worker (always male) to sacrifice "his tranquility, his freedom and his happiness." As Gilman wrote, from that "pitiful conception of labour as a curse comes the very old and androcentric (i.e., male-centered) habit of despising it as belonging to women and then to slaves. . . . For long ages men performed no productive industry at all, being merely hunters and fighters. . . . They assume as unquestionable that 'the economic man' will never do anything unless he has to . . . and will, inevitably, take all he can get and do all he can to outwit, overcome, and if necessary destroy his antagonist."[54]

Perhaps because women's traditional labors, however unpaid, yielded clear results and were not "alienated," as many men had come to think was inevitable in factories where fragmented tasks lacked even the satisfaction of finishing one process or product, many female activists brought with them into the public sphere a belief in the possibility of humanized, satisfying, even joyful work. Many hoped the Marxist promises of communalizing homemaking would be the answer to women's isolation and powerlessness within the household; or that eliminating private property would eliminate the ownership of women as reproductive property; or that subordinating sex and race to class would bring some magical, automatic liberation in a classless society. It was in response to women's demand for inclusion in class-bound Marxist theory that Engels wrote *The Origin of the Family, Private Property, and the State.* He drew a parallel between the rise of private property and the subordination of women as property, and became one of the very few male economic thinkers to include the interplay between production and reproduction. The tasks that those generations of suffragists and abolitionists performed included the official elimination of slavery as an economic system, achieving a legal identity as persons and citizens for females of all races, and bringing many women into the paid labor force. What they couldn't do was get beyond theory about the definition of productive work, the solution to women's double burden of salaried and unsalaried work, or changing the semantic slavery of "women who don't work."

It remains for this feminist wave to create viable substitutes for the patriarchal values underlying economics. It won't be easy. As the Nobel Prize Committee commented in 1984 when it awarded Sir Richard Stone the Nobel Prize for inventing a system that rendered half the world's work and all of its environment invisible: "The system has become accepted as so self-evident that it is hard to realize that someone had to invent it."

That's exactly the problem. We have to make what's wrong visible before it will be moved aside. Our willingness to rebel against our role of managing consumption, whether as a homemaker or as Superwoman, should be increased by realizing that our rebellion will help balance the world's consumption. As Hazel Henderson wrote:

> As a result of the changing role of the American woman, who no longer has time to serve as the "heroic consumer," the world's economies can no longer look to the United States to be the consumption-led "locomotive." . . . Over 60 percent of U.S. women who are now in the workforce have drastically changed their consumption habits to basic needs, fewer goods and more services, e.g., education, day care, energy and shelter. Already we see how such shifts have changed basic patterns of production and consumption. Daycare is one of our fastest growing industries as parenting became monetarized. Cooking is now in the money economy with fast food eateries, while all those other time-consuming chores, from food shopping and cleaning to cooking and waiting for the appliance repairman, babysitting and home maintenance, are shared by men. For example, one Madison Avenue survey leads to the conclusion that advertisers must now sell washing powders and toilet bowl cleaners with real respect, since almost 50 percent of their users are now men.[55]

This change is not yet creating a new definition of productive work. It is only fitting more of women's tasks into the old one by turning them into paid jobs. But it is creating an economy more focused on creating services than on manufacturing objects—which is all to the good, for women, for the environment, and for men too.

If the simple act of refusing to be an obsessed consumer can challenge the values at the heart of the maze, imagine what else we can do. Every time we balance our checkbooks in a new way, or vote on budget values, or invest charitable dollars in creating self-sufficiency, we challenge those values. Every time we insist on comparable worth, or compare notes with coworkers on how much we make —the one fact employers try to keep us quiet about—we are recreating them. Every time we value those living natural resources that would otherwise be counted only when dead, we're facing down a minotaur. Every time we refuse to be misled by experts who are themselves lost in the maze and instead follow our Ariadne's thread of values, we're getting closer to the heart of it. Every time we speak out, we bring others along. For instance, here is the latest letter from Saskatoon homemaker Carol Lees:

> I want to tell you of a local TV interview that I did on Sunday. Before the TV crew arrived, I prepared a clear glass bowl containing water, salt, sugar, shortening and yeast and I used this in the interview to illustrate my point.
>
> Voice-over footage of me filling a bowl: "Carol Lees is putting the ingredients for bread into a bowl, but she is purposely leaving out a key ingredient—flour. The point is to make an analogy. She says it's a lot like how the federal government leaves out a group of workers in its census forms."
>
> Shot of me sitting at my kitchen table with the bowl in front of me: "This is a bowl of bread. I've put everything in except the flour—so, of course, it is not really a bowl of bread. And that's a parallel for what the government is trying to do. They're trying to present measures of the labour force and productivity but they're leaving out half of what should be included."
>
> More interview: "If that work is not counted on the census, I'm going to try and initiate a national boycott of the section on work on the 1996 census, and I'm going to ask all Canadians to refuse to complete that census unless the work of all Canadians is included."
>
> In the wind-up footage, I'm adding flour and mixing up the dough. The crew did a good job of it all—it was on national TV too.

To those who refuse to revalue economics, we need to say: Half the world's labor and all of its resources will not be invisible anymore. To those who add environmental values only, we need to say:

Unless women control reproduction, population pressures will keep on degrading the environment. Unless the male/female, Man/Nature paradigm ends, domination will continue. We are here to issue a Declaration of Interdependence.

Postscript

I always trust the microcosm over the macrocosm. So let me leave you with news of an important and growing part of the women's movement—and a small but growing part of the U.S. national economy—that the media haven't noticed yet. It has already created more jobs than the Fortune 500 corporations. For the future, it has the potential for innovating a new economic form. Even as an economic alternative, it's flowering in the cracks left by inflexible, environment-damaging behemoths, and providing exactly the kind of communal, satisfying, productive workplace so many people are hungering for. It creates jobs that are recognized and measurable within the current census and GDP/GNP standards, thus making previously invisible work visible, but because it is controlled by its workers, it also provides for family-centered concerns that are not yet valued in conventional workplaces. It creates its own definitions of success, and doesn't reward unlimited growth and unreasonable return on capital.

I'm talking about the women's economic development movement —or empowerment, since development does sound more like hydro-electric dams—that is nurturing women's cooperatively owned businesses in many parts of this country, from the most isolated rural setting to the most depersonalized urban one. It is growing and changing too rapidly to be captured within the covers of a book, but every group and center of information mentioned here can be contacted through addresses in the notes to Part 5.

Even when one individual example has been noticed—for instance, when *60 Minutes* did a report on the Women's Economic Development Corporation in Minnesota (now called Women-

Venture[56]), a local feminist group that nurtures such businesses by giving them access to expertise, low-interest loans, and communal support—it was treated as an isolated circumstance rather than part of a national movement. In fact, these businesses and the umbrella groups that often nurture them are a conscious and growing part of feminism, with their own national get-togethers and such semi-underground media as *Equal Means,* a multi-cultural magazine for women forging new grassroots economic models.[57] Consisting mostly of businesses started and cooperatively owned by previously low-income or no-income women, this grassroots contagion is nothing less than the first economic base for the women's movement. After all, if we're going to agitate freely for our rights, some of us need to have jobs we can't be fired from, just as immigrant and other "out" groups need businesses they themselves control. As psychic immigrants who are also a majority and so have a better chance of transforming the mainstream, women of all groups need experimental laboratories for new economic forms and values.

This cooperative economic paradigm is neither capitalist nor socialist. Unlike the women business owners who are climbing the ladder Horatio Alger style—and also acquiring politically valuable independence, though usually in a more conventional economic form—these enterprises are usually owned and managed by those who work in them in a way that allows new flexibility and styles of working. The "Small Is Beautiful" or Gandhian village-level economy most resembles their inclusion of family needs, interdependent values, and human relationships in economic life. Some are small businesses that begin with a little capital created by several women who pool their savings, others are groups of pink-collar workers who start or take over companies to become their own employers, and still others are handicraft or other cooperatives that expand production, eliminate the marketing middleperson, and train new workers/owners as they grow. Many have been nurtured by revolving loan funds and other expertise supplied by feminist groups organized for the purpose. That's where local groups like WomenVenture or the Women's Self-Employment Project in Chicago[58] come in. Their goal is to help low- and moderate-income women become economically self-sufficient through self-employment, and their services range from loans and help with business plans to personal development and support groups. It's no accident that their loan programs usually follow the group lending approach that has worked so well in developing countries. Named after the Grameen Bank that originated this model in Bangladesh, it combines loans with flexibility and constant group support.* Nationally, the Ms. Foundation for Women has been an umbrella for many groups in this economic empowerment movement for a decade. Under the leadership of Marie Wilson, it has pioneered in putting together collaborative loan funds. (Write the Ms. Foundation for national information, or groups in your area.[59]) Altogether, their goals are good jobs and investment in people, not the 25 percent return on capital of venture capitalists.

In their total economic activity, these enterprises have already created hundreds, perhaps thousands, of jobs, exactly where they are needed most—often among women who are getting off welfare or out of battered-women's shelters, or are laboring in poorly paid, pink-collar jobs that have been yielding unfair profits for someone else. Since the much-admired Fortune 500 companies have actually lost jobs for U.S. workers since the late 1960s, this should be hopeful news; yet you're unlikely to read about these grassroots income-generating and job-creating groups in *Forbes* or *Fortune*.

Though their different work and management patterns haven't been described in terms rooted in economics yet, they resemble the culturally female styles described by Carol Gilligan in *In a Different*

---

* At a 1993 Washington conference, "Hunger, Poverty, and the World Bank," Professor Muhammad Yunus of the Grameen Bank spoke about this model, which gives small loans in thousands of villages, 94 percent to women, and has an almost perfect repayment record: "We take quite a bit of time preparing our borrowers to learn how to make decisions within their five-member groups. . . . We repeat the following advice many times to them . . . 'Please never get angry with the person who cannot pay the installment. Please don't put pressure on her to make her pay. Be a good friend, don't turn into an enemy. . . . First find out the story behind the non-payment. . . . When you get the full story, you'll see how stupid it would have been to twist her arm to get the money. She can't pay the installment because her husband ran away with the money. As a good friend, your responsibility will be to go and find her husband and bring him back, hopefully, with the money. It may also happen that your friend could not pay the installments because the cow which she bought with the loan money died. As good friends, you should promptly stand by her side, give her consolation and courage at this disaster. . . . Ask Grameen to give her another loan, and reschedule and convert the previous loan into a long-term loan.' . . . The borrowers own the bank. We lend out $30 million each month in loans under $100 on average. . . . Studies tell us that the borrowers have improved their income, widened their asset base, moved steadily toward a life of dignity and honour. Studies also tell us that nutrition level in Grameen families is better . . . child mortality is lower . . . adoption of family planning practices is higher. . . . All studies confirm the visible empowerment of women."

After years of ignoring the successful Grameen example, the World Bank came through with a small $2 million grant to help start the Grameen Trust, which will begin 30 to 40 such micro-credit programs in other countries in the next five years.

Voice, or the all-female classrooms, described by Myra and David
Sadker in *Failing at Fairness,* that are being used to conquer intimi-
dation by such traditionally male subjects as math or science.[60] Like
those groups and classrooms, these businesses are committed to mutual support, flexibility, cooperation, and helping individual members develop. Like them, these businesses will eventually provide a
new paradigm that the mainstream can learn from, just as women
have learned assertiveness, daring, and many other useful tools from
a culturally male paradigm.

Until there are proper phrases to describe this growing feminist
economics, think of it this way: Since women as a group share the
characteristics of a developing country, it's not surprising that this
economic form most resembles a developing paradigm. As a result,
there is a growing exchange of information between women's economic empowerment groups in the United States and those in the
developing world, with women of the north seeking the greater
expertise from women of the south in a healthy reversal of the colonial pattern. Those with a scholarly bent might think of the local
production model of old-fashioned anarchist theory, but with wom-
en's cultural values added.

Even before the right terminology emerges, however, we can see
these local groups as small but bright pieces in a growing national
and international economic quilt with these characteristics:

1. They tend to arise first among women at the very bottom of
the larger economy, as if the view from there is more clear and the
absence of temptation toward old versions of women's economic
roles is a blessing in disguise. Washington poverticians never imagined that women could get off welfare by starting their own businesses, but that's what's happening. The pioneering feminist groups
that act as go-betweens also help change restrictive welfare regulations, intercede with local banks, or offer revolving loan funds (often
made up of contributions from foundations, individual donors, and
investors looking for some return on their money plus a different
kind of bottom line). They also provide continuing services so that
a woman who's out there on the edge of personal and economic
history has some support. In these alliances between feminists with
economic expertise and grassroots economic adventurers, it's the
women doing the work who are calling the shots.

2. These new groups integrate economic techniques like job
training, sophisticated marketing, management tools, and advanced

technology with such innovative techniques as flexible schedules, child care, language workshops for new immigrants, assertiveness training, help in getting a driver's license, a link to political activity in the larger community, and even songs, poems, and ceremonies that fill a deeper need than the usual workplace practices. Like some of the labor-organizing groups of the 1930s, they tend to see life as a whole, with work and family, economics and culture, united— only this time, with women making their own decisions.

3. The groups put a premium on autonomy and independence. Like the Ramah Navajo women weavers in New Mexico,[61] they may already have a skill and a product, and just need help with bypassing the profiteering middlepeople. Or like the 240 African-American and Latina workers who own and govern the Cooperative Home Care Associates of the Bronx in New York,[62] they may assure training, benefits, and career opportunities to each other, while setting an industry standard of good service to the homebound ill and elderly. The point is that the people who do the work also make the decisions. As a result, these groups value a small-is-beautiful size over bigness, but that doesn't mean they can't reach national and international markets. The 700 workers of the Watermark Association of Artisans of North Carolina[63] produce many of the most prized handmade items now marketed through catalogs, cable television, and international companies, yet they can work at home, create their own schedules, and share in management decisions and profits. These women, whose success built a headquarters in the middle of cornfields two hours from the nearest airport, chose as their motto: "Rarely are orders too large or too small for us to handle."

4. These grassroots groups are also gaining the confidence and expertise to analyze and replace the values of the economic mainstream. After the challenge made by women's groups from developing countries to economic policies at the 1985 United Nations World Women's Conference, in Nairobi, Kenya, U.S. and other women from overdeveloped countries began to realize that they could and must understand and take on their own economies. Indeed, just using the term "overdeveloped" implied the need for a healthy process of change and achieving balance, just as "underdeveloped" did at the other end of the scale. Since then, efforts to demystify economics and promote "economic literacy" have sprung up at the grass roots. Now, international conferences turn into information exchanges and organizing meetings on the various

experiments in women's economic empowerment—both in over-developed and underdeveloped countries. In the United States, a new group founded in 1992, An Income of Her Own,[64] helps teenage women, especially but not only from low-income groups, to train for and even start their own businesses, with conferences, an entrepreneurial summer camp, and its own publications.

Since all the examples of this new economic paradigm strive to value what is important in our lives, from humane work patterns and child rearing to personal development and economic independence, perhaps the best definition comes from Rebecca Adamson of First Nations Development Institute,[65] which also nurtures businesses following a modernized Native American paradigm that includes the principles of communal ownership and balance rather than accumulation and exclusivity. Her updated definition of economics is this: "The science of dealing with the production, distribution, and consumption of wealth in a naturally holistic, reciprocal manner that respects humankind, fellow species, and the ecobalance of life."

Or perhaps we just need the words of Alice Walker's poem "We Alone":

> This could be our revolution:
> To love what is plentiful
> as much as
> what is scarce.[66]

Doing
Sixty

Doing Sixty

> I belong to a generation of women who have never ex-
> isted. Never in history . . . women who are outside of
> family, and whom society would like to silence. In so
> many ways, growing old contradicts the stereotype of the
> woman hunched over. It is a time for raising your head
> and looking at the view from the top of the hill, a view of
> the whole scene never before perceived.
>
> BARBARA MACDONALD (1913–) [1]

Age is supposed to create more serenity, calm, and detachment from the world, right? Well, I'm finding just the reverse. The
older I get, the more intensely I feel about the world around me,
including things I once thought too small for concern; the more
connected I feel to nature, though I used to prefer human invention;
the more poignancy I find not only in very old people, who always
got to me, but also in children; the more likely I am to feel rage
when people are rendered invisible, and also to claim my own place;
the more I can risk saying "no" even if "yes" means approval; and
most of all, the more able I am to use my own voice, to know what
I feel and say what I think: in short, to *express* without also having
to *persuade*.

Some of this journey's content is uniquely mine, and I find excitement in its solitary, edge-of-the-world sensation of entering new
territory with the wind whistling past my ears. Who would have
imagined, for instance, that I, once among the most externalized of
people, would now think of meditation as a tool of revolution (without self-authority, how can we keep standing up to external authority)? or consider inner space more important to explore than outer
space? or dismay even some feminists by saying that power is also
internal? or voice thoughts as contrary to everything I read in the
newspapers as: The only lasting arms control is how we raise our
children?

On the other hand, I know my journey's form is a common one.
I'm exploring the other half of the circle—something that is espe-

cially hard in this either/or culture that tries to make us into one thing for life, and treats change as if it were a rejection of the past. Nonetheless, I see more and more people going on to a future that builds on the past but is very different from it. I see many women who spent the central years of their lives in solitary creative work or nurturing husbands and children—and some men whose work or temperament turned them inward too—who are discovering the external world of activism, politics, and tangible causes with all the same excitement that I find in understanding less tangible ones. I see many men who spent most of their lives working for external rewards, often missing their own growth as well as their children's, who are now nurturing second families, their internal lives, or both —and a few women who are following this pattern too, because they needed to do the unexpected before they could feel less than trapped by the expected.

I'm also finding a new perspective that comes from leaving the central plateau of life, and seeing more clearly the tyrannies of social expectation I've left behind. For women especially—and for men too, if they've been limited by stereotypes—we've traveled past the point when society cares very much about who we are or what we do. Most of our social value ended at fifty or so, when our youth-related powers of sexuality, childbearing, and hard work came to an end—at least, by the standards of a culture that assigns such roles— and the few powerful positions reserved for the old and wise are rarely ours anyway. Though this growing neglect and invisibility may shock and grieve us greatly at first and feel like "a period of free fall," to use Germaine Greer's phrase, it also creates a new freedom to be ourselves—without explanation. As Greer concludes in *The Change,* her book about women and aging: "The climacteric marks the end of apologizing. The chrysalis of conditioning has once and for all to break and the female woman finally to emerge."[2]

From this new vantage point, I see that my notion of age bringing detachment was probably just one more bias designed to move some groups out of the way. If so, it's even more self-defeating than most biases—and on a much grander scale—for sooner or later, this one will catch up with all of us. Yet we've allowed a youth-centered culture to leave us so estranged from our future selves that, when asked about the years beyond fifty, sixty, or seventy—all part of the average human life span providing we can escape hunger, violence, and other epidemics—many people can see only a blank screen, or one on which they project fear of disease and dependency. This incomplete social map makes the last third of life an unknown country and leaves men stranded after their work lives are over, but it ends so much earlier for women that only a wave of noisy feminists has made us aware of its limits by going public with experiences that were once beyond its edge, from menopause as a rite of passage into what Margaret Mead called "postmenopausal zest," to the news that raised life expectancies and lowered birth rates are making older people, especially older women, a bigger share of many nations, from Europe to Japan, than ever before in history. I hope to live to the year 2030, and see what this country will be like when one in four women is sixty-five or over—as is one in five of the whole population. Perhaps we will be perennial flowers who "re-pot" ourselves and bloom in many times.[3]

More and more, I'm beginning to see that life after fifty or sixty is itself another country, as different as adolescence is from childhood, or the central years of life are from adolescence—and just as adventurous. At least it would be, if it weren't also a place of poverty for many, especially women over sixty-five, and of disregard for even more. If it's to become a place of dignity and power, it will require a movement that parallels many others—something pioneers have been telling us for a long time. In 1970, when Maggie Kuhn was sixty-four, she founded the Gray Panthers, and also understood that young people were more likely to be allies of the very old than were the middle-aged, who assume a right to decide for both their children and their parents. Activist and writer Barbara Macdonald used her view as a lesbian living off the patriarchal map to warn us that feminism had failed to recognize women beyond family age as a center of activism and feminist theory.[4] Generations of what Alice Walker called "the Big Mama tradition" in the black community have provided us with role models of energized, effective, political older women. A few pioneering studies have told us to confront fears of aging and look at a new stage of life; for instance, Carnegie Corporation's Aging Society Project, which predicted a decade ago of this country's future: "The increase of about thirty-five years in life expectancy in this century is so large that we have almost become a different species."[5]

We may not yet have maps of this new country, but parallels with other movements can give us a compass. Progress seems to have similar stages: first rising up from invisibility by declaring the existence of a group with shared experiences; then taking the power to name and define the group; then a long process of "coming out" by individuals who identify with it; inventing new words to describe previously unnamed experiences (for instance, "ageism" itself); bringing this new view from the margins into the center by means ranging from new laws and language to building a political power base that's like an internal nation; and maintaining a movement as an imaginative stronghold for what a future and inclusive world could look like—as well as a collective source of self-esteem, shared knowledge, and community.

Think about the pressure to "pass" by lying about one's age, for instance; that familiar temptation to falsify a condition of one's birth or identity and pretend to be part of a more favored group. Fair-skinned blacks invented "passing" as a term, Jews escaping anti-Semitism perfected the art, and the sexual closet continues the punishment, but pretending to be a younger age is probably the most encouraged form of "passing," with the least organized support for "coming out" as one's true generational self. I can testify to some of this undermining temptation because I fell for it in my pre-feminist thirties, after I had made myself younger to get a job and write an exposé of what was then presented as the glamorous job of Playboy bunny—and was in reality an underpaid waitressing job in a torturing costume.[6] In the resulting confusion about my age, the man I was living with continued the fiction with all good will (he had been married to an actress and believed a woman would have to be crazy to tell her real age), as did some of my sister's children, who thought she and I were two years younger. I perpetuated this difference myself for a couple of miserable years. I say miserable, because I learned that falsifying this one fact about my life made me feel phony, ridiculous, complicit, and, worst of all, undermined by my own hand. It all had to do with motive, of course, because lying to get the job and write the exposé had been the same kind of unashamed adventure I undertook as a teenager when I made myself much older to get work selling clothes after school or dancing in operettas. Falsifying oneself out of insecurity and a need to conform is very different from defeating society's age bias. It's letting the age bias defeat you.

That was why, when I turned forty, I did so publicly—with enormous relief. When a reporter kindly said I didn't look forty (a well-meaning comment but ageist when you think about it), I said the first thing that came into my head: "This is what forty looks like. We've been lying so long, who would know?" That one remark got so many relieved responses from women that I began to sense the depth and dimension of age oppression, and how strong the double standard of aging remains. Since then, I've learned that for many women, passing and worrying about being found out is as constantly debilitating as an aching tooth—since one has to conceal the pain, perhaps more painful.

I've met women who broke the law by forging their passports; who limited their lives by refusing to travel so they wouldn't have to get a passport; who told the men they married or lived with that they were as much as a decade younger than they really were; who had grown children whom they deceived; or who had mothers whose ages were not known until their deaths—with all the years of pretense each of those must have meant. I've listened to women who were working without health or pension plans because they feared they would have no jobs at all if their real ages were known; several who concealed academic degrees because their dates would have put them over a mandatory retirement age; and one amazing seventy-three-year-old who had successfully convinced her employer that she was fifty and wanted to be paid as a consultant rather than be on the payroll—"for tax reasons." As I write this, newscasters are telling the story of a nameless woman in Israel who convinced her doctor that she was forty-eight in order to become eligible for the implantation in her womb of a fertilized egg, and so gave birth—at sixty. Her doctor said he never would have provided this service if he had known her real age. Meanwhile, France has just passed a law against "medically assisted procreation" for post-menopausal women—on the grounds that this possibility might cause women to further delay having children, and the government is already concerned about France's falling birthrate. It makes you understand why women lie.

If all the women now pressured to lie were to tell their ages, our ideas of what fifty-five or sixty or seventy-five looks like would change overnight—and even doctors might learn a thing or two. More important, women telling the truth without fear would be a joyous "coming out." Yet, as with lesbian women and gay men who have given the culture that phrase as a paradigm of honesty, only people who freely choose to "come out" can diminish the fear others feel.

Those are only the beginning of the parallels with other social justice movements. There is also the political impotence that comes from invisibility as a constituency, one we increase when we deny our generational peers. We lose their power and comfort, they lose the added talents we could bring, and everyone is diminished. Conversely, once we identify, we both get and give strength. After a conference on women and aging in Boston, for instance, I asked participants what in its program had been useful. More helpful than all the information, they said, had been the act of walking past a sign in the hotel lobby that clearly announced a meeting of women over fifty. "For the first time since I was thirty-five," said one woman, "I felt proud of my age. I saw all those other terrific women walking in —as if it were the most natural thing in the world." Which, of course, it was.

On the other hand, segregation by age is just as unfair as that by race, sex, or anything else. We may decide to be with peers, but it has to be free choice. The ability to do the job, pay for the apartment, or pass the entrance exam is the point—and it's no one's business why or how we decided to take that action. Yet feminist groups, too, judge older women by age instead of individuality, and are more concerned about attracting the young than including the old—to put it mildly. I myself have written many feminist statements that touch on different constituencies in order to be inclusive, but in retrospect, I think almost every racial, ethnic, or occupational group has got more mentions than women over, say, sixty-five. Moreover, in nearly twenty-five years of feminist press conferences and questions from reporters, I can't now think of one that focused on women over sixty.

The results of feeling alone, isolated, and no longer viable in society's eyes stretch from the largest and most obviously political to the deepest and most supposedly personal. As Barbara Macdonald has pointed out, major parts of our conversation at any age are about our bodies. Adolescent girls compare notes about breast development and menstrual periods, young women about contraception and pregnancy, and all of us about sexuality and general health. Yet older women are made to feel that their version of such discussions is somehow embarrassing, not worthy of younger listeners, or proof of the myth that older people talk constantly about aches and pains —though personally, I know of no evidence that an older woman who breaks her hip talks about it more than a young woman with a leg in a cast from a ski accident, or a middle-aged man with a tennis elbow. Until a feminist generation began to talk about menopause or life after fifty, neither was an open topic of conversation; yet the interest must have been there. It has made a perennial best-seller of *Ourselves, Growing Older,* by the Boston Women's Health Book Collective, and recent best-sellers of books by Germaine Greer, Gail Sheehy, and Betty Friedan. It's in everyone's best interest that women past fifty or sixty or even ninety continue health and body discussions. Not only does the group in question gain the community no one should be without, but they help younger women to fill in the blank screen of imagined futures.

But the resistance to this movement is familiar too. Older employees are stereotyped as out of touch or less able to work, though the former is an individual question at any age and statistics on the latter show that to the contrary, older employees are less likely to be absentee and more likely to be responsible. The usual tactic of divide and conquer is going full steam too, with younger people being told that older ones who resist retirement are taking their jobs away, just as women of every race were said to be taking away the jobs of men of color, or immigrants were said to be causing unemployment among the native born. Looking at each situation shows the facts to be quite different; that jobs and skills are rarely competing. With age especially, this tactic is usually employed by companies trying to fire experienced employees who earn more and replace them with younger employees who earn less.

In recent years, I've noticed that even my accidental statement— "This is what forty looks like. We've been lying so long, who would know?"—has lost its second sentence when quoted. Instead of the plural that implied we are all fine as we are—which was the point— only the singular was left, as if there were only one way to look. Small as this may be, it's a symbol of the will to divide. So is a telephone call I just got from *Redbook.* For an article on aging, the reporter was asking, "How do you stay young?"

There is no such thing as being individually free in the face of a collective bias, just as with racism, or anti-Semitism, or prejudice against all but the able-bodied. Instead of treating my age as just another attribute, which was the goal, I found myself announcing it in any speech or public setting, whether age was relevant or not. It is one of the many ways we honor restrictions by striving to do their opposite.

. . .

In the past, I also put energy into trying to live up to society's expectations *and* trying to resist them. From my teenage years into my mid-thirties, the goal was to conform (or at least to appear to). I felt an uncertainty, a lack of self-authority, that came from a big dose of the "feminine" role, textbooks from which the female half of the human race was almost totally missing, and a conviction that living a conventional life would be better than my mother's fate of being poor, depressed, and alone with a child to rear. (Having not yet sorted out myth from reality, I didn't realize that her fate *was* conventional.) After feminism arrived in my thirties to show me that women had a right to every human choice, I began conscious resistance to all that. I found such usefulness and pleasure, such relief and companionship, in taking a different path that I assumed I was becoming as radical and rebellious as I could get.

After all, not only were I and other feminists treated as crazies—which we were, in the sense of wanting something that had never been—but unlike most feminists and women in general, I had skipped the years of raising a family and had created a chosen family of friends, lovers, and colleagues instead. Furthermore, I'd begun to work full time in this longest of all revolutions, and I felt lucky to be spending my days on what I cared about most, work so infinitely interesting, worthwhile, and close to the bone of my own and other women's hopes and survival that it rarely seemed like work at all. Because I was traveling around the country as an organizer and as part of a speaking team, I was seeing women flower and change in a miraculous way that continues on a far larger scale now, but was then a surprise every day, from the first sanity-saving realization "I am not alone" to the talent-freeing discovery "I am unique." Whether I was with Dorothy Pitman Hughes, a pioneer of community child care, or lawyer and feminist activist Florynce Kennedy, or organizer and writer Margaret Sloan, the most important thing we did was to make a space for women to come together—in groups that might be anything from a few dozen in a church basement to a few thousand in a lecture hall—and hear experiences confirmed by each other's lives. That our team was a black woman and a white woman together made audiences much more diverse and seemed to spread an implicit faith in crossing boundaries. In discussions that lasted longer than our speeches, women answered one another's questions, and men in the audience heard women telling the truth.

What I remember most about those years was being flooded with the frequent feeling: *If I'd done only this in my life and nothing more, it would have been enough.* Each day, I thought the next couldn't possibly be more intense and satisfying—and then it was.

After the first year or so of organizing had proved this changing consciousness was a contagion, *Ms.* magazine became one of the many local and national groups to be born from the energy. Though I had stoutly maintained I was entering into this group effort for only two years, and then going back to my life as a freelance writer, working on *Ms.* magazine, helping to start other feminist groups, and traveling as an organizer became my life.

After almost two decades of no week without traveling, speaking, fund-raising, brainstorming, deadlining, begging, arguing, and the incredible intensity of hope that any good movement is built on, I couldn't imagine a future that could be more rebellious or satisfying or stretched further from the rules. But I was also fragmented and burned out, realizing at the margins of my consciousness that the world was fading from color to shades of gray. Though not down-trodden, I felt down*pressed*—by pressures I myself had chosen. Even my cast-iron constitution was beginning to give way, and I felt more sharply than ever the unfairness of the pinched resources on which women at *Ms.* and other parts of the movement were required to perform daily miracles, while testosterone-fueled corporations lavished millions on, say, one magazine prototype that failed, or a corporate takeover that lost jobs. Of course, there was always the joy of working with the people and possibilities I loved, but the very intensity of my feelings made me more conscious of what they deserved—and weren't receiving. Nevertheless, as many women do, I went right on responding, explaining, responding again, reexplaining, and re-reexplaining as required, even if I was sometimes doing it on automatic pilot.

At about the same time—perhaps because I was so drained, something in my unconscious knew I needed to look at this—I began thinking about the need to link self-esteem to revolution. In almost two decades of traveling, plus the years of reading letters to *Ms.* of such intensity and diversity that the Schlesinger Library has since cataloged them as a populist record of the movement,[7] I'd come to know the stories of brave and talented women of all classes, ages, races, sexualities, and abilities, too many of whom assumed they were somehow "not good enough," even though they were performing miraculous feats under hard circumstances. I'd read and heard too many valuable sentences prefaced with phrases like: "It's probably only me, but . . . ," suitable words, I sometimes thought, for almost any woman's epitaph. Sure enough, when I finally had a little quiet in which to think and write (thanks to the fact that two Australian feminists had come along with investment money to keep *Ms.* going when our shoestring had worn to a thread), I discovered I'd been responding to outside emergencies for so long that I'd lost what little I had of the muscle that allows us to *act* instead of *react*.

Though I'd been countering my childhood and "feminine" conditioning with an activism that was half the battle—it still was only half. I didn't regret one second of the years spent chipping away at a sexual caste system that oppresses women's spirits and distorts men's too, but I'd been submerging myself, not in the traditional needs of husband and children, true, but in the needs of others nonetheless. Having been bred by class and gender to know what other people wanted and needed better than I knew my own wants and needs, I had turned all my antennae outward. Focusing on women as a group had been a giant leap forward, for their needs were mine too. But no one could know my unique talents and demons unless I took them seriously enough to express.

It wasn't a question of getting back into a balance between the internal and the external, the self and others. As a well-socialized woman, I'd never been in balance. I wouldn't have known balance if I'd tripped over it. Even thinking about it was a new event.

For three years, *Revolution from Within*,[8] the book that resulted from this exploring that began a few years after I turned fifty, was a living, breathing presence in my life. It helped me to know with certainty that our inner selves are no more important than an outer reality—but no less important either. Could I have learned this earlier? I don't know. Certainly, I would have been a more effective activist if I had. I would have been better able to stand up to conflict and criticism, to focus on what I could uniquely do instead of trying to do everything, and to waste less time confusing motion with action. But perhaps I couldn't explore internally until I stopped living in an external pressure cooker. Or perhaps I had to exhaust myself on half the circle before I could appreciate the other half. In a larger sense, it doesn't matter. The art of life isn't controlling what happens, which is impossible; it's using what happens.

Gradually, I discovered I was researching and writing what I needed to learn. What I started out to address in other women, I myself shared: the need to treat ourselves as well as we treat others. It's women's version of the Golden Rule.

In fact, I have yet to meet a woman who has completely kicked the habit of leading a derived life. Even if we've refused to be hyper-responsible for the welfare of a family, we often feel too responsible for what goes on at work. Even if we're no longer trying to surgically transplant our egos into the body of a husband or children, we still may be overly dependent on being needed—by coworkers and bosses, lovers and friends, even by the very movements that were intended to free us of all that.

For myself, learning this lesson was definitely a function of age. I wasn't ready to admit how deeply into my brain cells and viscera the social role had permeated while I was still within the age range of its grasp.

Once I began to listen to my own authentic voice—or at least to realize I had one—I discovered a new answer to my earlier rhetorical question: How much more rebellious could I get? The answer was: A lot. I found anger as a source of energy within myself, or in the wonderful phrase of Patricia Williams—writer, law professor, and African-American feminist—"a gift of intelligent rage."[9]

As it turns out, love and anger are both emotions of the free will, yet only love is acceptable for the powerless to express. For women or any category of people whose fair treatment would upset the social order, anger becomes the most punished and dangerous emotion. Therefore, showing it is also a sign of freedom. It's an honesty without which love, too, eventually becomes a sham. So for me, it was and is a step forward to say: I feel anger when I remember how much time I had to spend explaining myself; explaining what was wrong; explaining "what women want"; or explaining at all. I feel anger that I had to fight against living in a culturally deprived, white-only box of the sort this society creates to limit our friends and keep our labels clear. I feel anger that I've studied history, watched television, and obeyed governments in which I saw so little that looked like my half of the human race, or the diversity of the country. I feel anger that all of the above are still happening in varying degrees of painfulness; for instance, that I and others still require adjectives, while those who define go unadorned. Just what is the difference between a *woman* writer and a writer? a *black* surgeon and a surgeon? a *lesbian* athlete and an athlete? a *disabled* mathematician and a mathematician? Why does the operative definition of a *special issue* turn out to be any issue not important to the speaker? And why is the word "qualified" applied only to those who have to be more so? Why are women raped far away (say, Bosnia) called *victims,* while those raped nearby (say, a local campus) are playing *victim politics?*

Finally, I feel angry that the righteous anger I did manage to express in the past was denigrated as unprofessional or self-defeating, or more subtly suppressed when others praised me as calm, reasonable, not one of those "angry feminists." (How do we fall victim to the "good girl" syndrome? Let me count the ways.)

But it's a healthy anger that warms my heart, loosens my tongue, leaves me feeling ever more impatient and energized, and gives me a what-the-hell kind of courage. At last, I'm beginning to ignore the rules altogether—by just *not paying tribute to them,* whether by conforming *or* confronting. Now, messages I once heard only with my head go straight to my heart.

For instance, these words from a woman whose birth year I share, the late and well-loved poet Audre Lorde:

> I speak without concern for the accusations
> that I am too much or too little woman
> that I am too Black or too white
> or too much myself[10]

Or these from writer and scholar Carolyn Heilbrun, now in her mid-sixties, about the heroine of the mysteries she writes as "Amanda Cross"—who is therefore herself:

> . . . she has become braver as she has aged, less interested in the opinions of those she does not cherish, and has come to realize that she has little to lose, little any longer to risk, that age above all, both for those with children and those without them, is the time when there is very little "they" can do for you, very little reason to fear, or hide, or not attempt brave and important things.[11]

In other words, I'm becoming more radical with age.

I don't know why I'm surprised by this. When I was forty-five, I wrote an essay about the female journey as being the reverse of the traditional male one.[12] Men tend to rebel when young and become more conservative with age, while women tend to be more conservative when young and become rebellious and radical as we grow older. I'd noticed this pattern in the suffragist/abolitionist era, when women over fifty, sixty, even seventy were a disproportionate number of the activists and leaders—think of Sojourner Truth and Susan B. Anthony, or Elizabeth Cady Stanton and Ida B. Wells—but I'd assumed it was due to the restrictions placed on younger women by uncontrolled childbirth and a status as household chattel: hard facts that limited all but a few single or widowed white women, and all but even fewer free women of color. Yet when I looked at the current wave of feminism, I was surprised to find that the age of self-respecting activism wasn't all that different. The critical mass were still women of thirty, forty, fifty, or beyond—only a decade or so younger than their suffragist counterparts. I realized that most women in their teens and twenties hadn't yet experienced one or more of the great radicalizing events of a woman's life: marrying and discovering it isn't yet an equal (or even nonviolent) institution; getting into the paid labor force and experiencing its limits, from the corporate "glass ceiling" to the "sticky floor" of the pink-collar ghetto; having children and finding out who takes care of them and who doesn't; and, finally, aging, still the most impoverishing event for women of every race and so potentially the most radicalizing. To put it another way, if young women have a problem, it's only that they think there's no problem.*

I wrote that essay because I was angry with the media—though you probably would have had to be on LSD to sense it from my calm prose—for assuming that the male cultural pattern of rebelling in youth and growing more conservative with age was the only one. Indeed, reporters still look for the red-hot center of feminist activism on campus—and in the male style of dropping out of the system, though it's often more radical for women to drop in—thus missing the activist centers of battered women's shelters, rape crisis hot lines, child support and custody actions, economic development groups,

---

* Which makes the many organizations of young women active on their own behalf more remarkable. Their number is growing. For instance, Students Organizing Students (SOS, 1600 Broadway, Suite 404, New York, N.Y. 10019), a national feminist student and youth movement; the Third Wave (185 Franklin Street, New York, N.Y. 10013), a multiracial, direct-action group, whose first activity was Freedom Summer, 1992, a bus caravan that crisscrossed the country to register voters in poor areas; and the Young Women's Project (1511 K Street, N.W., Suite 428, Washington, D.C. 20005), a national organization that promotes political activism. There are many more such groups at a local level.

pink-collar organizing, and many other sources of energy. If my essay had little impact on journalists, however, I have to admit that it also had little impact on my sense of my own life. I still thought I was reporting on others, and failed to sense that this cultural pattern of growing more radical with age was also happening within myself.

I don't know what I imagined the last thirty or forty years of my life were going to be. Perhaps just more of the same, for I thought I had already disobeyed the rules. After all, I'd left my childbearing years behind without following a traditional pattern. Furthermore, I was constantly aware that very few people, male or female, could work full-time at what they loved without starving. Or perhaps I'd just been confronted so often in my life with people who insisted, "You're so different from those other ———" (fill in the blank with the group of your choice), that I'd fallen into thinking I was an exception to the trends I myself observed.

What I'd forgotten is that patriarchy creates megapatterns that affect us all—even as we forge different individual choices within them—just as do the megapatterns of nationalism or racism. This amnesia on my part was all the more remarkable because I knew I'd shared many of the experiences leading up to that more-rebellious-with-age conclusion. For instance:

• I, too, believed when I was in high school and college, as my textbooks led me to, that everything had been solved decades earlier by worthy but boring, asexual suffragists about whom I knew very little, except that I didn't want to be like them. *Today's young women are encouraged to feel somewhat the same way about feminists who preceded them, a conscious or unconscious way of stopping change by cutting off the supply of changemakers.*

• I, too, thought marriage would shape my life more than any other single influence—which was why I kept putting off what seemed to be the death of choice. *Young women now can be more honest about delaying marriage or choosing a different path. But if they do marry, they still end up with a life more shaped by marriage than their husband's life is likely to be.*

• I, too, identified with every underdog in the world before realizing there was a reason, that women are primordial underdogs. *Today, many young women still take injustice more seriously if it affects any group except women, and support other causes before having the self-respect to stand up for their own.*

There's a lesson here about who's encouraged to have a sense of belonging and who isn't. Whether the category is as specialized as "physicians" or as generalized as "white males," members of a powerful group are raised to believe (however illogically) that whatever affects it will also affect them. On the other hand, members of less powerful groups are raised to believe (however illogically) that each individual can escape the group's fate. Thus, cohesion is encouraged on the one hand, and disunity is fostered on the other.

Though I would have been delighted to think that I, too, could grow more radical and rebellious with age, for instance, the habit of exempting myself won out. With few role models of daring, take-no-shit older women in my history books, or my family history as transmitted to me (though both held many in reality)—and with even the rebellious older women I had written about consigned to the category of "other" prescribed by my reporter's role—my own future remained a hazy screen.

Since "radical" is often turned into a word as negative as "aging," perhaps I should explain why, as a person who came of age in the conservative 1950s, I came to believe it was a good thing. There were two experiences that shaped its positive meaning for me, one of them a decade before feminism came into my life, the other in the way it finally arrived.

The fall after graduating from college, I went to India on a year's fellowship. (Remember my tactic of delaying marriage? Well, India was not only a place I'd always wanted to go to, but an escape from a very kind and tempting man to whom I was engaged, but knew I shouldn't marry.) To my surprise, I found that I felt more at home and involved there than I ever had in any other country not my own. I stayed for another year doing freelance writing. In that diverse country that welcomes foreigners with the same equanimity that allowed it to absorb foreign cultures for centuries and yet remain unique, the students at the women's college of the University of Delhi accepted me as one of two Westerners to live there. They taught me to wear saris and were generally more instructive about India than was the curriculum, which was still shaped by the English system. In the same period, I was also befriended by a group of gentle activists and intellectuals known as the Radical Humanists. From listening to their energetic analyzing of world events, I learned that "radical" didn't have to mean violent, extremist, or crazy, as a reading of U.S. newspapers had led me to believe. It could mean exactly what the dictionary said: going to the root.

Though many Radical Humanists, women and men, had started out as members of the Communist Party of India when it was supporting the Indian Independence Movement, they had left once the Party did an about-face during World War II and supported the British Raj—an evidence of its allegiance to Soviet needs rather than Indian members. Like many friends who were Gandhians, and who also were to show me new alternatives, these activists felt they had progressed beyond such Marxist tenets as "the end justifies the means." Their experiences caused me to rethink my romance with Marxism, which had started in college when Joseph McCarthy's persecution of actual or imagined Communists made them seem admirable by comparison. As the Radical Humanists pointed out, the means we choose dictate the ends we achieve—so much so that one might more accurately say, "the means *are* the ends." M. N. Roy, one of their founders, wrote that "the end justifies the means . . . eventually brought about the moral degeneration of the international communist movement."[13]

As Gandhians explained, the goal was *swaraj*—a Hindi word meaning both freedom and self-rule. Gandhi also used natural imagery: "the means may be likened to a seed, the end to a tree."[14]

I remember my first hands-on experience with activism that consciously reflected a future goal in its present tactic. I'd been traveling through South India on my own, having passed beyond the friendly chain of Radical Humanists in the north. As I made my way down the coast from Calcutta, I discovered that a Westerner in a sari was no more strange than someone from a distant part of India might have been, and that my English-with-a-little-Hindi was as useful (or useless) as some of the other fourteen major languages of India. In the women's car of third-class trains and in public hostels, I found myself struggling to respond to the very un-British, thoroughly Indian habit of asking personal questions. In my case, this meant probing everything from why I wasn't married to whether I knew how to have fewer children—by methods their husbands couldn't discover.

When I went inland by rickety bus to visit one of the ashrams started by Vinoba Bhave—a disciple of Gandhi who was asking village landowners to give part of their acreage to the poor—Bhave and most of his coworkers had already left; not on one of their usual pilgrimages to ask for land donations, but walking from village to village through Ramnad, a nearby rural area where caste riots had broken out. Government officials in faraway Delhi had responded by embargoing all news coming out of the area and closing it off in the hope that burnings and killings could be kept from spreading. Nonetheless, Bhave's teams had walked in on their own. Instead of asking people to stay in their houses, they were holding village meetings. Instead of a chain of vengeance, they were offering Gandhian nonviolence. Instead of weapons, they were carrying only a cup and a comb, knowing that if villagers wanted peace, they would feed and house the peacemakers, thus becoming part of the process.

Their problem was that no woman was left in the ashram to join a last team of three. Men couldn't go into the women's quarters to invite women out to meetings, and if there was no woman at the meeting, other women were unlikely to come. The question was: Would I go with them? Bhave's coworkers assured me I wouldn't seem any more odd than others from outside the area. They themselves were trusted only because of their work in creating land trusts for the poor. Besides, part of their mission was to show villagers that people outside this isolated area knew and cared what was happening to them.

For the next few days, we walked from one village to the next—sitting under trees for meetings in the cool of the early morning, walking during the heat of the day, and holding more meetings around kerosene lamps at night. Mostly, we just listened. There were so many stories of atrocities and vengeance, so much anger and fear, that it was hard to imagine how it could end. But gradually, people expressed relief at having been listened to, at seeing neighbors who had been too afraid to come out of their houses, and at hearing facts brought by Bhave's team, for the rumors were even more terrible than the events themselves. To my amazement, long and emotion-filled meetings often ended with village leaders pledging to take no revenge on caste groups whose members had attacked their group in a neighboring village, and to continue meetings of their own.

Each day, we set off along paths shaded by palms and sheltered by banyan trees, cut across plowed fields, and waded into streams to cool off and let our homespun clothes dry on us as we walked. In the villages, families shared their food and sleeping mats with us, women taught me how to wash my sari and wash and oil my hair, and shopkeepers offered us rice cakes and sweet milky tea in the morning. I found there was a freedom in having no possessions but a sari, a cup, and a comb, and, even in the midst of turmoil, a peacefulness in focusing only on the moment at hand. I remember this as the first time in my life when I was living completely in the present.

Toward the end, when the violence had quieted down, my unseasoned feet had become so blistered that infection set in, and I hitched a ride in an oxcart back to the bus route, and to the ashram. But I ended those days with regret. I had also learned the truth of what I once disdained as an impractical and impossibly idealistic Gandhian saying: *If you do something the people care about, the people will take care of you.*

From our team leader, a no-nonsense man in his seventies who had devoted his life to this kind of direct action—to tactics that were a microcosm of their goal—I also remember this radical advice:

If you want people to listen to you, you have to listen to them.

If you hope people will change how they live, you have to know how they live.

If you want people to see you, you have to sit down with them eye-to-eye.

Most of us have a few events that divide our lives into "before" and "after." This was one for me.

When I finally traveled back home to my own country, these lessons didn't seem very portable. If "radical" is often misunderstood now, consider how it sounded in 1958, with Eisenhower still President and fears of McCarthyite persecution still in the air. At least at a visible level, there was no populist movement against the Cold War; no women's movement; not even an understanding yet that hunger existed in this country; and only a few groups working on such issues as fallout from nuclear testing, plus civil rights events that had not yet become a movement. As for India, it hadn't yet appeared on this nation's media radar as anything other than a place of former British power and present poverty. Even the Beatles hadn't discovered India yet (indeed, there were no Beatles), and if I brought up India, an island of polite silence would appear in the conversation—and then the talk would flow right on around it.

I was in shock myself, for I was seeing my own overdeveloped country through the eyes of the underdeveloped world for the first time. In search of imagery for this revelation, I remember saying to all who would listen, "Imagine a giant frosted cupcake in the midst of hungry millions." What really ran through my head like a naive mantra was: *This can't last.*

Because India had accustomed me to seeing a rainbow of skin colors, I was also realizing belatedly that in my own multiracial country, you could go snowblind from white faces in any business area or "good" neighborhood. True, skin color in India often carried the cruelty of caste, but a South Indian Brahman might have darker skin than a North Indian harijan (the Gandhian term for "untouchable"), and since all had suffered collectively under British rule, there was at least a striving for a shared identity. Furthermore, Indians described nuances of color as unselfconsciously as any other aspect of appearance. It made me realize that the deafening silence about color in my own upbringing had not been polite but just another way of saying that being anything other than white was impolite. I began to see how caste-divided this country was, how dishonest we were in discussing it, and how effective was this training that I had to experience a different society in order to see.

Sometimes my culture shock took surrealistic forms. In New York, where I had been sleeping on my friends' living room floors while trying to find a job, I remember insisting on riding in the front seat with taxi drivers. My sense memory of sitting in an Indian tonga —a two-wheeled cart pulled by a man riding a bicycle or running between the staves—was so strong that I felt engulfed by the unacceptable experience of being driven by another human being. Of course, a Calcutta tonga wallah had little to do with a New York taxi driver, but the images of the recent past were still imprinted on my eyes, and the world looked very different when viewed through them. I alternated between trying to explain what I'd experienced in India and leaving gatherings I couldn't handle because the contrast was too painful.

In other words, I must have been a terrible pain in the ass.

The more I became acclimated to my own country, however, the more India began to seem like two years dropped out of my life—a time whose intensity and lessons I would never be able to match or make use of. Some of my trying to explain was really trying to catch what was slipping away. Though I attempted to work in student politics, it also didn't yet exist as a movement. I was far too broke and impatient to consider any graduate school.

Finally, I began to work as a freelance writer, but the assignments I could get as a "girl reporter" often widened the gap between what I was working on and what I cared about. I was drawn to the civil rights and anti-Vietnam movements that were becoming public events by then, but they were not the assignments given to girl reporters. I found myself paying the rent with humor and advice pieces for women's magazines (while going to a school desegregation rally in Virginia or a civil rights march in Washington); writing about the mayor's wife or a fashion designer because I was impressed to get a freelance assignment from *The New York Times* (while lobbying for Peace Corps volunteers to go to communities in India); profiling actors, dancers, and other celebrities for various magazines and newspapers (while organizing with writers and editors to refuse to pay that portion of our taxes going to the Vietnam war); and writing about the "ins" and "outs" of pop culture for *Life* (while trying to get Cesar Chavez and his new United Farm Workers on the cover of *Time* as protection against threats on his life from California growers). It wasn't that I disliked what I was doing. On the contrary, I liked Mary Lindsay, the mayor's wife, I loved writing satire for an *Esquire* campus issue or *That Was the Week That Was* on television, and I enjoyed learning about people while profiling them, from James Baldwin and Margot Fonteyn to Dorothy Parker and Truman Capote. But I never felt fully engaged, as if I were leading other than a derived life. Some of the tactics of those anti-Vietnam days made me feel more estranged than I had in India, for I had absorbed the idea that violent means are unlikely to reach a peaceful end—that ends and means are a seamless web—and this philosophy wasn't always guiding the most public events of the peace movement.

When *New York* magazine was founded—aided by a group of us who were to be its regular writers—this gap between work and interest narrowed somewhat. At least I could write about electoral politics, social justice movements, and neighborhood organizing in New York; all assignments that other magazines and newspapers usually gave to male reporters. But I was still a long way from the hands-on, organic, personal kind of activism I had glimpsed in India. Indeed, I had put it out of my mind.

In the movements of the 1960s, there was a saying: "You only get radicalized on your own concerns." That was to prove true again in the way feminism arrived in my life.

It wasn't the first brave, reformist variety of the mid-1960s that woke me up. Though I was old enough to be part of the *Feminine Mystique* generation, I wasn't living in the suburbs, wondering why I wasn't using my college degree. I'd ended up in the workforce many of these other women were then trying to enter. Though college had taken me out of my blue-collar Toledo neighborhood and made me a middle-class person, I shared the reaction of many working-class women and women of color: *I support women who want to get out of the suburbs and into jobs,* I thought to myself, *but I'm already in the workforce and getting screwed. The women's movement isn't for me.* Given the contrast between India and this country's share of the world's resources, I also had another reservation: *Sure, women should get a fair share of the pie, but what we really need is a new pie.*

By the end of the 1960s, younger women were coming out of the civil rights and peace movements with similar feelings. They also had a new phrase, "women's liberation," which addressed all women as a caste. Instead of integrating current systems, they were taking on the patriarchy and racism at their base. Instead of trying to make "feminine" equal to "masculine," they were joining all human qualities into a full circle that was available to everyone. At their speak-outs, I listened to stories of experiences I, too, had known, but had never put into words. When I covered as a reporter an early feminist hearing on abortion, I heard personal testimonies to the sufferings brought on by having to enter a criminal underworld. I had had an abortion too, but I'd been lucky enough to be in England, where laws were slightly less punishing. It was just after college, but I never forgot the weeks of panic before I found a doctor, or how it changed my life to be able to continue the trip to India that was about to begin; yet I'd never spoken to anyone about this major experience in my life. Since one in three or four women had undergone an abortion even then, I began to wonder *why* it was illegal; *why* our reproductive lives were not under our own control; and *why* this fundamental issue hadn't been part of any other social justice movement. It was a time of epiphanies. I remember sitting amazed in front of my television set watching Anne Koedt, Anselma Dell'Olio, Betty Dodson, and other early feminists talk about sexuality on an obscure local show. It was the first time I'd ever heard women be sexually honest in public (it was rare enough in private) or take on Freud's myth of the vaginal orgasm (about which Koedt had just written an essay that was to become a classic).[15] I started asking *why* women were supposed to have sex but not talk about it; *why* Freud got away with calling women "immature" for failing to have a male-fantasy orgasm; and *why* the so-called sexual liberation movement of the 1960s had been mostly about making more women sexually available on male terms.

God may be in the details, but the goddess is in the questions. Once we begin to ask them, there's no turning back. Instead of trying to fit women into existing middle-class professions or working-class theory, these radical feminist groups assumed that women's experience should be the root of theory. Whether at speak-outs or consciousness-raising groups, "talking circles" or public hearings, the essential idea was: *Tell your personal truth, listen to other women's stories, see what themes are shared, and discover that the personal is political—you are not alone.*

I'm not sure feminism should require an adjective. Believing in the full social, political, and economic quality of women, which is what the dictionary says "feminism" means, is enough to make a revolution in itself. But if I had to choose only one adjective, I still would opt for *radical* feminist. I know patriarchs keep equating that word with *violent* or *man-hating, crazy* or *extremist*—though being a plain vanilla *feminist* doesn't keep one safe from such epithets either, nor does "I'm not a feminist, but . . ." Nonetheless, *radical* seems an honest indication of the fundamental change we have in mind and says what probably is the case: the false division of human nature into "feminine" and "masculine" is the root of all other divisions into subject and object, active and passive—the beginning of hierarchy. Since that division comes from the patriarchal need to control women's bodies as the means of reproduction—a control that racial "purity" and caste and class systems are built on—digging out the "masculine/feminine" paradigm undermines all birth-based hierarchies, and alters our view of human nature, the natural world, and the cosmos itself. Just a few little things like that.

Everything comes together once we've found the work for which experience and temperament suit us. I've been traveling around this country every week for most of the last twenty-five years, working with many women and some men in the kind of direct-action organizing I first saw and was so magnetized by in India. Only recently have I understood the resonance between what I have been doing and that long-ago and long-buried turning point. I find the wisdom of our Ramnad team leader still holds true: *you have to listen. . . . you have to know . . . you have to sit down eye-to-eye.*

As for the Gandhian adage *If you do something the people care about, the people will take care of you,* I have to admit there is a big difference here. Walking from village to village could get you arrested, and having to pay for your own airline ticket is very different from hitching a ride on a bullock cart. But like other traveling feminists or organizers for other movements who bring hope in anything like a commonsense way, I do notice that the ticket clerk sometimes saves three seats across so I can sleep; flight attendants may slip me a healthier meal from first class; airport cleaning women stop to tell me about the latest woman candidate from their neighborhoods; women now able to mother other women stock our car with spring water and apples; and even such brief contact as seeing women standing in highway toll booths yields good advice about the traffic or the weather. "It's going to rain, honey," one of them said kindly to me last week. "Want to borrow my umbrella?" A movement is only composed of people moving. To feel its warmth and motion around us is the end as well as the means.

Even our faults can be useful if we're willing to expose them. Because I was scared to death of public speaking, for instance, I often began lectures by explaining that only the women's movement had given me a reason worth making a damn fool of myself, that I'd never spoken publicly at all until I was in my mid-thirties, and that if I could do it, anyone could. It was this fear that led me to speaking in teams in the beginning—which turned out to be a helpful tactic. It's this fear now that makes me look forward to a discussion time in which the audience takes over and creates its own organizing meeting. Invariably the result is better than anything I or any single speaker could produce. In this way, I learned that being able to use all of ourselves, whether positive or negative, is a good sign that we're doing the right thing.

I've learned from the collective wisdom of these audiences, from the late-night groups that gather after meetings, individuals who stop me in the street to tell me stories of changes in their lives, people who write letters that should be books, populist researchers who send clippings with crucial passages marked, strangers who share what might be difficult to say to friends, and people in groups everywhere who are especially valuable as advisers about what I or others could be doing better.

I've always been hooked on this "found wisdom," as I've come to think of it. When I went back to India almost twenty years after my student days, I realized it was a form of populist teaching to be preserved. I met with Indira Gandhi—then prime minister, though she had been a lonely and uncertain young woman when I first saw her—and she told me the story of her own third-class travels around India as a young mother in crowded women-only railway cars like the ones I remembered. On learning that she had only two children, women invariably asked her: "How did you do it?" And often: "How can I keep my husband from knowing? How can I keep him from thinking I'll be unfaithful?"

As prime minister, she defied population experts who insisted that poor and illiterate women didn't want birth control, or couldn't understand it until they became literate, or would accept it only if their husbands approved. She instituted family planning programs that were the first to offer women contraception in private. She also offered small financial rewards for men who agreed to be sterilized, and told health workers to explain to them that this way, husbands would know if their wives were being unfaithful. Those measures were very controversial, but often more effective than the conventional ones. She received delegations of grateful women, and also criticism within her own country and in international circles for encouraging male sterilization. But the day we talked, she seemed unperturbed. She had never forgotten the words or the desperation of her populist women teachers.

On this same trip in the late 1970s, I was often told by academics, reporters, and others in India's big cities that feminism was a Western phenomenon, that it had no roots in India. I later learned that unknown to many in the cities, a movement called Stree Shakti Jagritti (Women's Power Awakening) had been organizing conferences and padyataras (foot journeys) through rural India. Combining women's issues with the teachings of Gandhi and Vinoba Bhave, both of whom honored their populist women teachers by saying that only awakening the inner strength of women could overcome India's obstacles, this movement had been working since the 1950s on everything from literacy campaigns to giving women small loans so they could produce and sell vegetables or handicrafts, and wouldn't be forced into prostitution. At the time I was being told feminism was peculiar to the West, 10,000 members of this loose federation of women workers were marching from village to village, asking women about their problems, helping them to organize, offering the principles of self-strength and nonviolence—just as we had done in a much smaller way two decades before. Though most of the funds and women came from the poor areas in which the work was being done, 75,000 women participated in the second padyatara.[16]

Now there is much more acknowledgment of the role of Indian feminist groups, urban as well as rural, in working for many forms of empowerment and against everything from sexual harassment in the workplace (often called Eve teasing in the Indian media) to the dowry murders that still take place when a husband or his family, wishing to acquire a second dowry, cause the "accidental" death of his first wife. But the truth is that every country has its own organic feminism. Far more than communism, capitalism, or any other philosophy I can think of, it is a grassroots event. It grows in women's heads and hearts.

Each day or week or month seems like a morass of confusion, missed plans, happenstance, and bewildering detail. One of the great advantages of age is a longer view that suddenly reveals patterns. An internal voice, an intrinsic set of values, a DNA that is powerful and unique within each of us—something has been organizing and occasionally prevailing over that morass of detail. It took me years to see the connections between discussions with Indian women in a third-class railroad car and the feelings that finally gave me the courage to speak in public, or the links between walking in Ramnad and getting on planes to unknown places with Dorothy or Flo or Margaret—but they were there. I'm looking forward to the still longer views that reveal more patterns, for they tell us what is true within us. That means we know what should be continued in the future.

I also see patterns of my resistance to what I knew in my heart I should do. Some people hang on to the familiar and the things they already know out of fear. Others do it out of defiance. The latter has always been my drug of choice. It's taken me a long time to realize that when I said so defiantly at fifty, "I'm going to go right on doing everything I did at thirty or forty," this was not progress. I was refusing to change, and thus robbing myself of the future. I'm indebted to Robin Morgan for reminding me that for women like us, defiance for defiance's sake is a political version of a face-lift—a denial of change.

Probably, hanging on to the past brings more destruction than any other single cause. It's the strict constructionists who prefer a literal U.S. Constitution to the mechanisms for change that were the greatest creation of its framers. It's the Muslim fundamentalists who worship the past and ignore the reformist spirit with which Muhammad viewed women. It's the backward-looking Christian literalists who interpret religious teachings in a way that consolidates their power. It's the fearful politicians who cite the "good old days" and tell us we're going to hell in a handbasket. Nostalgia may be the most tempting and deceptive form of opposition to change. In truth, no day or situation is identical with any other. To resist this constancy of change is to be as ridiculous as I was when I sat in front with a New York taxi driver. It's to be as dangerous as fundamentalists who bring glorification of death out of the past and into a nuclear present.

Clinging to the past is the problem. Embracing change is the solution. If we remember that our tactics must always reflect our goals, there will be a flexible structure of continuing values—not to mention greater success. There's no such thing as killing for peace, strengthening people by making their decisions for them, or suppressing dissent to gain freedom.

There's also no such thing as being fully conscious in the present while preoccupied with the past *or* the future. When I was in my twenties and thirties, I had a habit of mind that I just accepted then but realize now was robbing me of living the present. I used to fantasize pleasurably about being very old. Some part of my consciousness must have decided that only an acerbic, independent old lady would finally be free of the vulnerability and lack of seriousness that attach to female human beings. Only much later would I no longer be an interchangeable moving part, "a pretty girl," a group rather than an individual. Fortunately, by the time I was in my late thirties, feminism had helped me to understand that I could fight the role instead of wishing my life away. It makes no more sense to wish for age than to fear it. But not until I was past fifty did I read Carolyn Heilbrun's *Writing a Woman's Life* and understand that many women become ourselves after fifty, and that my odd habit of mind had a good political reason.

What we all need, whatever our age, are personal role models of living in the present—and a change that never ends. We need to know that life past sixty or seventy or eighty is as much an adventure as it ever was, perhaps more so for women, since we are especially likely to find new territory once the long plateau of our role is over. Explorers of this region have always existed in some number, but now their lights dancing on the path ahead will guide many more.

I think of Frieda Zames, who at the age of sixty-two is now answering reporters' questions about how she successfully integrated the Empire State Building, part of a class action suit against a number of hotels and office buildings that were not accessible to the disabled. In 1980, her work also helped put lifts on New York buses so disabled passengers could ride, and in 1984, she helped to make New York polling places accessible to disabled voters for the first time. Having retired as a professor of mathematics, she has more time for Disabled in Action, the civil rights group with which she works.[17] Felled early by polio, she spent her childhood in a hospital, and then became a mathematician—only to be told that high schools would not hire disabled teachers. She got an advanced degree, but discovered that being a woman was even more of a disability than getting around on crutches or a motorized scooter—at least, in the eyes of the all-male technological institute where she taught—so she became an activist twice over. She is now writing a book on the disability movement, and her scooter can often be seen at the head of demonstrations.

I think of Charlotta Spears Bass, who was a pioneering newspaper reporter into her sixties, and who then used her expertise on issues to begin another career. At the age of seventy, she became the Progressive party's candidate for Congress from California. At seventy-two, she ran on that party's ticket against Richard Nixon—thus becoming the first black woman to run for the vice-presidency of the United States. I wish I had known her when I was struggling against being a "girl reporter" in the 1960s, for she had begun work as a journalist in 1900 at the age of twenty. She became the editor of a small newspaper and crusaded against the Ku Klux Klan and segregated housing, for women in political office and for early efforts to ban the atomic bomb. As a candidate, her slogan was "Win or lose, we win by raising the issues." She died in 1969 at the age of eighty-nine, knowing she had helped to put civil rights, women's rights, and peace on the national agenda.[18]

I think of Mary Parkman Peabody, a Boston Brahmin by birth and marriage. In 1964, at the age of seventy-two—without telling her son, who was then governor of Massachusetts—she left for a civil rights demonstration in Florida organized by Martin Luther King. When she was jailed for sitting in at a segregated motel dining room, she made national headlines because of her illustrious family and her status as the widow of an Episcopal bishop. At a press conference, she commented cheerfully that the jail was very clean, there were beautiful flowers outside it, and she had enjoyed eating hominy grits with her fingers. Well into her eighties, she continued to demonstrate for civil rights, against the war in Vietnam, and against military spending. When she died at eighty-nine, obituaries called her "a prominent civil rights and antiwar activist," and only later mentioned her illustrious family. To this day, she is a symbol of rebellion for women born into a class trained not to rebel.[19]

I think of Edith Big Fire Johns, who began a new career four years ago at seventy-five. As a representative of Travellers and Immigrants Aid at Chicago's O'Hare Airport, she receives babies arriving from Korea and Romania for adoption, helps African students and Asian immigrants coming to this country for the first time, and talks to runaways who feel they have no home but the airport. Having earned her nursing degree in 1937—one of the first Indian women to do so—she had a long career in that profession, and was one of the first staff members of the Native American Educational Services College, the only private Indian college in this country. At sixty-five, she joined the Peace Corps as a nurse on the island of Dominica, and traveled to meet with indigenous peoples in Australia and New Zealand. Now she also teaches the Indian beadwork at which she is expert as a member of both the Winnebago and Nez Percé tribes, helps others in the Indian community to maintain tribal values in the midst of urban life, and looks forward each week to "meeting people from parts unknown."

I think of Carrie Allen McCray, whose fresh and true poetry I have just discovered—which is not surprising, since she only began to write seriously at seventy-three and is publishing and giving poetry readings at eighty. The daughter of one of the first black lawyers and a mother who was a charter member of the National Association for the Advancement of Colored People in 1917, she herself was a social worker and professor of sociology in South Carolina and Alabama. With a memory that stretches from the Harlem Renaissance to the poetry of Sonia Sanchez and Sharon Olds, she is now at work on a novel about her mother, her grandmother who was a former slave, her grandfather who was a Confederate general, and the surprises she has found in researching their stories. Widowed by a husband whose work as a journalist she admired but who said, "I'm the writer in the family," she now writes every day. As she says, "I get up writing." Here are some of her words:

Nobody wrote a poem
about me
In ugly tones they
called me "Yaller Gal"
How lovely to have been
born black or brown
Pure substance the artist
could put his pen to
Not something in between—
diluted, undefined, unspecific
I search the poets
for words of me
Faint mention in Langston Hughes'
Harlem Sweeties, *I think,*
yet I'm not sure
So full of "caramel treats,"
"brown sugars" and "plum
tinted blacks," it was
Soft, warm colors
making the poets sing
I, born out of history's
cruel circumstance,
inspired no song
and nobody wrote a poem

At last, Carrie Allen McCray is writing her own poem—and a novel besides.[20]

I think of Esther Peterson, born in 1906, a tall, slender young woman with brown braids encircling her head, who came out of Utah to become a labor organizer in the sweatshops of New England and the South. In the lonely years between suffrage and modern feminism, she carried the heart and conscience of the women's movement—learning from Eleanor Roosevelt to "draw a wider circle" around issues, and in her fifties becoming head of the Women's Bureau under President Kennedy, a man she had educated on labor issues when he was a young Congressman. In the Johnson and Carter administrations she was a voice for consumers, and at eighty-six she was appointed by President Clinton to represent the United States at the first United Nations session of his administration. She knew the U.N. well, having pioneered its international listing of products considered dangerous in their country of manufacture but "dumped" in other countries nonetheless, a listing opposed by many U.S. corporations and the Reagan administration. I see her now at eighty-seven, her snow-white braids encircling her head, speaking on international consumer issues, women's equality, and the needs of the United Seniors' Health Cooperative, a new organization she founded to help older people become informed consumers of health care and health insurance.[21] As always, she is on the path ahead.

Now that I am finally retrieving the importance of India in my life, I think most of all of sitting on a New Delhi veranda in the 1970s, drinking tea with Kamaladevi Chattopadhyay, whose first name was (and is) enough to identify her in many countries of the world. Biographical dictionaries list her as "freedom fighter, social worker, writer." In the 1950s, when I first met her, she was also in her fifties and already a legend for her leading role in the Freedom Struggle with Gandhi and Nehru—an activism for which she spent five years in British jails—and for her pioneering of the Indian handicraft movement. Our meeting was arranged by my oldest friend in India, Devaki Jain, because we wanted to ask Kamaladevi's advice. Since Gandhi's nonviolent tactics were so well suited to women's movements around the world, we were thinking of studying his letters and writings, distilling what was most useful, and creating a kind of Gandhian/feminist handbook.

Kamaladevi listened patiently. Only at the end did she say, "Of course Gandhi's tactics were suited to women—that's where he learned them." It was a sudden understanding that made us all laugh; one more instance of history lost, and then being attracted to what once was ours.

When I returned home, I lost track of Kamaladevi. I knew only that she had continued to travel the world into her eighties, helping other countries to preserve their creativity and culture in a handicraft industry, too, and also writing many books. But I always remembered this woman who taught us women's history over a cup of tea, while continuing to make history herself.

She died at the age of eighty-five on her way to make a speech, effective to the last. Devaki Jain wrote a moving tribute: "I weep for her absence—a central support for realistic idealism. . . . She made museums appear like bread or water—things without which one could not live." She described how Kamaladevi, asked to join dignitaries on a podium and light a lamp celebrating the golden jubilee of the All India Women's Conference, had said, just a year before she died, "I have never gone on to a raised platform, it connotes hierarchy, distance." As Devaki explained, "She lit the lamp at the back of the hall, to the delight of the last rows."[22]

I don't mean to say that all of us have to do illustrious deeds; quite the contrary, all our deeds are illustrious. How we speak to each other, how our bodies feel, what we wear, how we work, what we buy, what we eat, whom we love—all these are part of the impact of our lives. Indeed, I'm not sure we have any idea which of our actions is important while we are doing it. Therefore, to get us out of any sober, historic, or otherwise intimidating mood, I'll risk placing a poem here—nothing is accomplished without making fools of ourselves, and poetry for me is like singing in the shower. I well understood while writing it that groups of women mentioned here might have little choice as to how they dressed or acted—but this poem refused to be politically correct. Even its title is only the answer that popped out when someone asked me what I planned for my old age: "I Hope To Be an Old Woman Who Dresses Very Inappropriately."

Women in business
Dress in man-style suits
And treat their secretaries
In a man-style way.

Women on campus
Wear "masculine" thoughts
And look to daddy for
Good grades.

Married women
Give their bodies away
And wear their husbands'
Wishes.

Religious women
Cover sinful bodies
And ask redemption from god
Not knowing
She is within them.

That's why I'll always love
The fat woman who dares to wear

A red miniskirt
Because she loves her woman's body.
The smart woman who doesn't go to college
And keeps possession of her mind.
The lover who remains a mistress
Because she knows the price of marrying.
The witch who walks naked
And demands to be safe.
The crazy woman who dyes her hair purple
Because anyone who doesn't love purple
Is crazy.

Dear Goddess: I pray for the courage
To walk naked
At any age.
To wear red and purple,
To be unladylike,
Inappropriate,
Scandalous and
Incorrect
To the very end.

As you can see, I'm just beginning to realize the upcoming plea-sures of being a nothing-to-lose, take-no-shit older woman; of look-ing at what once seemed outer limits as just road signs. For instance:

• I used to take pleasure in going to a feminist Seder every year, subverting that ancient ceremony by including women in it. In our Women's Haggadah, we honored not only Deborah, Ruth, and other heroines of the Bible, but also our own foremothers. "Why have our Mothers on this night been bitter?" we read together. "Because they did the preparation but not the ritual. They did the serving but not the conducting. They read of their fathers but not of their mothers." [23]

Lately, however, I've been wondering: Why start with anything that must be so changed, so fought *against*? Why not begin with the occasions of our own lives and create the ceremony we need for births or marriages, adopting friends as chosen family or setting off on a new adventure, recognizing the life passage of divorce, or a new home? Having learned the pleasures of ritual, I'm thinking of found-ing a service: "Ceremonies to Go."

• I used to pass urban slums, or rows of poor houses anywhere, and compulsively imagine myself living there: *What would it be like?* It was a question of such fearsome childhood power that I only recently realized it had fallen away. It's simply gone. The deep groove worn by such imaginings has finally been filled by years of words written and deeds done, crises survived and friends who became family, work done for others and thus an interdependence. In other words, I no longer fear ending up where I began.

• I used to indulge in magical thinking when problems seemed insurmountable. Often, this focused on men, for they seemed to be the only ones with power to intercede with the gods. Now it has been so long since I fantasized a magical rescue that I can barely remember the intensity of that longing. Instead, I feel my own strength, take pleasure in the company of mortals, and no longer believe in gods. Except those in each of us.

• I used to think that continuing my past sex life was the height of radicalism. After all, women too old for childbearing were supposed to be too old for sex, and becoming a pioneer dirty old lady seemed a worthwhile goal—which it was, for a while. But continuing the past even out of defiance is very different from advancing. Now I think: Why not take advantage of the hormonal changes age provides to clear our minds, sharpen our senses, and free whole areas of our brains? Even as I celebrate past pleasures, I wonder: Did I sometimes confuse sex with aerobics?

• I used to be one of the majority of Americans whose greatest fear was dependency in old age—a fear that must have roots other than economic, for it is no more prevalent among women or the racial groups of men most likely to be poor. Then I listened to the historian Gerda Lerner question that fear among a group of middle-aged women gathered to talk about aging. As she pointed out, we don't fear dependency in the early years of life. On the contrary, we understand that being able to help children find what they need can be a gift in itself. Why shouldn't we feel the same about the other end of life? Why shouldn't the equally natural needs of age be an opportunity for others to give? Why indeed? Now I wonder if women's fear of dependency doesn't stem from being too much depended upon. Perhaps if we equalize the caretaking and the giving—with men, with society—this will bring a new freedom to receive.

• I used to think that uprooting negative childhood patterns was an activity reserved for individuals. Now I wonder if this familiar healing process wouldn't benefit countries and races too. In the country in which I live, there is a glorification of violence and a willful denial of how much it hurts—not to mention how much of this hurt is passed on to future generations. I wonder if we're collectively doomed to keep repeating these violent patterns until we admit the hurt that took place in this nation's childhood: the reality of genocide that wiped out millions of indigenous peoples and all but destroyed dozens of major cultures, plus the still only half-admitted realities of slavery and its legacy within each of us. I'm happy about the new Holocaust Museum in Washington, for I know our government refused to admit thousands of Jews until it was too late. But we also need to have a Native American Museum, which finally admits that the "uninhabited" Americas were home to as many people as Europe, and a Middle Passage Museum to memorialize the beginning of the massive injustice of slavery that's still playing out. We need this remembrance not for guilt or punishment —which only creates more of the same—but to root out the patterns of our national childhood.

• I used to think nationalism was the only game in town. The most radical act was to support poor countries in their rights against rich ones. Now I look at artificial boundaries—lines that can stop no current of air or drought or polluted river—and mourn the violence lavished on defending them. Long ago, in times suspiciously set aside as "prehistory," we were mostly nomadic peoples who claimed nothing but crisscrossing migratory paths. Cultures were the richest where different peoples and paths were most intermingled. We're still a nomadic species; indeed, we move and travel on this earth more than ever before. Yet we insist on the destructive fiction of nationalism, one that becomes even more dangerous when it joins with religions that try to create nations in the sky.

As a group who can never afford the expensive fiction of having a nation—and whose bodies suffer from nationalism by being restricted as its means of reproduction—women of all races and cultures may be the most motivated to ask: How can we create a future beyond nationalism? After all, it has been around for less than five percent of humanity's history. Surely there are other ways of sharing this spaceship Earth.

• Lest this all seem too impractical, let me add one more: I used to think I would be rewarded for good behavior. Therefore, if I wasn't understood, I must not be understandable; if I wasn't successful, I must try harder; if something was wrong, it was my fault. More and more now, I see that context is all. When someone judges me, anyone, or anything, I ask: *Compared to what?* When I see on television a series about children of divorce, for instance, I find myself asking: *What about a series on children of marriage?* When a woman fears the punishment that comes from calling herself a feminist, I ask: *Will you be so unpunished if you don't?* When I fear conflict and condemnation for acting a certain way, I think: *What peace or praise would I get if I didn't?*

I recommend the freedom that comes from asking: *Compared to what?* Hierarchical systems prevail by making us feel inadequate and imperfect, whatever we do, so we will internalize the blame. But once we realize there is no such thing as adequacy or perfection, it sets us free to say: *We might as well be who we really are.*

By the time you read this, I'll be sixty. I realize now that fifty felt like leaving a much-loved and familiar country—hence both the defiance and the sadness—but sixty feels like arriving at the border of a new one. I'm looking forward to trading moderation for excess, defiance for openness, and planning for the unknown. I already have one new benefit of this longer view:

I've always had two or more tracks running in my head. The pleasurable one was thinking forward to some future scene, imagining what should be, planning on the edge of fantasy. The other played underneath with all too realistic fragments of what I should have done. There it was in perfect microcosm, the past and future coming together to squeeze out the present—which is the only time in which we can be fully alive. The blessing of what I think of as the last third or more of life (since I plan to reach a hundred) is that these past and future tracks have gradually dimmed until they are rarely heard. More and more, there is only the full, glorious, alive-in-the-moment, don't-give-a-damn yet caring-for-everything sense of the right now.

I was about to end this with, *There's no second like the next one,* in much the same spirit that I ended the preface of this book, *I can't wait to see what happens*—which remains true. But this new state of mind would have none of it: *There's no second like this one.*

Notes

PART ONE   *What If* Freud *Were* Phyllis?

1. Gloria Steinem, "If Men Could Menstruate," in *Outrageous Acts and Every-day Rebellions* (New York: Holt, Rinehart & Winston, 1983), pp. 337–40.

2. Sigmund Freud, "Some Psychological Consequences of the Anatomical Distinction Between the Sexes" (1925), in *Standard Edition of the Complete Psychological Works,* vol. XIX, trans. and ed. James Strachey (London: Hogarth Press, 1961), pp. 257–58.

3. Peter Gay, *Freud: A Life for Our Time* (New York: Anchor/Doubleday, 1988), p. 217.

4. Ibid., p. 39.

5. Lisa Appignanesi and John Forrester, *Freud's Women* (New York: Basic Books/HarperCollins, 1992), p. 3.

6. Ethel Spector Person, "Women in Therapy: Therapist Gender as a Variable," *International Review of Psycho-Analysis,* vol. 10 (1983), pp. 193–204.

7. For the results of this survey, the first of its kind, see Nanette Gartrell, M.D., et al., "Psychiatrist-Patient Sexual Contact: Results of a National Survey," Part I, "Prevalence," *American Journal of Psychiatry,* vol. 143, no. 9 (September 1986), pp. 1126–31.

For the saga of the APA's efforts to block the survey—a parable of use to anyone trying to change an establishment institution from within—see Nanette Gartrell et al., "Institutional Resistance to Self-Study: A Case Report," in *Sexual Exploitation of Clients by Health Professionals,* ed. A. Burgess (Philadelphia: Praeger, 1986), pp. 120–28.

8. Nanette Gartrell, M.D., et al., "Reporting Practices of Psychiatrists Who Knew of Sexual Misconduct by Colleagues," *American Journal of Orthopsychiatry,* April 1987, pp. 287–95.

9. Jeffrey Moussaieff Masson, trans. and ed., *The Complete Letters of Sigmund Freud to Wilhelm Fliess, 1887–1904* (Cambridge, Mass.: Belknap Press of Harvard University Press, 1985), pp. 277, 281, 291, and 299.

10. Gay, *Freud,* p. 97 n.

11. Ibid., p. 96

12. Frank J. Sulloway, *Freud: Biologist of the Mind* (Cambridge, Mass.: Harvard University Press, 1992), p. 19.

13. Ibid., p. 18.

14. John Kerr, *A Most Dangerous Method: The Story of Jung, Freud, and Sabina Spielrein* (New York: Knopf, 1993), p. 137.

15. Frederick Crews, "The Unknown Freud," *New York Review of Books,* November 18, 1993, p. 65 n.

16. C. G. Jung, "Sigmund Freud," in *Memories, Dreams, Reflections,* trans. Richard and Clara Winston (New York: Vintage/Random House, 1989), p. 158.

17. Sándor Ferenczi, *The Clinical Diary of Sándor Ferenczi,* trans. Michael Balint and Nicola Zarday Jackson, ed. Judith Dupont (Cambridge, Mass.: Harvard University Press, 1988), p. 93.

18. Quoted by Helen Walker Puner in *Sigmund Freud: His Life and His Mind,* foreword by Erich Fromm, with a new introduction by Paul Roazen and an afterword by S. P. Puner (New Brunswick, N.J.: Transaction Publishers, 1992), p. 130.

19. Gay, *Freud,* p. 8.

20. Giovanni Papini, "A Visit to Freud," in *Freud as We Knew Him,* ed. Hendrik M. Ruitenbeek (Detroit: Wayne State University Press, 1973), pp. 98–99.

21. Jung, "Sigmund Freud," pp. 152, 167, 150.

22. Puner, *Sigmund Freud,* p. 26.

23. Ibid., p. 212.

24. Gay, *Freud,* p. 559.

25. Jung, "Sigmund Freud," pp. 156–57.

26. With thanks to Suzanne Braun Levine for the phrase.

27. Matt Moffett, "The Women of Juchitan, Mexico, Control the Economy and the Men," *Wall Street Journal,* April 2, 1991.

28. Sherwood Anderson, *Dark Laughter* (New York: Liveright, 1970).

29. Juliet Mitchell, *Psychoanalysis and Feminism: Freud, Reich, Laing and Women* (New York: Vintage/Random House, 1975), p. 433.

30. David Stafford-Clark, *What Freud Really Said* (New York: Schocken Books, 1966), p. 82.

31. ". . . penis envy . . . women . . ." Sigmund Freud, "Femininity," in *Freud on Women: A Reader,* ed. and with an introduction by Elisabeth Young-Bruehl (New York: W. W. Norton, 1990), p. 360.

32. ". . . women . . ." Ibid., pp. 361–62.

33. ". . . beautiful . . ." Gay, *Freud,* p. 522.

34. Ibid., p. 565.

35. Puner, *Sigmund Freud,* pp. 119–20.

36. All words in the paragraph are Freud's own except ". . . women . . . herself . . ." and ". . . feminine . . . genital deficiency." Sigmund Freud, "Femininity," *Freud on Women,* p. 360.

37. Ernest Jones, *The Life and Work of Sigmund Freud,* vol. I (New York: Basic Books, 1953), pp. 17–18.

38. Peter J. Swales, "Freud, His Teacher, and the Birth of Psychoanalysis," in *Freud: Appraisals and Reappraisals,* vol. I, ed. Paul E. Stepansky (Hillsdale, N.J.: The Analytic Press, 1986), p. 3.

39. Sulloway, *Freud,* pp. 79 and 57.

40. Josef Breuer, "Fräulein Anna O.," in Josef Breuer and Sigmund Freud, *Studies on Hysteria,* in *Complete Psychological Works of Sigmund Freud,* vol. II, trans. and ed. James Strachey (London: Hogarth Press, 1968), pp. 21–47.

41. Appignanesi and Forrester, *Freud's Women,* pp. 77–80.

42. Sulloway, *Freud,* p. 84 n.

43. Ibid., pp. 51–89.

44. Breuer, "Fräulein Anna O.," in Breuer and Freud, *Studies on Hysteria.*

45. Sulloway, *Freud,* pp. 83–100.

46. Appignanesi and Forrester, *Freud's Women,* p. 80.

47. Lucy Freeman and Dr. Herbert S. Strean, *Freud and Women* (New York: Continuum, 1987), p. 137.

48. Puner, *Sigmund Freud*, p. 60.

49. Ibid., pp. 64–65.

50. Appignanesi and Forrester, *Freud's Women*, p. 85.

51. Masson, *Complete Letters*, p. 57.

52. Appignanesi and Forrester, *Freud's Women*, p. 176.

53. Gay, *Freud*, pp. 296 and 103 n.

54. Ibid., pp. 137–38.

55. That's Peter Gay, of course, in *Freud*, p. 296.

56. Appignanesi and Forrester, *Freud's Women*, pp. 421–22.

57. Ibid., p. 45.

58. Masson, *Complete Letters*, p. 280.

59. "woman . . ." Kate Millett, *Sexual Politics*, (New York: Touchstone/Simon & Schuster, 1970), p. 193.

60. Sigmund Freud, "Femininity," in *Freud on Women*, p. 344.

61. In part from the first English translation of Freud's "Femininity," quoted by Kate Millett, *Sexual Politics*, p. 193.

62. Sigmund Freud, "The Acquisition of Power Over Fire," in *Collected Papers*, vol. V, ed. James Strachey (New York: Basic Books, 1959), p. 294.

63. Sigmund Freud, "Some Psychological Consequences of the Anatomical Distinction Between the Sexes," in *Collected Papers*, p. 191.

64. Gay, *Freud*, p. 163.

65. Sigmund Freud, " 'Civilized' Sexual Morality and Modern Nervous Illness," in *Freud on Women*, p. 173.

66. Gay, *Freud*, p. 59.

67. Puner, *Sigmund Freud*, p. 120.

68. Gay, *Freud*, p. 163.

69. Impressionable young wives, of course; in this case, Wilhelm Fliess's wife. Gay, *Freud*, pp. 62–63.

70. ". . . adult woman . . ." Ibid., p. 501.

71. Philip Rieff, *Freud: Three Case Histories* (New York: Collier/Macmillan, 1963), p. 7.

72. Sigmund Freud, "Some Psychological Consequences of the Anatomical Distinction Between the Sexes," *Collected Papers*, p. 194.

73. Puner, *Sigmund Freud*, pp. 30–31.

74. Marianne Krüll, *Freud and His Father*, trans. Arnold J. Pomerans (New York: W. W. Norton, 1979), p. 112.

75. Masson, *Complete Letters*, p. 287.

76. Allen Esterson, *Seductive Mirage: An Exploration of the Work of Sigmund Freud* (Chicago: Open Court, 1993), p. 245.

77. Sigmund Freud, "L'Hérédité et l'étiologie des nervoses," *Revue neurologique*, March 30, 1896, trans. Jeffrey Masson, in *The Assault on Truth: Freud's Suppression of the Seduction Theory* (New York: HarperPerennial, 1992), p. 91.

78. Gay, *Freud*, p. 95.

79. Krüll, *Freud and His Father*, p. 155.

80. Eric Miller, *Passion for Murder: The Homicidal Deeds of Dr. Sigmund Freud* (San Diego: Future Directions, 1984). See p. 306 for copy of birth registry.

81. Ibid., pp. 30 and 27.
82. Esterson, *Seductive Mirage*, p. 121.
83. Miller, *Passion for Murder: The Homicidal Deeds of Dr. Sigmund Freud*, and Dr. Paul Scagnelli, *Deadly Dr. Freud* (Durham, N.C.: Pinewood Publishing, 1994).
84. Sigmund Freud, "The Aetiology of Hysteria," in Masson, *Assault on Truth*, p. 275.
85. Breuer and Freud, *Studies on Hysteria*, pp. 100–101 n.
86. Masson, *Assault on Truth*, pp. 76–78.
87. Masson, *Complete Letters*, pp. 309–10.
88. Wilhelm Fliess, *New Contributions to the Theory and Therapy of the Nasal Reflex Neurosis*, trans. and excerpted in Masson, *Assault on Truth*, pp. 75–76.
89. Ibid., pp. 87–9.
90. All true. See Masson, *Complete Letters*, pp. 116–18.
91. Masson, *Assault on Truth*, pp. 68.
92. ". . . her episodes . . . hysterical . . . the woman . . ." Emma refused to supply the dates of either her bleeding episodes or her menstrual periods to see whether they conformed to Fliess's periodicity theory. This and following quotations on Emma Eckstein's case are from ibid., pp. 68–70, 99–101. For more discussion of the case, see ibid., chaps. 3 and 4, appendix A, index references.
93. Ibid., pp. 70, 249, 257.
94. Masson, *Complete Letters*, p. 227.
95. ". . . Emma . . . her . . . her . . ." Masson, *Assault on Truth*, p. 99.
96. Gay, *Freud*, p. 276.
97. Jones, *The Life and Work of Sigmund Freud*, vol. I, pp. 291 and 302.
98. Gay, *Freud*, p. 86.
99. Krüll, *Freud and His Father*, p. 192.
100. Masson, *Assault on Truth*, p. 216.
101. Ibid., pp. 139–42.
102. ". . . his . . ." Gay, *Freud*, p. 89.
103. ". . . hysteria . . . hysteria . . . six men and twelve women . . ." Freud, "The Aetiology of Hysteria," in Masson, *Assault on Truth*, pp. 276, 271, 268, 272–273.
104. Ibid., pp. 284 and 283.
105. Sigmund Freud to Wilhelm Fliess, *Complete Letters*, pp. 183–184.
106. Masson, *Complete Letters*, p. 231.
107. Masson, *Assault on Truth*, pp. 230, 135, 27.
108. Masson, *Complete Letters*, p. 184.
109. Ibid., p. 185.
110. ". . . old man's . . . him . . . unmarried sister . . . him . . ." Quoted in Krüll, *Freud and His Father*, p. 41.
111. Ibid., p. 40.
112. ". . . old man's . . . He . . ." and . . . barber shop . . . , Masson, *Complete Letters*, p. 202.
113. Ibid., p. 238.
114. Ibid., p. 220.
115. Ibid., pp. 230–31.
116. Jones's quotes from Scagnelli, *Deadly Dr. Freud*, pp. 511, 514, 515, 525.

See Kerr, *A Most Dangerous Method*, p. 379, on blackmail. Also see Sulloway, *Freud*, p. 460.

117. Masson, *Complete Letters*, p. 254.

118. Jung, "Sigmund Freud," p. 161.

119. Krüll, *Freud and His Father*, pp. 57–58.

120. ". . . the *father* . . . hysteria . . ." Masson, *Complete Letters*, p. 264.

121. Ibid., p. 265.

122. Ibid., pp. 268–69.

123. For full text, see ibid., pp. 269–70.

124. ". . . his . . . him." Masson, *Assault on Truth*, p. 11.

125. Krüll, *Freud and His Father*, p. 222.

126. Anna Freud's own words except: ". . . the Electra and the less important . . ." Letter from Anna Freud to Jeffrey Masson, September 10, 1981, in Masson, *Assault on Truth*, p. 113.

127. Gay, *Freud*, pp. 112–13.

128. Peter J. Swales, "Freud, Katharina, and the First 'Wild Analysis,' " in *Freud: Appraisals and Reappraisals*, vol. III, pp. 81–164.

129. Masson, *Assault on Truth*, p. 133.

130. Sándor Ferenczi, "Confusion of Tongues Between Adults and the Child," trans. Jeffrey Masson and Marianne Loring, ibid., pp. 291–303.

131. ". . . Sigmund . . . His . . ." Steven Marcus, *Freud and the Culture of Psychoanalysis* (Winchester, Mass.: Allen & Unwin, 1984). He also coedited a one-volume version of Ernest Jones's biography of Freud with Lionel Trilling—who considered Freud the prime mover of modernism.

132. Daniel Goleman, "As a Therapist, Freud Fell Short, Scholars Find," *New York Times*, March 6, 1990.

133. Gay, *Freud*, pp. 255–56, 260–61.

134. Puner, *Sigmund Freud*, p. 214.

135. Sigmund Freud, " 'A Child Is Being Beaten': A Contribution to the Study of the Origin of Sexual Perversions," in *Freud on Women*, p. 235.

136. Jeffrey Masson, *Final Analysis: The Making and Unmaking of a Psychoanalyst* (New York: HarperCollins, 1990), p. 55.

137. ". . . penis . . ." Robert J. Campbell, ed., fifth ed., *Psychiatric Dictionary* (New York: Oxford University Press, 1981), p. 32.

138. ". . . she . . . herself . . . She . . . herself . . . she . . . she . . ." Ibid., pp. 82–83.

139. Linda Meyer Williams, "Recall of Childhood Trauma: A Prospective Study of Women's Memories of Child Sexual Abuse," paper presented at the annual meeting of the American Society of Criminology, October 27, 1993, to be published by *Journal of Consulting and Clinical Psychology*. (Contact Linda Meyer Williams, Family Research Laboratory, University of New Hampshire, Durham, N.H. 03824.)

140. Goleman, "As a Therapist, Freud Fell Short, Scholars Find."

141. Gay, *Freud*, p. 563.

142. Goleman, "As a Therapist, Freud Fell Short, Scholars Find."

143. Gay, *Freud*, p. 565.

144. ". . . him . . . his . . . his . . . he . . . his . . ." Peter Neubauer, in Goleman, "As a Therapist, Freud Fell Short, Scholars Find."

145. ". . . his creation." Gay, *Freud,* pp. xviii–xix.

146. ". . . mother's womb . . ." Maurice Lever, *Sade: A Biography* (New York: Farrar, Straus & Giroux, 1993). For a woman's defense of Sade, see the review of this book by Francine du Plessix Gray, *The New Yorker,* September 6, 1993. For a feminist view, see Andrea Dworkin, *Woman Hating* (New York: E. P. Dutton, 1974).

147. "In the phallic phase, phantasies of piercing, penetration, or dissolution of . . ." Campbell, *Psychiatric Dictionary,* p. 327.

148. Harold Bloom, "Freud, The Greatest Modern Writer," *New York Times Book Review,* March 23, 1986, p. 27.

149. Quotes in this paragraph and the next from Sigmund Freud, as excerpted by Ann Salyard in "Freud as Pegasus Yoked to the Plough," *Psychoanalytic Psychology* 5:4 (1988), pp. 403–29.

150. Sándor Ferenczi, in *Journal clinique* (January–October 1932), translated from the German by Le Groupe de Traduction du Coq-Heron (Paris: Payot, 1985); translated from the French by Jeffrey Masson, in *Against Therapy* (Monroe, Maine: Common Courage Press, 1994), p. 19.

151. Jung, "Sigmund Freud," p. 152.

PART TWO   *The Strongest Woman in the World*

1. Adrienne Rich, *Of Woman Born* (New York: W. W. Norton, 1986), p. 285.

2. Gloria Steinem, "Coming Up: The Unprecedented Woman," *Ms.,* July 1985, pp. 85–86, 106–8.

3. For some typical male/female experiences in the Achilles Track Club, a group of runners who challenge the restrictions of artificial limbs, wheelchairs, and cancer and other life-threatening diseases, see Dick Traum and Mike Celizic, *A Victory for Humanity* (Waco, Tex.: WRS Publishing, 1993).

4. On foot binding, see Andrea Dworkin, "Gynocide: Chinese Footbinding," in *Woman Hating* (New York: E. P. Dutton, 1974), pp. 95–117. On clitoridectomy (the surgical excision of all or a major part of the clitoris) and infibulation (the excision of the clitoris plus cutting off the labia minora and labia majora, then sewing together the scraped sides of the vulva so they grow into a chastity belt of flesh that must be torn open and resewn for every insemination and birth), see Robin Morgan and Gloria Steinem, "The International Crime of Genital Mutilation," in Robin Morgan, *The Word of a Woman* (1979; updated, New York: W. W. Norton, 1992), pp. 90–101. Also Alice Walker and Pratibha Parmar, *Warrior Marks: Female Genital Mutilation and the Sexual Blinding of Women* (New York: Harcourt Brace, 1993). On self-starvation, plastic surgery, and other Western limits on female strength, see Naomi Wolf, *The Beauty Myth: How Images of Beauty Are Used Against Women* (New York: William Morrow, 1991); and Joan Jacobs Brumberg, *Fasting Girls: The Emergence of Anorexia Nervosa as a Modern Disease* (Cambridge, Mass.: Harvard University Press, 1988).

5. Deborah Pike, "Redefining the Body," *Vogue,* January 1994, pp. 105, 166–167.

6. Charles Gaines and George Butler, *Pumping Iron II: The Unprecedented Woman* (New York: Simon & Schuster, 1984).

7. Peter McGough, "A Career in Focus," *Flex,* August 1993, pp. 65–66, 150–56.

PART THREE   *Sex, Lies, and Advertising*

1. Robin Morgan, *The Word of a Woman: Feminist Dispatches 1968–1992,* reprinted with a new introduction (New York: W. W. Norton, 1992), pp. 49–69.

2. INFACT: Campaign for Corporate Accountability, 256 Hanover Street, Boston, Massachusetts 02113. "Deadly Deception," INFACT's Oscar-award winning documentary on GE's environmental, defense, and worker safety record, can be ordered for $15 by calling (800) 688-8797.

3. *National Boycott News,* 6506 28th Avenue, N.E., Seattle, Washington, 98115.

4. Editorial, *National Catholic Reporter,* April 26, 1991. For this and other reports, contact FAIR, 130 West 25th Street, New York, N.Y. 10011.

5. Todd Putnam, "The G.E. Boycott: A Story NBC Wouldn't Buy," *EXTRA!,* January/February 1991, p. 5.

6. Michael Hoyt, "When the Walls Come Tumbling Down," *Columbia Journalism Review,* March/April 1990, p. 35.

7. Randall Rotherberg, *New York Times,* January 18, 1989.

8. Jan Ferris, "BUTT OUT: Publishers and Their Tobacco Habit," *Columbia Journalism Review,* January/February 1994, pp. 16–18.

9. Joanne Lipman, *Wall Street Journal,* July 30, 1991.

10. Jon Swan, "The Crumbling Wall," *Columbia Journalism Review,* May/June 1992, p. 23.

11. Text by Philip Shenon, produced by Polly Hamilton, photographs by Marie Laure De Decker, "The Mist of Perfume River," *The New York Times Magazine,* November 21, 1993.

12. Jon Swan, "The Crumbling Wall," *Columbia Journalism Review,* p. 23.

13. G. Pascal Zachary, *Wall Street Journal,* February 6, 1992.

14. For membership and publications, contact Center for the Study of Commercialism, 1875 Connecticut Avenue N.W., Suite 300, Washington, D.C. 20009-5278. Telephone: 202-797-7080; FAX 202-265-4954.

PART FOUR   *The Masculinization of Wealth*

1. This quote has been attributed to me, but I first heard it while organizing in the South in the early 1970s, and was told it had been said by a black woman of the abolitionist and suffragist era to her white Southern sisters. If any reader knows its source, I would love to have it.

2. M. M. Marberry, *Vicky: A Biography of Victoria C. Woodhull* (New York: Funk & Wagnalls, 1967), p. 70.

3. Ibid., p. 83

4. For more by and about Victoria Woodhull, see Madeleine B. Stern, *VW Reader* (Weston, Mass.: MNS Publishers, 1974); Emanie Sachs, *The Terrible Siren: Victoria Woodhull, 1838–1927* (New York: Harper & Brothers, 1928). In her later stage of seeking a rich husband in Europe, Woodhull was the model for Nancy Headway in *The Siege of Paris,* by Henry James.

5. Susan A. Ostrander, *Women of the Upper Class* (Philadelphia: Temple University Press, 1984), p. 151.

6. Robin Morgan, *The Demon Lover* (New York: W. W. Norton, 1989), p. 159.

7. This is a fifteen-year study that began in 1981. A ten-year report has now been published. Karen D. Arnold, "Academic Achievement—A View from the Top: The Illinois Valedictorian Project," North Central Regional Educational Library, 1900 Spring Road, Suite 300, Oak Brook, IL 60521. "Higher Education: Colder by Degrees," Myra and David Sadker, *Failing at Fairness* (New York: Charles Scribner's Sons, 1994), pp. 161–96.

8. Joan Jacobs Brumberg, *Fasting Girls* (Cambridge, Mass.: Harvard University Press, 1988), pp. 12–13.

9. Linda Tschirhart Sanford and Mary Ellen Donovan, *Women and Self-Esteem* (New York: Anchor Press/Doubleday, 1984), p. 74.

10. Ibid., p. 47.

11. "Relating to Our Family, Money and Communities," Selected Highlights of the Third Annual Women Managing Wealth Conference, 1990. A program of the Ms. Foundation for Women, 141 Fifth Avenue, New York, N.Y. 10010.

12. G. William Domhoff, *Who Rules America Now?* (New York: Simon & Schuster/Touchstone, 1983), p. 42.

13. Aileen S. Kaditor, *The Ideas of the Woman Suffrage Movement: 1890–1920* (New York: W. W. Norton, 1981), pp. 153–54, 241.

14. Ibid., p. 153n.

15. Madeleine B. Stern, *Queen of Publishers' Row* (New York: Messner, 1965), p. 186.

16. For information about local or national meetings of women managing wealth, contact: Resourceful Women, 3543 18th Street #9, San Francisco, CA 94110, 415-431-5677, fax 415-431-9634.

National Network of Women's Funds, 1821 University Avenue, Suite 409 North, St. Paul, MN 55104, 612-641-0742, fax 612-647-1401.

Funding Exchange, 666 Broadway, Suite 500, New York, N.Y. 10012, 212-529-5300.

PART FIVE   *Revaluing Economics*

1. Meridel Le Sueur, "Women Are Hungry," *Ripening: Selected Works, 1927–1980* (Old Westbury, N.Y.: The Feminist Press, 1982), pp. 140–41.

2. Eighteen years ago, Sheila Tobias, then a provost at Wesleyan University, identified and named math anxiety as a problem largely but not only of female students. (See "Why Is a Smart Girl Like You Counting on Your Fingers?," *Ms.*, September 1976.) She developed clinics and other remedial methods that are now used on many campuses or in classrooms, as well as by individuals. See her books *Overcoming Math Anxiety* (New York: W. W. Norton, 1978; rev. 1994); and *Succeed with Math: Every Student's Guide to Conquering Math Anxiety* (The College Board, 1987).

3. Robert L. Heilbroner, "The Heresies of John Maynard Keynes," *The Worldly Philosophers* (New York: Touchstone/Simon & Schuster, 1992), p. 287.

4. John Kenneth Galbraith, "The Higher Economic Purpose of Women,"

Annals of an Abiding Liberal, ed. Andrea D. Williams (Boston: Houghton Mifflin, 1979), pp. 38–9, 41. Interview with John Kenneth Galbraith by Gloria Steinem, "The Economics of Housework," *Ms.,* April 1983, pp. 27–31.

5. For a discussion of the Superwoman and the two-job burden, see Arlie Hochschild with Ann Machung, *The Second Shift* (New York: Avon Books, 1989).

6. Shelley Coverman, "Women's Work Is Never Done: The Division of Domestic Labor," in *Women: A Feminist Perspective,* ed. Jo Freeman (Mountain View, Calif.: Mayfield Publishing, 1989), pp. 356–68.

7. Noam Chomsky, " 'Mandate for Change' or Business as Usual," *Z* magazine, February 1993, p. 40.

8. Caroline Bird, *What Women Want: The National Women's Conference* (New York: Simon & Schuster, 1979). For the agenda and the official report, see *The Spirit of Houston: The First National Women's Conference* (Washington, D.C.: National Commission on the Observance of International Women's Year, 1978); for sale by the Superintendent of Documents, U.S. Government Printing Office, Washington, D.C. 20402, Stock Number 052-003-00505-1.

9. For information on such groups, many of which are still active, write to the National Women's Conference Committee, P.O. Box 455, Beaver Dam, WI 53916.

10. Jimmy Carter's own book on the White House years, *Keeping Faith: Memoirs of a President* (New York: Bantam, 1982), leaves out this incident, as well as most women's constituency concerns. As an exemplary ex-President, he has organized technical assistance for elections in newly democratic countries, helped to create low-income housing through Habitat for Humanity, and coordinated anti-poverty groups through the Atlanta Project. The point is not one man's shortcomings but the need for women of all races to be decisionmakers.

11. Bella Abzug, with Mim Kelber, *Gender Gap: Bella Abzug's Guide to Political Power for American Women* (Boston: Houghton Mifflin, 1984), p. 74.

12. *Getting It Done: From Commitment to Action on Funding for Women and Girls,* April 1992, third in a series of Far From Done Reports, Women and Foundations/Corporate Philanthropy, 322 Eighth Avenue, Room 702, New York, N.Y. 10001.

For information on a women's fund near you, or on starting your own, write to: National Network of Women's Funds, 1821 University Avenue, Suite 409 North, St. Paul, MN 55104; 612-641-0742, fax 612-647-1401.

13. Cathy N. Davidson, *36 Views of Mount Fuji* (New York: Dutton, 1993), pp. 75–76.

14. For general information on "women's work" by country, see: Joni Seager and Ann Olson, *Women in the World: An International Atlas* (New York: Simon & Schuster/Touchstone Books, 1986). Robin Morgan, ed., *Sisterhood Is Global: The International Women's Movement Anthology* (New York: Doubleday/Anchor Press, 1984).

15. Julie Johnson, "Prospect of Racial Parity Called Bleak," *New York Times,* August 8, 1989.

16. Barbara F. Reskin, "Bringing the Men Back In: Sex Differentiation and the Devaluation of Women's Work," in *Feminist Frontiers III,* ed. Laurel Richardson and Verta Taylor (New York: McGraw-Hill, 1993), pp. 205–6.

17. Paula Ries and Anne J. Stone, *The American Woman 1992–93: A Status Report* (New York: W. W. Norton, 1992), p. 341.

18. Ronnie J. Steinberg, "Radical Changes in a Liberal World: The Mixed Successes of Comparable Worth," *Gender & Society* 1 (1987), pp. 466–75.

19. Patricia A. Rees, "Women in the Composing Room: Technology and Organization as the Determinants of Social Change," paper presented at 1986 meeting of the American Sociological Association. Cited in Reskin, "Bringing the Men Back In," *Feminist Frontiers III*, p. 205.

20. Evelyn Nakano Glenn and Roslyn L. Feldberg, "Clerical Work: The Female Occupation," in *Women: A Feminist Perspective*, pp. 300–301.

21. "The Annual Report on the Economic Status of the Profession," *Academe: Bulletin of the American Association of University Professors*, March/April 1993.

22. Gary Rhodes, "Playboy Bunny on the Move, but Miami Students Hopping Mad," *Cincinnati Post*, October 1, 1991. Private communication from Andrea Dworkin, February 5, 1994.

23. For information about how to support, join, or organize locals of this union organized by and for clerical workers—or to stay informed on issues of this part of the labor force via its Working Woman Education Fund—contact: 9to5, 238 West Wisconsin Avenue, Suite 806, Milwaukee, WI 53203-2308, 414-272-7795, fax 414-272-2870. (Projects include worker-safety measures for the use of word processors, sexual harassment hot lines, and legislative alerts.)

24. For a sample pledge covering full-time, part-time, and live-in workers, plus benefits, mutual obligations, etc., see "A Working Relationship—The Household Employer and Employee Pledge," *Ms.*, October 1979. (Previously published February 1973.)

25. Michael Hanlon, "Women's 'Unpaid' Work Worth Billions, House Chores Full-time Job, Studies Show," *Toronto Star*, May 9, 1993.

26. Sekai Holland, Zimbabwe Association of Women's Clubs, as quoted in a press release, "Overcoming Global Hunger," World Bank NGO Conference, Washington, D.C., November 30, 1993.

27. Hazel Henderson, "Redefining Wealth and Progress," *WorldPaper*, March 1994.

28. Robin Morgan, *Sisterhood Is Global: The International Women's Movement Anthology* (New York: Doubleday, 1984), p. 697.

29. Raj Krishna, *Women and Development Planning: With Special Interest to Asia and the Pacific*. Quoted in Marilyn Waring, *If Women Counted: A New Feminist Economics*, introduction by Gloria Steinem (New York: Harper & Row, 1988; published in U.K. as *Counting for Nothing*), pp. 283–84.

30. Berit Ås, "A Five-Dimensional Model for Change: Contradictions and Feminist Consciousness." Quoted in Marilyn Waring, *If Women Counted*, pp. 42–43.

31. Galbraith, "The Higher Economic Purpose of Women," pp. 39–41.

32. Gail J. Koff, Esq., *Love and the Law* (New York: Simon & Schuster, 1989), p. 193.

33. Lenore Weitzman, *The Divorce Revolution* (New York: Free Press, 1985), p. 323.

34. Ries and Stone, *The American Woman*, pp. 385–86.

35. Christine A. Littleton, "Restructuring Sexual Equality," *California Law Review* 75 (1987), p. 228.

36. Maria Mies, *Patriarchy and Accumulation on a World Scale: Women and the International Division of Labour* (London, England, and Atlantic Highlands, N.J.: Zed Books, 1986), p. 45.

37. Jonathan Glover et al., *Ethics of New Reproductive Technologies: The Glover Report to the European Commission* (DeKalb, Ill.: Northern Illinois University Press, 1989).

38. Waring, *If Women Counted*, p. 46.

39. Galbraith, "The Higher Economic Purpose of Women," pp. 41–46.

40. Letter from Carol Lees to Commissioner Benoit Bouchard, March 8, 1991.

41. Telephone interviews, January–February 1994.

42. "Woman: Challenges to the Year 2000" (New York: United Nations, 1991), p. 39.

43. Waring, *If Women Counted*, pp. 142–43.

44. Telephone interviews, January 1994.

45. Muriel Rukeyser, "Kathe Kollwitz," *No More Masks* (New York: Harper Perennial, 1993), pp. 81–86.

46. Galbraith, "The Higher Economic Purpose of Women," p. 38.

47. Adam Smith, *The Wealth of Nations* (New York: Random House, 1965), p. 14.

48. Simon Kuznets, "Towards a Theory of Economic Growth," in *Economic Growth and Structure* (New York: W. W. Norton, 1965), p. 173.

49. Raul Solorzano et al., "Accounts Overdue: Natural Resource Depreciation in Costa Rica" (Washington, D.C.: World Resources Institute, December 1991).

50. Hazel Henderson, "Needed: A Score Card on National Growth," *Christian Science Monitor,* May 3, 1993.

51. Fatima Mernissi, *The Veil and the Male Elite* (Reading, Mass.: Addison-Wesley, 1991), p. 18.

52. Charlotte Perkins Gilman, *Women and Economics* (New York: Harper Torchbooks, 1966).

53. Olive Schreiner, *Women and Labour* (London: Virago, 1978).

54. Charlotte Perkins Gilman, *The Man-Made World or Our Androcentric Culture* (New York: Johnson Reprint, 1971), pp. 232–36.

55. Hazel Henderson, *Paradigms in Progress: Life Beyond Economics* (Indianapolis: Knowledge Systems, Inc., 1991), pp. 14–15.

56. For information, write WomenVenture, 2324 University Avenue, St. Paul, MN 55114.

57. For information on annual economic development institutes, and to subscribe to this three-times-yearly magazine of the women's economic empowerment movement, write *Equal Means,* 2512 Ninth Street, Suite 3, Berkeley, CA 94710.

58. For information, write Women's Self-Employment Project, 166 West Washington, Chicago, IL 60602.

59. For information about this national economic empowerment movement and groups in your area, write Sara Gould, Ms. Foundation for Women, 141 Fifth Avenue, New York, N.Y. 10010.

60. Carol Gilligan, *In a Different Voice* (Cambridge, Mass.: Harvard University Press, 1982). Myra and David Sadker, *Failing at Fairness: How America's Schools Cheat Girls* (New York: Scribner, 1994).

61. For information, write Ramah Navajo Weaving Association, P.O. Box 486, Pine Hill, NM 87357.

62. For information, write Cooperative Home Care Associates, 349 East 149th Street, Bronx, N.Y. 10451.

63. For information and catalogs of products (handicrafts also created or copied to order), write Watermark Association of Artisans, Inc., 150 US Highway 158 East, Camden, NC 27921 (fax 919-338-1444).

64. To become an adult member ($50), to sponsor or become a teen member ($20), and for other information about programs for schools and community groups, write An Income of Her Own, P.O. Box 8452, San Jose, CA 95155-8452 (1-800-350-2978).

65. For information, write First Nations Development Institute, 69 Kelley Road, Falmouth, VA 22401.

66. Alice Walker, "We Alone," in *Horses Make a Landscape Look More Beautiful, Poems* (New York: Harcourt Brace and Company, 1984), p. 329.

Suggested reading:

Christine Delphy and Diana Leonard, *Familiar Exploitation* (Cambridge, England: Blackwell/Polity Press, 1992).
Maria Mies, *Patriarchy and Accumulation on a World Scale* (Atlantic Highlands, N.J.: Zed Books, 1986).
Joni Seager, *Earth Follies* (New York: Routledge, 1993).
Vandana Shiva, *Staying Alive* (Atlantic Highlands, N.J.: Zed Books, 1989).
Marilyn Waring, *If Women Counted: A New Feminist Economics* (New York: Harper & Row, 1988).

PART SIX   *Doing Sixty*

1. Barbara Macdonald, "Politics of Aging: I'm *Not* Your Mother," *Ms.*, July/August 1990, p. 56.

2. Germaine Greer, *The Change: Women, Aging and the Menopause* (New York: Alfred A. Knopf, 1992), pp. 8, 387.

3. Paula Ries and Anne J. Stone, *The American Woman 1992–93: A Status Report* (New York: W. W. Norton, 1992), p. 212.

"The 21st Century Family," Winter/Spring 1990 special issue of *Newsweek*, pp. 24, 63.

4. Barbara Macdonald with Cynthia Rich, *Look Me in the Eye: Old Women, Aging and Ageism* (Minneapolis: Spinsters Ink, 1991).

5. James E. Birren, "The Process of Aging: Growing Up and Growing Old," in Alan Pifer and Lydia Bronte, eds., *Our Aging Society: Paradox and Promise* (New York: W. W. Norton, 1986), p. 267.

6. Gloria Steinem, "I Was a Playboy Bunny," in *Outrageous Acts and Everyday Rebellions* (New York: Holt, Rinehart & Winston, 1983), pp. 29–69.

7. The Schlesinger Library at Radcliffe College, 10 Garden Street, Cambridge, MA 02138; 617-495-8647. For a sampling, see *Letters to Ms. 1972–1987,* ed. Mary Thom (New York: Henry Holt, 1987).

  8. Gloria Steinem, *Revolution from Within* (New York: Little, Brown, 1992).

  9. Patricia J. Williams, *The Alchemy of Race and Rights* (Cambridge, Mass.: Harvard University Press, 1991), p. 216.

  10. Audre Lorde, "Prologue," in *Undersong: Chosen Poems Old and New* (New York: W. W. Norton, 1992).

  11. Carolyn Heilbrun, *Writing a Woman's Life* (New York: Ballantine Books, 1988), p. 123.

  12. Gloria Steinem, "The Good News Is: These Are *Not* the Best Years of Your Life," *Ms.,* September 1979, p. 64. Republished as "Why Young Women Are More Conservative," in *Outrageous Acts and Everyday Rebellions,* pp. 211–18.

  13. M. N. Roy, *The Russian Revolution* (Calcutta: Renaissance Publishers, 1949), p. x.

  14. Gandhi's response to a reader in *Hind Swaraj,* a newspaper of which he was editor, quoted in *The Collected Works of Mahatma Gandhi* (New Delhi: Government of India, 1958–1984), vol. 10, p. 43.

  15. Anne Koedt, "The Myth of the Vaginal Orgasm," reprinted in *Radical Feminism,* ed. Anne Koedt, Ellen Levine, and Anita Rapone (New York: Quadrangle Books, 1973), pp. 198–207.

  16. To contact the recently formed Prathisthan or coordinating body for these grassroots groups, write: Principal Coordinator, Nirmala Deshpande, A-223 Pandara Road, New Delhi, India.

  17. A group dedicated to improving the legal, social and economic conditions of people with disabilities so they may achieve complete integration into society. Contact the New York group to find or start groups in your area: Disabled in Action, Post Office Box 30954, Port Authority Station, New York, New York 10011–0109; 718-261-3737.

  18. *Black Women in America: An Historical Encyclopedia,* vol. 1, ed. Darlene Clark Hine (Brooklyn, N.Y.: Carlson Publishing, Inc., 1993), p. 93.

  19. For a profile of Mary Peabody written by her granddaughter, Pulitzer Prize–winning author Frances FitzGerald, see "My Most Unforgettable Character," *Reader's Digest,* September 1965.

  20. Carrie Allen McCray, "Nobody Wrote a Poem," in *Piece of Time* (Goshen, Conn.: A Crimson Edge Chapbook of Chicory Blue Press, 1993), p. 2. Order from Chicory Blue Press, 795 East Street North, Goshen, CT 06756.

  Poet Sondra Zeidenstein began Chicory Blue Press with a special commitment to publishing women who began their major creative work after forty-five. For an anthology of twelve such women, edited by Zeidenstein and published by Chicory Blue in 1988, see *A Wider Giving: Women Writing After a Long Silence.*

  21. United Seniors' Health Cooperative, 1331 H Street N.W., Suite 500, Washington, D.C. 20005; 202-393-6222, fax 202-783-0588.

  22. Devaki Jain, "Remembering Kamaladevi," *Indian Express,* March 11, 1988.

  23. For those who would like to continue a feminist Seder, see the Women's Haggadah, by E. M. Broner and Naomi Nimrod, plus the author's personal account of our experiences, in E. M. Broner, *The Telling* (San Francisco: HarperCollins, 1993).